Fred and Elizabeth Brenchley … red is Canberra correspondent for *The* … editor of the *Australian Financial Revie* … irfax's Sydney newspapers.

STOKER'S SUBMARINE

STOKER'S SUBMARINE

FRED & ELIZABETH BRENCHLEY

HarperCollins*Publishers*

HarperCollins*Publishers*

First published in Australia in 2001
by HarperCollins*Publishers* Pty Limited
ABN 36 009 913 517
A member of the HarperCollins*Publishers* (Australia) Pty Limited Group
http://www.harpercollins.com.au

HarperCollins*Publishers*
25 Ryde Road, Pymble, Sydney, NSW 2073, Australia
31 View Road, Glenfield, Auckland 10, New Zealand
77–85 Fulham Palace Road, London W6 8JB, United Kingdom
Hazelton Lanes, 55 Avenue Road, Suite 2900, Toronto, Ontario M5R 3L2
and 1995 Markham Road, Scarborough, Ontario M1B 5M8, Canada
10 East 53rd Street, New York NY 10022, USA

National Library of Australia Cataloguing-in-Publication data:

Brenchley, Fred, 1942– .
Stoker's submarine.
Bibliography.
ISBN 0 7322 6703 X.
1. Stoker, H. G. (Henry Gordon). 2. Australia. Royal Australian Navy – History – World War, 1914–1918. 3. A.E.2 (Submarine). 4. Great Britain. Royal Navy – Officers – Biography. 5. World War, 1914–1918 – Campaigns – Turkey – Gallipoli Peninsula. I. Brenchley, Elizabeth. II. Title.
940.45994

Cover and internal design by Matt Lobina, HarperCollins Design Studio
Cover photographs from the Stoker Collection
Typeset by HarperCollins in 11.5/16pt Berkeley Book
Printed and bound in Australia by Griffin Press on 79gsm Bulky Paperback White

5 4 3 2 1 01 02 03 04

Acknowledgements

This book, like many a story, started at a cocktail party.

David Evans, Australia's ambassador to Turkey, attended a cocktail party at the Rahmi M. Koç Museum in Istanbul just before Christmas 1994. Not surprisingly, he met Selçuk Kolay, the Director of the Museum. Selçuk is a maritime buff. The conversation turned to the long missing Australian submarine *AE2*, scuttled in Turkey's Sea of Marmara on April 30 1915, after an extraordinary mission up the Dardanelles Strait through minefields to attack the Turkish Gallipoli supply lines from the rear.

Selçuk left the encounter to secure permission from his boss, Rahmi Koç, the Turkish industrialist, to find *AE2*. David and his wife, Pamela, shortly left for a holiday in France, where they told the authors of new attempts to find *AE2*. Like most Australians, we had been unaware that Australia even had a submarine at Gallipoli, much less of what it had achieved. For the next three years while based in London, we followed Selçuk's ups and downs as he scoured the Marmara for *AE2*. Equipment didn't work; a promising find proved mistaken. Yet Selçuk never gave up; if anything failure increased his determination.

Those years also enabled us to learn something about Dacre Stoker, the captain whose similarly indefatigable spirit led the *AE2* to perform one of the most daring and strategically significant missions in the history of the Australian navy. We have drawn liberally from Stoker's *Straws in the Wind*, published in the early 1920s, and thus redolent with the language and ethos of that era. When Stoker was called 'gay', it meant he was fun loving. Our particular thanks to Stoker's closest remaining relative in Britain, his niece Primrose Stoker, who helped us find Stoker's full personal records through first a Canadian, then an American branch of the family. Sadly, Primrose died in late 2000, aged 90. Documentary film producer Andrew Solomon was also invaluable in hunting up Stoker memorabilia.

One of the joys of writing this book was the unstinting help we received from a group of submariners. 'Submarines must come first, always first with me, through pride at ever having been associated with the Service,' said Stoker late in life. That love of submarines was particularly evident in the help we received from the Submarine Association's members, especially Peter Smith, Dave (Fess) Parker, Sam Walker and Phil Solomon. Vice-Admiral Ian MacDougall, Admiral Gerry Carwardine, Admiral Briggs, Captain Mark Sander, Commander Les Roberts and Commodore Adams were also supportive.

We received outstanding assistance from Lieutenant Commander Greg Swindon, Commander Tony Vine, ex-RAN imagery specialist Steve Dent, Captain Peter Hugennot, Professor Tristram Cary and Dr Michael White, QC, of the University of Queensland. In the UK curator Margaret Bidmead of the Royal Navy Submarine Museum was very helpful, as were Lieutenant Commander Barrie Downer RN, Commodore Dacre Smyth and Mrs Jenny Smyth, Mrs Gwen Simpson, Professor Robert O'Neill of the Department of War History, Oxford, and Bill Sellars in Istanbul.

Thanks also to Dr Gül Izmir, who translated from Turkish a book by Captain Riza, whose ship *Sultanhisar* damaged *AE2* in a battle in the Sea of Marmara before the submarine was scuttled, and to Dr Mark Spencer, who led the Australian diving team to confirm Selçuk's discovery.

Thanks are due to the families of all the men of the *AE2*, and those who generously allowed us access to a wealth of primary source material. They are listed at pages 247–49.

A valuable source into the personalities and social life of the prisoners of war was Greg Kerr's book, *Lost Anzacs: A Tale of Two Brothers*. This, together with his grandfather's recently transcribed shorthand diary now in the Australian War Memorial, provided a unique perspective. Thanks are due to the War Memorial's Ashley Ekins for his advice and guidance. Special thanks also to Peter, John and Andrew Lundy, Dr Jamie Kassler, Helen Lundy and Virginia Knox who all helped in research.

Acknowledgements

In writing this book it was surprising to learn how Australia appears to have wiped *AE2* and Dacre Stoker from its Gallipoli legends. Even the War Memorial's Gallipoli exhibit has no mention of *AE2*. We hope this book goes some way in bringing to light the incredible bravery of the crew of *AE2*, and the indelible stamp of the amazing Dacre Stoker on those tragic but heroic events at Gallipoli.

Elizabeth and Fred Brenchley, Canberra, November 2000

Contents

4

'It's Got To Be Tried and You Shall Do It'

5

'Run Amuck!'

6

'It's Done the Trick!'

7

'E14, By All the Gods!'

8

'How I Sank the *AE2*'

9

Tales of the Trade

10

Noble Is As Noble Does

11

'What About Me?'

12

The Fourth Man

13

'Look for a Man Carrying *The Times*'

14

Monkey Tricks

15

The Place All the Straws Led To

16

'North! North!'

17

Stoker's men

Introduction

It has lain upright in soft mud on the floor of the Sea of Marmara for 85 years, lost for most of that time. Its daring feats and its influence on the course of the Gallipoli invasion are largely forgotten.

Its hatch is ajar, just as it was left by the last of its crew when they scrambled out on 30 April 1915. The only occupant these days is a large conger eel, which has made a home in the heavily encrusted conning tower.

The painted '*AE2*' on the side which once proudly identified it as an Australian submarine—indeed, the second one bought by the new Australian navy—has long since faded and disappeared. These days the vessel carries only a coating of fishing nets. Many Turkish fishermen over the years must have cursed its hidden presence as they jagged their nets on the submarine hull.

They were not the first Turks to curse it. For the *AE2* was the Allied craft that exposed the rear of the Turkish defence of Gallipoli. To do this it undertook what many believed was an impossible mission—an underwater passage of the Narrows of the Dardanelles Strait, the treacherous, winding slice of water that connects the Mediterranean to the Sea of Marmara. The then Turkish capital of Constantinople (now Istanbul), and the prize of the Gallipoli landing, lay at the opposite end of the Marmara to the Dardanelles Strait.

Some liken the Dardanelles Strait to a river. At just 1274 metres across at its narrowest point, with dangerous currents flowing in and out, the strait has strong natural defences. To these, the Turks had added minefields, a string of heavily armed forts along both sides and searchlights. British and French submarines had already come to grief in the strait, with crews either lost or captured.

The military prize, however, was judged worth these losses, and perhaps more. In early 1915, with the war bogged down in bloody trench warfare across the Western Front in France, the British War Council assembled a massive navy and army force off Gallipoli, the foot-like peninsula of Turkey stretching into the Aegean, with the Dardanelles Strait at its base.

The Allied aim was to relieve the hard-pressed Russians by striking Turkey out of the war, exposing the soft underbelly of the Central Powers, Germany and Austria-Hungary. The War Council's original plan, a naval attack through the Dardanelles Strait, clearing mines along the way, and advancing across the Sea of Marmara to Constantinople, suffered a crushing reverse on 18 March 1915, when the massed armada swept into the mouth of the strait only to hit an unknown minefield. Seven hundred sailors drowned when three Allied battleships sank. Admiral de Robeck, the British navy commander, lost his nerve to resume the attack and handed the Dardanelles campaign to the army.

As British, French and Anzac forces prepared to land, it quickly became apparent that a submarine threat inside the Marmara could seriously disrupt Turkish supply lines to the isolated Gallipoli peninsula. But this was not just a matter of sailing submerged up the heavily mined strait, dodging Turkish fire from forts and mobile howitzers along the way. There was the problem of uncertain battery power for the long underwater voyage, and the dangers of the currents around the Narrows, where the strait doglegs for a final run up to the Sea of Marmara. Yet against incredible odds, the *AE2*, under the command of the debonair Irish captain Dacre Stoker, successfully navigated the strait, breached the Narrows and showed other Allied submarines the path into the Marmara. Over the next few months these marauders virtually cut off Turkish sea supply lines to Gallipoli, forcing the Turks and Germans to use inefficient and inconvenient rail and road links to service their troops on the peninsula.

Yet *AE2*'s daring feat remains unsung, even in its own country. Britain was generous with VCs for its Marmara submarine commanders. The commander who crept up to the Narrows in an older B class submarine, sinking a Turkish cruiser, and the two who followed Stoker in the newer E class submarines right through into the Marmara, were all awarded the Empire's highest award for gallantry. But Stoker, for all his trailblazing, received the lesser Distinguished Service Order (DSO). He never complained, although he must have bitten his lip at the injustice.

Gallipoli, says the conventional wisdom, was the formation of Australian nationhood. Australia's official war historian, C. E. W. Bean, was the first, but not the last, to say that 25 April 1915 marked the birth of consciousness for the Australian nation, then just 14 years old. And for good reason. The troops who performed so valiantly that day came from a new nation untested in battle, with no history of military operations.

Yet the very same day, against equally daunting odds, the *AE2* achieved a magnificent naval feat. Submarines from Britain and France, with their long naval histories, had failed to breach the Narrows. But a submarine from an infant navy of a new country, captained by an Irishman, found a way through the mines and past the forts.

If the ability of the Anzac force to hold on to the clifftops after landing was a test of character for the new nation Australia, so too was the underwater passage of the Narrows. Twice the *AE2* was grounded and almost destroyed. Twice Stoker and his crew managed to escape. Despite incredible odds, *AE2* even managed to fulfil its kamikaze orders to 'run amuck' in the Narrows, sinking a Turkish cruiser.

The *AE2*'s reward, however, has been virtual oblivion. Few Australians even know their country had a submarine at Gallipoli, much less that it achieved daring feats, sunk an enemy craft, and possibly played a pivotal role in their troops staying on the beachhead for eight months. The modern imagery of Gallipoli is of heroic fighting on the cliffs; the bravery of Simpson and his donkey; valiant Australian efforts sometimes thwarted by incompetent English commanders. The final point may be overdone, but Gallipoli remains an army preserve. The *AE2* and its story has been lost for 85 years.

Now the tiny submarine has been located, and in this book its story is resurrected. Incredibly, the submarine is largely intact, the only known E class submarine in such a state. Even though it still lies on the floor of the Marmara, *AE2* is the most tangible relic of Australia's role at Gallipoli, the crucible of nationhood.

The *AE2* may now be raised and restored. If so, Australians will have a second chance to properly acknowledge their little submarine, with a half English and half Australian crew, captained by an Irishman, that wrote a unique chapter in the history of submarine warfare.

How long can a nation forget its heroes?

1

Straws in the Wind

In 1901, both the new Commonwealth of Australia and submarines as a naval weapon were about the same vintage. January of that year had seen the merger of the six Australian colonies into a single nation. Ten months later the Royal Navy launched its first submarine, *Holland 1*, slightly behind both the United States and France, but five years ahead of Germany.

Like the new nation, submarines had been talked up for years. Not everyone was in favour of them. Admiral Sir Arthur Wilson's famous comment that they were 'underwater, underhand and damned un-English' summed up traditionalist naval suspicion that there was something sinister and sneaky about submersibles. Wilson also sniffed that submariners caught in wartime should be hung as pirates. To this day submariners often fly the Jolly Roger as a mark of their status.

Submersibles in fact had been around for a couple of centuries. In 1580 the Englishman William Bourne published details of 'a boate that may go under the water'. David Bushnell's *Turtle* in the American War of Independence, akin to a large barrel with a single person inside, sneaked up on the British flagship *Eagle* in New York Harbour, but its charge failed to penetrate the hull. George Washington labelled Bushnell's *Turtle* 'an effort of genius'.

The US navy recently recovered the Confederate submersible *H. L. Hunley* that had disappeared off Charleston in February 1864, after torpedoing the USS *Housatonic*, a feat not repeated by a submarine until 1914.

Modern submarines began with the Irish-American John Philip Holland, whose early submersibles were avidly supported by Fenians in the United States as a means to attack British naval dominance in Ireland.

Amidst much New York bar room intrigue, disgruntled Fenians captured the *Fenian Ram* submersible in 1879, equipped with an underwater gun that fired a 1.8-metre projectile, and tried to sell her to the Russians.

Ironically, it was a Holland design, already adopted by the US navy, which the Royal Navy picked for its first submarine in 1901. The walrus-moustached Holland, although of Irish birth, obviously had no qualms about selling his technology to the British.

Reportedly there were no crowds and little ceremony as HM Submarine Torpedo Boat No 1 (*Holland 1*) was launched at the Vickers Sons and Maxim yard at Barrow-in-Furness in 1901. The mighty Royal Navy might have been a touch nervous about what it was doing. Submarines could threaten its great fleet of battleships. Earl St Vincent had sounded the warning a century before: 'Pitt is the greatest fool that ever existed to encourage a mode of warfare which those who command the seas do not want, and, if successful, will deprive them of it.'

But the Sea Lords obviously had a duty to determine whether new-fangled submersibles really did pose a threat to their fleet. While some still dismissed submersibles as playthings, Admiral (later Lord) Fisher was a fervent supporter, and when he became First Sea Lord in 1904 began to write submarines into naval building plans.

The 63 foot [19 metre], slug-like *Holland 1*, and four sister ships soon proved their worth, despite numerous explosions of their dangerous petrol engines. Submarines were deemed particularly useful for harbour defence, their main role before World War I.

Just as submarine technology was rapidly developing—the 30-metre A class was launched in 1901 and the 40-metre B class in 1905—the fledgling Australian nation was in the throes of a lively debate on acquiring its own navy. The ragtag collection of colonial navies had been transferred to the new Commonwealth, but a revolving door of early federal governments and mixed signals from London on dominion navies delayed the formation of an Australian navy. Public support for a national force, however, was high, as evidenced by the huge crowds that gathered to welcome the US navy's Great White Fleet when it visited Sydney in 1908.

Australia was under the protective wing of the Royal Navy. But many Australians feared that Britain's eyes were largely on events in Europe, with the Pacific a very secondary theatre. The new nation contributed to an auxiliary fleet attached to the Australia station of the Royal Navy. The Admiralty stuck to the notion that in the era of the dreadnoughts a powerful navy should not split its fleet with dominion navies.

It was not until 1908 that the Admiralty conceded that the dominions could have naval forces for their own defence. A special Imperial Defence Conference in July–August 1909 agreed that Australia could create and control its own navy, but in an emergency the ships would come under the command of the Royal Navy. Even as late as 1914 Churchill, the First Sea Lord, was talking about an imperial squadron, built around a Canadian nucleus, to be based in Gibraltar. The ships would take 23 days to reach Vancouver on Canada's west coast and 28 days to reach Sydney. Obviously they could reach European waters quickly. The scheme collapsed after Canada refused to co-operate.

As in Britain, sections of Australia's early naval brass were hotly opposed to acquiring any of the revolutionary new submarines. Captain (later Vice-Admiral) William Rooke Creswell, the early Commander of Commonwealth Naval Forces, strongly favoured destroyers ahead of submarines. Creswell, an ex-Royal Navy lieutenant, migrated to Australia in 1879, becoming a pioneer in Queensland and the Northern Territory. He was appointed head of several of the colonial and state naval forces before becoming director of the new Commonwealth naval force. Peter Firkins in *Of Nautilus and Eagles: History of the Royal Australian Navy* said Creswell was always an advocate of a strong, local, independent navy manned by Australians.

But when it came to submarines, Creswell, according to Michael White in *Australian Submarines*, had a closed mind. In one letter Creswell wrote that submarines would be 'useless for Australia under present conditions or against any attacks possible', and 'unusable under weather and sea conditions of common occurrence with us'. Creswell cited the rip outside Port Phillip as 'impassable to submersibles'.

Sent to England in 1906 to report on what Australia might acquire, Creswell recommended to the Deakin government a force of torpedo boats and destroyers for coastal defence. This seemed to be accepted. The next year, a special report on advanced naval defences also came down against submarines, claiming they 'would constitute both a costly and inefficient means of naval defence of Australia'.

But the prime minister, Alfred Deakin, thought otherwise. Deakin had attended an Imperial Conference in London in 1907. British politicians and the Royal Navy had convinced him that Australia should include submarines in its new fleet. Deakin saw a submarine in operation. On his return, a paper issued to parliamentarians argued the case for submarines. It cited the US navy's Admiral Dewey, who snatched the Philippines from Spain in 1898, as claiming that if the Spanish navy had possessed just two of the Holland-type submarines he could not have held Manila Bay.

Reports began to leak into the press that the Commonwealth government, acting on Admiralty advice, would acquire submarines. An angry Creswell, then director of naval forces for Deakin's government, wrote cuttingly to the defence minister that he had 'not been privileged to see the views on which the prime minister has based his reasons for a change so radical in the Australian naval defence proposals before the government'.

Deakin, however, ignored objections. He told parliament the submarine would be the best weapon for harbour defences, and said the government planned to buy nine of the new C class submarines. However, the new Australian fleet which took shape just before the war included a battle cruiser (HMAS *Australia*), three light cruisers, three destroyers, two submarines and some small torpedo boats as well as remnants from the colonial navies.

Costs of the new submarines escalated, a phenomenon still evident today. Nine planned submarines became two. C class submarines were to have cost £55 000 each, the new D classes £85 000, and the latest

E classes £115 000. The E class boats were equipped with safer diesel engines, larger crews and greater torpedo capacity. The E class later proved the real submarine workhorse for the British navy in the Baltic and Marmara campaigns. Later submarine design owed a lot to their versatility.

Compared to modern submarines, however, the Es were small, cramped museum pieces. At 54 metres long and 589 tonnes surfaced (716 tonnes underwater), Es could run at some 15 knots on the surface, with a diving speed of 9 knots. They had four torpedo tubes, and carried eight torpedoes. For Dardanelles missions extra torpedoes were sometimes lashed to the interior casing.

The earlier E model, including the two Australian submarines, were not armed with guns. They had a crew of about 30, living in incredibly cramped conditions, often sleeping between torpedoes. Three officers shared two bunks. There were buckets for washing, and the entire crew shared two toilets. Privacy on board was provided by a few curtains. The Es had a small kitchen with an electric cooker.

Ordered from Vickers at Barrow-in-Furness, the two Australian E boats (with an 'A' in front of the 'E' to distinguish the Australian subs from their British counterparts) quickly ran behind schedule. They were not ready when the battle cruiser flagship *Australia*, and the cruiser *Sydney*, left for Australia, to triumphantly lead the new Australian fleet into Sydney Harbour on 4 October 1913.

Crewing was another problem. With no submarine experience Australia advertised amongst British submariners, ending up with a mixture of Australian and loaned Royal Navy crews. Australia added a telegraphist to bring the total crew of each submarine to 32.

One Royal Navy officer who heard the call was Henry Hugh Gordon Stoker, born in Dublin on 2 February 1885. Stoker's parents hastened to also call him 'Dacre' after a godfather of that name threatened to cut the child out of 'great wealth' if he was not named after him. The name Dacre stuck throughout his life, although the rich godfather went to South Africa to dabble in diamonds and was never seen again. Stoker's father was a physician, head of a prosperous and prominent Dublin family, which included many doctors.

Stoker applied for a transfer to the Australian navy because he heard that in Sydney there was a rich Australian who sponsored polo, then one of Stoker's favourite pastimes. This was typical Stoker. Life, for him, was summed up by the title of his 1920s memoirs, *Straws in the Wind* (1925). Fun-loving, irreverent and a bit of a dandy, Stoker found it hard to take life too seriously. 'With indulgent smile and jest on lip, I like to wave an airy hand and murmur: "Look at it all. What funny little folk we are—how seriously we take ourselves! We live, we laugh, we love, we weep, we war, we waste away—oh! So seriously! As if the world hinged on our petty doings!"'

This easygoing façade masked another Stoker: a hard worker with an attention to detail that commanded lasting loyalty from his men. In modern terminology, Stoker would be called a 'good communicator'. In fact, his innate talents gave him a flair that extended from his naval days through to a multi-artistic career of author, actor, playwright and stage director.

Of slight build, with angular features, sharp, lively eyes and an ironic sense of humour, Stoker appears to have done a lot of laughing and loving in his early days. A self-confessed philanderer, Stoker was also an enthusiast for most sports, and very popular amongst his fellow officers. On a posting in Gibraltar in 1913 as captain of one of the B class submarines, Stoker reflected on his life: 'Sun and moon, cricket and football, horses and hounds, bands and beauteous ladies—all at the same moment. What more could anyone ask?'

The answer, apparently, was someone to pay him to play polo. 'Polo is the finest game in the world,' said Stoker, 'but a regrettably expensive one, and I had never been able to afford it. But one day a straw came blowing down the wind, and caused me to meet a man who had a remarkable bit of news: to wit, that at Sydney, Australia, lived a rich man who would mount you and pay all expenses of the game if you'd only go and play polo with him. I felt I would like to go to Sydney to meet this rich man; in fact, I felt he was the man I'd been waiting to meet all my life. And then I remembered hearing that the Australian government was going to have two submarines built in England . . . RN officers were to be lent to the Australian navy to man them, so [I] immediately applied to be given command of one.'

Stoker was straight from central casting to accomplish a military feat for the new nation of Australia. He was bred with the optimism that lay behind the formation of a nation from six colonies. Moreover, his wicked sense of humour and his determination to 'have a go' were very Australian traits. *AE2*, then being built at Barrow-in-Furness was Stoker's new command. Australia was fortunate to attract him, as events proved. For all his happy-go-lucky, sports-loving appearance, Stoker was a formidable submarine commander. G. C. Brodie, a fellow officer in the Dardanelles campaign, described Stoker as 'Irish, gay [in the sense of happy], the best of companions, with an eye like a hawk for a ball or a periscope, he would have been the choice of any board of generals, historians or novelists for a dashing enterprise. More important, he would have been the choice of all his own crew, and so many of his old messmates.' A pre-war ferry ride with Stoker in Gibraltar, Brodie wrote, was an unforgettable experience. 'Every soul on board, of whatever sex or seniority, English or Spaniard, wanted to shake him by the hand, and he passed gaily round, delighting his old friends and forgetting none.'

A 'periscope eye' in those days was the submarine's main attack weapon. With none of the modern electronically guided systems, the captain's 'eye' for a moving target was everything.

Curiously, there was nothing in Stoker's family to attract him to a life in the navy. As a boy in Dublin he had never even seen one of the queen's naval ships. For Stoker, it was the first of his straws in the wind. When Dacre was 12, a friend's younger brother failed in his bid to enter the navy. But he had brought the possibility of a naval career to Dacre's attention. 'The idea was born that I would like to go into the navy,' he said. 'It was such a light straw in the wind.'

Dr Stoker sent his son to a tutor. 'His report stated that I seemed an utter fool and quite unfit to pass the difficult and competitive navy examination,' said Stoker. The boy was furious—not at the evaluation of his knowledge, but at the assumption that he couldn't learn if he tried.

Stoker defied anyone under thirteen to be interested in Latin or Greek, 'or that exasperating fellow Euclid . . . I was just as learned as the tutor on problems of play and tactics in football, or cricket, or any really interesting thing.'

Stoker persuaded his father to send him to a small school in England that specialised in preparing boys for the navy examination. He was violently seasick crossing the Irish Channel, and life at the new school was a misery. The boys poked fun at his Irish brogue, the headmaster thought him impertinent, and the matron laughed at his clothes, 'collected, Irish fashion, in bits and pieces from any old place'. Despite the headmaster's report that he had little chance, Stoker passed the examination, and was inducted as one of Her Majesty's Naval Cadets.

Stoker seems to have adjusted well to the discipline of life on board the training ship *Britannia*, moored at Dartmouth. He figured in the tennis, cricket, rugby and hockey teams. 'I also learned a little about seamanship and naval matters,' he quipped. Stoker's fondest memory of the period was being selected amongst a group of cadets to attend the funeral procession in London of Queen Victoria in 1901.

As a junior midshipman he was transferred to the *Jupiter*, where the sub-lieutenants (aged 19) kept the youngsters firmly in line with regular beatings. Stoker describes it in his usual ironic manner, saying woe betide the poor junior midshipman who had one right-handed sub-lieutenant and another left-handed.

> From time to time, when the sub-lieutenant felt that the good of one's soul called for attention, one would be requested to attend in the gunroom at a given hour, an hour which gave ample period for uneasy anticipation. Arrived in the gunroom, one would be politely directed to smell a certain spot on the table, and the left-handed sub-lieutenant at one side and the right-handed senior midshipman at the other would strike with a cane, or dirk scabbard, that portion of one's body appointed for the purpose. It was extremely trying because the rapidity with which the

> alternative blows fell precluded all possibility of fitting in a breath and a bracing up between them. All of which resulted in a most extreme soreness of the sit-upon but an indisputable soothing of the soul.

At 16, Stoker was transferred to HMS *Implacable*, the newly commissioned and largest battleship afloat, under Prince Louis of Battenberg, a personal aide-de-camp to the new king. Prince Louis believed good gamesters made good workers, so he encouraged the crew to play sport. *Implacable* became known as 'the games ship'.

For Stoker, it was three years of heaven, as *Implacable* was sent on extended duty in the Mediterranean. 'We roamed the Mediterranean, visited a hundred foreign ports, played our cricket and football and hockey and rackets and tennis; we rode and we danced, and we lost our youthful hearts with ease and regularity, retrieving them only for the purpose of losing them again.'

Youthful hijinks abounded. In Rome, a hotel manager kept three of the midshipmen prisoner while he sent another back to the ship to raise money to pay for a dance the young men had hosted for a group of American girls on an educational tour of Europe. But play was mixed with a life of solid work, studying navigation, seamanship, gunnery and torpedoes. 'Work hard, play hard—there is no better recipe for happiness, and happy we were,' said Stoker. One irritation, however, was that Sir John Fisher, the Commander in Chief and later the First Sea Lord who walked out on Churchill over the Dardanelles campaign, kept pirating his dancing partners. Stoker was peeved that the ladies seemed to prefer an admiral to a midshipman.

By 1904 when he was promoted to acting sub-lieutenant, and sent to courses and examinations at the Royal Naval College at Greenwich, Stoker had lost his Irish brogue. Tongue in cheek, Stoker lamented that exams that would determine his career for the next 12 years were held so close to London's attractions. 'I feel sure that some situation might be found for the college more conducive to earnest study on the part of the young officers,' he wrote.

Stoker worked hard at Greenwich, and also found time to 'philander' in London. But money was a problem. This led him to volunteer for the new submarine service.

> Submarines were then in their earliest pioneering stage [wrote Stoker]. Accidents and disasters were of common occurrence, and, on the face of it, it did not appear to be a very pleasant life. But ... an officer was paid an extra six shillings a day for risking his life in them; and when you are a sub-lieutenant on full pay of five shillings a day the prospect of drawing an extra six shillings was a comprehensibly big inducement. And then there is that search of Adventure, which tempts man and boy—yes, and woman, too—under its pseudonym, Romance—into such queer paths.

In those days five shillings was enough for Stoker to go to the football and then spend a night in town. Six shillings extra was obviously a big attraction. Stoker applied and sat for the exams, but the new submarine service had proved surprisingly attractive despite the dangers. 'I found, to my intense discomfiture, that my sober-sided rivals had scored over me so much that they were taken and I was not.'

Stoker's disappointment was softened by a posting to rejoin Prince Louis on his flagship, the *Drake*. A cruise of Canadian and US ports rekindled all the fun of his Mediterranean days. 'The cruise ended in a blaze of glory at New York, midst daily mountains of oysters washed down with gallons of champagne—a diet to be stood by young men in excellent physical training.'

After a year on the *Drake*, Stoker received a letter from the Admiralty offering him a submarine position. He agonised. Prince Louis seemed doubtful. 'I acted against his unmistakable hint,' said Stoker. 'I suppose philanderers by nature are always attracted by the leap in the dark as opposed to the lighted and marked-out way—perhaps that was the reason. However—a straw in the wind again turned me off in a new direction; I bade Prince Louis goodbye, and joined the submarine headquarters at Portsmouth.'

Stoker's first submarine training was on one of the five original petrol-driven Hollands. 'The boats were tiny, tiny little cigar-shaped things filled with masses of machinery; rods and valves and pumps and cocks and gauges, and pipes and wheels and motors and switches appearing to the untrained eye to be jumbled together in utter confusion,' said Stoker in his memoirs. '[But] before long one was doing duty in one of the tiny cigars with just as much pride in the wee ship and its works as had ever been caused by the finest battleship.'

In his personal notebooks Stoker was less rosy-eyed about the first submarines. 'They were alarming boats to dive and there were frequent battery fires and explosions inside,' he wrote. 'We kept white mice inside that were supposed [to give] distress warnings of dangerous gasses—but they seldom did.'

Whether the white mice survived or not, Stoker certainly did. Two years later, aged 23, he was promoted to lieutenant and given his first command, HM Submarine *A10*. Stoker promptly ran it into the Devonport dockyard wall. The Navy appeared forgiving, and Stoker was promoted to a larger B class boat, and posted with two other submarines to open Britain's first foreign submarine station, at Gibraltar.

Happy days followed. Stoker and his submarine mates concocted a yarn around their 'special vintage port' on board the subs—exactly the same port as in the other messes—that had all the wine snobs drooling. 'I have never held quite the same respect for amateur wine experts since those days.' For two years Stoker practised 'attacks' on passing ships, besides avidly pursuing various sports, including his new love, polo.

It was polo, as we have seen, that led Stoker to apply, at 28, to join the submarine service of the new Australian navy. 'It is only another straw in the wind, but I seemed amazingly lucky to get such a command then,' he said. 'The boats were E class, the latest and by far the largest submarines that our steady process of development had produced. Only five of them were completed when I got my appointment, and all [the others] were commanded by men greatly senior to me.'

In late 1913 Stoker joined the new crew of *AE2* at Barrow-in-Furness. He chose Lieutenant Geoffrey Haggard, Royal Navy, as his first lieutenant.

Haggard, born in London in 1888, was three years younger than Stoker. Third officer, appointed later, was Lieutenant John Pitt Cary.

Whether the trio ever talked literature is not known, but they certainly had the right connections. Stoker's cousin was Bram Stoker, author of the popular *Dracula*, Haggard's uncle was Rider Haggard, author of *King Solomon's Mines*, and Cary's brother was Joyce Cary, later of *The Horse's Mouth* fame. It must have been the most literary boat in the navy's history. Lieutenant T. F. Besant, Royal Navy, born in Liverpool in 1883 and an experienced submariner, had been selected to captain *AE1* and appointed senior officer of the little Australian flotilla.

As the half British, half Australian crew assembled, Stoker was impressed with their 'shore spirits', seeing it as a good omen for future working relations. Houdini, the famous escape artist, was visiting Barrow and the crew placarded the town with a challenge, which read:

> We, the undersigned Petty Officers and Men of the Australian Submarines now building at Barrow, happening to have in our possession an old straightjacket which used to be used for the criminally insane, challenge Houdini to escape from the same. The only conditions we wish to enforce are that we should personally strap Houdini in the jacket, and that he should remain on the stage in full view of the audience during the whole time he is endeavouring to escape.

Houdini was to pay £250 should he fail to escape.

It was clearly a put-up job by Houdini's theatre organisers. Stoker, tongue-in-cheek, wondered why sailors should be roaming the world with an old straightjacket for the criminally insane. Nevertheless, a crowded theatre cheered as Houdini was strapped in by the Australian sailors. 'Such roars of laughter from the audience every time a sailor gave an extra heave!' Houdini of course struggled free, and the sailors cut up the straightjacket on stage, saying it was obviously useless.

The two new submarines sailed from Barrow on 10 February 1914 for Portsmouth. The 800-kilometre voyage without breakdown was a record for the new E boats, which were already experiencing problems with their new diesel engines. For Stoker, this made the long voyage to Australia 'look rather formidable'.

In Portsmouth, *AE1* and *AE2* were fitted with gyrocompasses. Newly developed Marconi wirelesses were hurriedly installed. Australia paid Marconi £75 for each of the sets installed on the two subs. Earlier submariners straying from their tender ships had used homing pigeons.

On 2 March 1914, in company with the tender ship *Eclipse* loaned by the Royal Navy—the tender HMAS *Penguin* was already in Australia—the two subs set sail for Australia. Three days out from Portsmouth *AE2* experienced vibrations, apparently from a damaged port propeller. *Eclipse* helped tow the two subs into Gibraltar, where *AE2*'s propeller was fixed and Stoker was much in demand from his old friends. For some years afterwards the Australian navy tried to negotiate compensation from Vickers, but gave it away by the end of the war. Another propeller had to be fitted at Aden.

'Then the long, long voyage,' wrote Stoker. 'Through a long list of mechanical difficulties and mishaps overcome by hook and crook, the miles were pushed astern.' Partly under tow, the two submarines visited Malta, Port Said and Aden before the long hike across the Indian Ocean to Colombo. To cut the searing heat inside, the *AE1* was painted white in Aden, and not repainted grey until Cairns. On the *AE2* Stoker mounted his bed on deck. 'The only exciting incident occurred when a flying fish flew into my bed,' he said. 'A fish in its proper place, at the end of your line or on a breakfast plate, is a most estimable animal; as a companion of your bed it is a failure.'

As the flotilla ploughed along, the starlit skies, dead smooth sea and phosphorescent water swishing musically by must have brought out the literary streak in temporary Sub-Lieutenant Hopkins, a former school teacher. Stoker said that every evening the red-haired, sentimental Hopkins would stand on deck, smoke his pipe and lean on the rails to declare: 'This is a night on which every woman wishes to be loved . . .'

'Such thoughts lose their value when in a submarine one thousand miles from the nearest point of land,' quipped Stoker.

In Singapore the Australian cruiser *Sydney* took over the tender role for the run to Australia. But *Sydney* had made no provision for support or accommodation of the submarine crews during the sweltering stopover in Singapore. The crews stayed on the submarines berthed alongside *Sydney*. 'An inferno it was when trying to do our work of overhauling and repairing machinery inside the submarine,' Stoker said. And on the run to Dutch Batavia (now Jakarta), *Sydney* burnt poor quality coal. The black smoke and cinders blowing back on the submarines meant the crew on watch had to wear goggles. Batavia impressed Stoker, who listed 'its portly and hospitable Dutch admiral, its startling glimpses of nude ladies bathing in canals, its sixteen-dish curry lunch at the Hôtel des Indes . . .'

Then, in the Lombok Strait, the two submarines were almost lost just short of their Australian landfall. On a dark night, *AE1* was under tow by *Sydney* while *AE2* followed astern. But *AE1*'s towline parted, and the submarine drifted right across *AE2*'s path. Stoker tried to swing to starboard, but, caught in an eddy, his submarine held to its course.

'It looked as if a collision was absolutely inevitable, as there could be no hope of the engines answering to the order of "Full Speed Astern" before the boats struck,' he said. 'As a last resort, we in *AE2* put the helm hard over the other way; a lucky swirl caught the boat's nose at the same moment, helping to swing her off to starboard—and we whizzed past *AE1*'s stern at a distance of some three feet.'

A very narrow escape. But the danger was not over. For a while *AE2* drifted towards the rocks of Lombok with a jammed helm. With this fixed, the two submarines moved ahead of the *Sydney*, and then waited for her to catch up. But the broken tow rope fouled the *Sydney*'s propeller, and the cruiser came straight at the submarines. 'By going full speed ahead immediately, we got out of the way in time to avoid being run down, but not by a sufficient margin to make one feel very comfortable,' noted Stoker wryly.

The flotilla reached its first Australian port, Darwin, on 5 May 1914. Stoker, expecting a dry and parched desert, was surprised to find the green tropical growth of 'Port Darwin'. Aborigines gazed in amazement at the strange craft. 'Their effort at describing our arrival was: "Big fellah [ie the *Sydney*] him come first, little fellah him follow after—all same emu",' wrote Stoker.

Stoker took a dim view of the White Australia policy, showing remarkable foresight in that era. 'Is the white man justified in holding this land, empty, to the excluson of teeming millions of blacks and yellows, over-crowded in their own countries?' he said.

From Darwin, the flotilla headed to Thursday Island and down through the Barrier Reef to Cairns. A Lord Mayor's banquet had been planned for the scheduled arrival in Sydney on 23 May 1914, but bad weather delayed the flotilla in Moreton Bay.

There were few welcomers in sight when the two submarines and *Sydney* passed through Sydney Heads at 6 am on the grey morning of Sunday 24 May, moving up the harbour to berth at the navy's Garden Island base. A suggestion that the flotilla wait outside the Heads for a grand entry later in the day was rejected.

The voyage from Britain had taken 83 days, 60 at sea. The two small submarines had sailed 13 000 miles [20,800 kilometres], about 9000 [14,400] of those under their own power. As they tied up at Garden Island, proudly unfurling large white ensigns, it was a world record for submarines. *The Times* listed it as 'manifestly the most remarkable [voyage] yet performed by any submarine'.

Stoker felt there were few people on earth more patriotic and proud of their country than Australians. But for a man who clearly enjoyed an argument and a joke, he had to bite his tongue 'for fear that philandering words would be taken seriously'. It was not long before the inevitable question, 'And what do you think of our harbour?', tested Stoker's diplomacy.

By moonlight, said Stoker, with the deep shadows, bays, and ferry lights picking out the sweeping curves of the shores, Sydney Harbour was 'as pretty a sight as the eye can desire'. But by daylight, Stoker queried whether 'the works of men have added to or detracted from what must have been the original picturesque grandeur of this magnificent example of God's handiwork'.

'And so, my Sydney friends, I cavil at that expression, "Our Harbour",' said Stoker. 'The Creator created that harbour and saw that it was good—are you really entitled to the praise for its beauties?'

Still, Stoker found Sydney 'the most attractive city to live in I have ever seen'. There was, however, one major disappointment. The polo sponsor he had come out to seek had become eccentric and it was feared he had been placed under restraint. 'They also feared most of his money was gone,' said Stoker. 'Sad, wasn't it? I felt very sorry for him. But somehow I was not altogether surprised.'

2

'Gentlemen, War was Declared on Germany at Midnight--Waiter, a Gin and Bitters, Please!'

As it happened, the two submarines arrived in Sydney as Australia celebrated Empire Day, 24 May 1914. In those days, when Australians took pride in being part of the great British Empire, this was a grand occasion. A combined church parade was held in Sydney's Domain. Farmer's, the big department store, advertised a special luncheon featuring a program of patriotic music. A Miss Dorrie Ward sang 'Land of Hope and Glory', while Mr A. K. Jamison rendered 'Rule Britannia'. If patrons were in a shopping mood after this, Farmer's advertised a clearance sale, with tweed coats reduced to 21s 6d ($2.15).

Down at Garden Island, the new submarines were creating quite a stir. Crowds could look at the exterior, but were not allowed to see inside. These submarines were still top secret. Even the *Sydney Morning Herald*'s reporter was denied access. 'It is said that the only civilian in the British Empire who has seen the inside of a submarine is Mr Winston Churchill, First Lord of the Admiralty,' said the obviously awed *Herald*'s reporter. 'The rule is that none but naval and army officers shall be allowed on board.' Under a sub-heading 'A House of Secrets', the *Herald*, forced to observe the new submarines from the deck of HMAS *Sydney*, explained their power.

'A submarine is a deadly thing. A battleship may ride in majesty on the waves, and in a moment be torn by a torpedo hurled by the stealthy, invisible foe beneath the water. You may see everything else around you, yet miss the submarine. It is because this type of vessel is so valuable in time of war that such pains are taken to guard its secrets.'

Sydney marvelled at the strange new craft. The *Daily Telegraph*, then a sober broadsheet newspaper, said the two submarines looked more like 'a pair of languid whales' as they crept up the harbour just after 6 am. But showing signs of its tabloid future, the *Telegraph*'s report continued:

> An old waterman not yet fully awakened from his slumbers rubbed his eyes and gazed at the two moving grey hulls. 'Two bosker whales,' he ejaculated. Then his eyes alighted upon the *Sydney*. 'Well, I'll be blowed!' he exclaimed. 'They're the bloomin' submarines the papers ha' been talkin' about so much lately!' But he consoled himself with the reflection that 'they look like whales, any'ow, and if they were prolin' down about Eden, instead of in Sydney 'Arbor, at this hour o' the mornin', they'd ship a harpoon or two, and wonder what 'ad 'appen 'em'.

As the senior officer, Lieutenant Commander Besant of *AE1* did all the media interviews, telling the *Daily Telegraph* the two subs had experienced no serious mechanical problems on the long voyage out. The press was very interested in life on board such small craft. Besant said it wasn't so bad, although he admitted to some monotony. 'There are books and things,' said Besant, 'and the men play draughts, and a couple of them have concertinas.'

The press was fascinated by the smoking ban. 'But, after all, when one thinks of it, with 26 pipes and two cigars going intermittently in that small underwater area, the atmosphere might very likely get into such a state that a steam shovel might be needed to remove it,' wrote one reporter.

The following day Sydney's Lord Mayor, Alderman Richards, turned on a civic reception for the officers of the two submarines, attended by the Admiral of the Australian Fleet, Sir George Patey. Besant told the audience that submarines were still evolving, and one hardly knew where development would stop. To applause, he said that 30 of the trained submariners brought out were Australians. He assured the reception that the submarines would be very valuable additions to the defence of the new Commonwealth.

That assurance was put to the test more quickly than most imagined. In the initial weeks after the arrival of the submarines, Stoker found Sydney full of 'delightful people' and 'hospitable clubs'. In between golf, tennis and race meetings he managed surf bathing at Sydney's Manly beach. 'There is every cheery pastime which the philanderer can wish to taste,' he said.

Two months after arrival, Stoker was in the mess sitting down to lunch when an officer walked in and announced, 'Gentlemen, war was declared on Germany at midnight, English time.' Silence fell, and the officer continued, 'Waiter, a gin and bitters, please.'

The submariners had mixed feelings. 'Since joining the navy we had believed that the sole reason of our existence, and main demand on our efficiency, was that one day we would fight the Germans,' said Stoker. 'The day had dawned—to find us in Australia, thousands of miles from the main scene of naval activity. It seemed cruel luck. The prospect of our ever getting a chance at the enemy seemed utterly remote; whilst our brethren in the North Sea would, in our imagination, be banging their torpedoes into dreadnoughts and things every odd hour of the day. We cursed the moment in which we had been lent to the Australian navy.'

That quickly changed when the two submarines were ordered into the Pacific to join the hunt for the German Pacific squadron under Admiral Graf von Spee. From three to six German cruisers were suspected to be in the German South Pacific colonies, then stretching across northern New Guinea through several island chains, including New Britain and Nauru. Although the Australian fleet was formally transferred to the control of the Admiralty, as decided in 1911, it was mutually agreed that destruction of the German fleet and capture of the German colonies were top priorities.

As it happened, Spee fled the area after a surprise raid on Apia, Samoa, on 14 September, where he had expected to catch the *Australia*, flagship of the new fleet. Having missed her, Spee raided French Polynesia before moving to South America, where he destroyed a British naval squadron at the Battle of Coronel, sinking the *Good Hope* and *Monmouth*. But the British fleet under Vice-Admiral Sir Doveton Sturdee defeated Spee off the Falklands in December.

The two Australian submarines were keen to have a crack at Spee's cruisers, believed to be still wandering the Pacific. Spirits were high as they moved towards Rabaul. Intelligence reports suggested that two of the largest German cruisers were in harbour there. According to Stoker, crews of the big ships cheered the smaller destroyers as they raced ahead to be the first to attack. Sailors tend to a laconic sense of humour, and Stoker reported the philosophism of one of the crew of the destroyers: 'Cheer! So would I b—— well cheer if I was in a b—— great ship like that!'

Rabaul Harbour, however, was clear of any German warships. After troops occupied the shore, the navy began patrolling the narrow St George's Strait between New Britain and New Ireland to catch any passing German ship. *AE2*, with a destroyer, performed the first day's patrol at the head of the strait, scouting for the enemy. *AE2* remained in harbour the next day as *AE1* took up patrol with the destroyer *Parramatta*.

One of the great mysteries of the Australian navy then unfolded. Aboard *AE1* everything appeared normal. Besant swapped signals with *Parramatta* throughout the patrol. About 2.30 pm, as a haze was gathering, *Parramatta* again sighted *AE1*, signalling to the submarine that visibility was then about 8 kilometres. The two stayed in sight for about the next hour before *Parramatta* scouted off.

The *AE1* was never seen again. *Parramatta*, believing that *AE1* would return to Rabaul, entered harbour about 6 pm to find that *AE1* had not been sighted. Rear Admiral Patey ordered a search, but over three days and nights nothing was found.

Patey quizzed Stoker for a possible explanation. Like everyone else, Stoker could only offer conjecture as to why the submarine had disappeared without trace. Enemy attack was ruled out. There was no evidence of enemy warships in the area. Subsequent German records confirmed this. Stoker theorised that it could have been an internal explosion, an accident while diving, or just an ordinary navigational accident.

Stoker believed that the absence of telltale remains on the surface pointed to mechanical failure or an accident while diving. But like others, Stoker had no explanation as to why the *AE1* should be diving that afternoon. 'The *Parramatta* was certain that no shipping approached which might have caused the *AE1* to dive for investigation,' he wrote. 'And also, her captain was a skilful, cautious and experienced submarine commander; he had expressed the utmost satisfaction with the capability of his officers and crew, and also with the manner in which his boat dived; so that it must have been a strange mischance which caused their loss in ordinary practice diving.'

A shocked Stoker could see the dangers if *AE1* had dived and struck trouble. 'The sinking submarine would slip away down into the vast depths existing in those parts, rapidly filling as the increasing pressure of water outside forced its way through the hull, bringing a quick and clean death to the crew, whose end might well have come before their steel tomb had reached the ocean's bed—there to rest undisturbed by man and his investigation.'

That last forecast proved right. *AE1*, the first Australian submarine, became the first Australian warship lost in World War I. It remains lost to this day. Sonar investigations in the 1970s found nothing. Many suggest the submarine must have struck a reef while diving, but all remains speculation.

Stoker was distressed. The two submarines had shared travels and adventure; the officers were friends. 'There seemed to me to lie but a straw in the wind 'twixt *AE2*, at anchor in Rabaul Harbour, and her sister ship, the steel tomb, hundreds of fathoms deep.'

There was more to Stoker's 'straw in the wind' allusion than meets the eye. *AE1*'s first officer was Lieutenant (the Honourable) Leopold Scarlett, younger son of Baron Abinger. Stoker had met Scarlett, (inevitably called 'Will'), during his happy sojourn at Gibraltar before the war. The two had become great friends. 'About the most loveable character I have ever known,' Stoker wrote of Will in his personal scrapbook.

But Scarlett contracted tuberculosis. He was invalided out of the Royal Navy in 1911, moving to Australia to live on a sheep station. 'When war came he rushed to Sydney, where I was in command of *AE2*, produced [somehow] a clean bill of health, and wanted to join me,' Stoker noted. 'The captain of *AE1* was, however, six months my senior, so exercised his undoubted right and grabbed Scarlett. Had Scarlett not been so outstandingly valuable as an officer he wouldn't have lost his life off Rabaul.' As we shall see, Scarlett would later figure in another baffling episode in Stoker's life.

As *AE2* lay in Rabaul harbour ready for action in case the Germans staged a reprisal raid, the Australians issued a proclamation to the newly conquered locals. Stoker was amused that it was proclaimed in pidgin English. No such thing as pidgin German existed.

AE2 remained in harbour for the next three weeks, practising diving on occasion. Natives, said Stoker, referred to the strange craft as 'devil fish'. Some disappeared into the hills until the submarine resurfaced.

* * *

In early October 1914, *AE2* accompanied the battleship *Australia* and the cruiser *Sydney* to Suva, Fiji, suffering another broken propeller on the way. 'At the start of the long voyage, as the shores of the St George's Strait disappeared from sight astern, the lingering hope that we might, even yet, get some clue as to the *AE1*'s fate seemed to die; and the other ships of the squadron did little to remove a sense of loneliness on the face of the waters to the one little submarine remaining,' Stoker wrote in somewhat maudlin fashion.

At Suva, *AE2* stayed in harbour as day guard while the flagship and its cruiser searched for German ships. Stoker was bewitched by the beauty of Fiji. 'Some of the islands have long, slowly shelving sandy beaches; and if on one of these, towards late afternoon, you lie as naked as may be, basking in the rays of a not too powerful sun, and feel the waters of the rising tide, warmed to surprising heat by their passage over the hot sand, come trickling first round your toes and slowly, inch by inch, covering your whole body—then an indescribable feeling of perfect peace is with you, which must be near akin to that which passeth all understanding.'

Stoker's sunny peace, however, was disturbed by two pieces of wartime news. He was appalled by propaganda reports that Spee had failed to save any lives from the sinking British ships in the Battle of Coronel. 'Foul tales, disgusting tales, were rife after this action,' said Stoker. Although he had never met the German commander, Stoker said his 'charm of manner and general character were vouched for by many English as well as people of all nations'. War could be waged cleanly, he argued. 'Is the martial fire of a nation such a sorry thing that lies must be used to fan it?'

Another harsh reality of war was the forced departure as First Sea Lord of his old captain, Prince Louis of Battenberg. Although retitled Marquess of Milford Haven to disguise his German origins, Prince Louis still had to step aside. Stoker labelled this prejudice as 'ignorant, petty' public opinion. 'I doubt if there was a single officer in the navy who would have seriously contended that he was not the right man in the right place as head of the British navy in the hour of its greatest test,' said Stoker. 'And then he was sacrificed to the ignorant, the petty, and the scandalmongers. The tragedy of it, for the navy as a whole, and the nation.'

Two years later, Prince Louis's youngest son, also Louis, joined the Royal Navy. He rose to become Earl Mountbatten, Chief of Combined Operations for D-day and later the last Viceroy of India, overseeing the separation and independence of India and Pakistan. He was assassinated by IRA terrorists in 1979. One of Prince Louis's grandsons, Philip, married the young Princess Elizabeth in 1947 and became consort to Queen Elizabeth II when she ascended the throne in 1952. Stoker, who in later life developed a genuine affection for English royalty despite his Irish background, took great pleasure in the Battenberg redemption.

With the South Pacific clear of German ships, the *AE2* was ordered back to Sydney for a refit. Stoker took the opportunity to write a report to the

Australian Naval Board on modifications that should be made to *AE2*—and future Australian submarines—for service in tropical Pacific, rather than cold English, waters. Apart from numerous mechanical specifications, Stoker was anxious to stress crew comfort, urging a 'properly fitted WC'.

But it was not all work while in dock in Sydney. One incident ashore demonstrated Stoker's mischievous sense of humour. The anecdote is best told in his own words.

> I wandered ashore one afternoon in Sydney, and with a sailor's distaste in the war's early days for uniforms ashore, had chanced to break the regulations and don plain clothes. It was December, and very hot; towards evening a strong desire for liquid refreshment caused me to pass through the swinging doors of the Australia Hotel [later to become one of the city's most fashionable hotels] and direct my weakening steps towards the cool and comfortable lounge bar.
>
> A goodly number of khaki-clad gentry were refreshing themselves after, doubtless, an arduous day's training and, threading my way through these, I chose a retired corner. A haughty-eyed Duchess presided behind the bar, and, with due humility, I craved an iced concoction prepared by her fair hands. Her Grace, without unbending, complied with my demand; after the first strengthening draught of nectar, I idly fingered my glass, meditating on the horrors of war, my experiences of the last few months, and the sadness of my return to Sydney without the companions whose utmost sacrifice war had already demanded.
>
> 'Now, you're a likely looking young chap! Why don't you volunteer?'
>
> I looked up. Yes; he was addressing me. He was somewhat red of face, he also held a glass in his hand, and he sported the uniform of private in an Australian infantry regiment. I looked at him a while without answering—being rather at a loss. He had obviously only volunteered a few days before himself, as he bore few signs of the military caste.
>
> 'Why don't you volunteer?' he repeated.

Then the spirit moved me, and I asked in turn: 'Why should I?'

A burst of eloquence came in reply. I listened with interest, thinking that his speech would have sounded more effective if uncoloured by the strong Australian accent, and if the words did not have such a distressing tendency to run into each other. I decided he must have had a very arduous day's training indeed. But his speech had some points; and, curiously enough, I began to like the fellow. But I also saw fit to be very dense.

He explained his ideas of the way King and Empire were calling me, and ended again with the question, 'So why don't you volunteer?'

'Oh, well,' said I, seeking an excuse, 'I think I'm not tall enough.' [Stoker was indeed shortish.]

'Not a bit of it,' quoth he. 'We have many chaps just as small as you.'

A grand answer—I liked him much more now, because, you see, it chanced that he himself was smaller than me.

'But I don't think I'd like to be a soldier,' said I musingly; 'It must be most awfully uncomfortable in the trenches.' He was horror-struck for the moment, and speech left him.

'Besides,' I went on, 'it must be dangerous.'

He only recovered speech sufficiently to call, in agonised tones, on the Duchess and ask if she'd ever heard anything like it.

'But surely it's true,' I insisted: 'You must know—you're a soldier!'

'Bah!' interposed the Duchess—my friend was speechless again.

'Bah! Some of you things that call yourself men make me sick!'

This was distressing. I couldn't bear that Her Grace's excessively well-developed form should waste away on my account. So I endeavoured to clear myself.

'After all,' I said, 'there must be many men who ought to go to the trenches before me.'

My friend had recovered slowly. 'Why?' he demanded, 'Why should there be? Every man is wanted, you just as much as anyone.'

'No,' I answered. 'I'm afraid I can't agree with you. What about my job—what is going to happen to that?'

He didn't seem pacified. 'People can't think of their jobs—suppose everyone put their own private business before the country's affairs—what then?' he demanded angrily of the bar at large.

I began to fear a public interest being taken in my miserable case, so said confidentially, 'Well, look here, I'll tell you how it really is. I wouldn't mind becoming a soldier a bit, but I'm afraid of the bosses in my business. I don't think they'd be pleased if I ran away.'

'That's all right,' said he. 'We can easily fix that up for you. Employers can't be allowed to stand in the way like that. You tell me who your employers are, and I'll see about having them spoken to.' (I have mentioned that he was a private.)

I placed my empty glass with care on the counter, and then spoke with deliberation.

'I'll make a bargain with you. If you will get me out of my present job, I will promise to volunteer.'

'What is your job?' He made ready to write it down.

'Well,' said I, speaking with the utmost English drawl I could produce, 'I happen to be captain of the only submarine there is at the present moment in the southern hemisphere.'

'Lor!' said the Duchess. But my friend was speechless again; to ease his discomfiture I went on chattily. 'There were two of us, you know, but in the recent operations up north the other boat was lost with all hands—you probably saw all about it in the papers.' I kept the chat on for some time, watching his face the while; it was an interesting study.

When speech at last returned he made the amende honourable indeed. 'Will you have me the honour of shaking your hand?' he asked, whereat I felt that my poor little joke wasn't so amusing as I had thought.

Feeling surprisingly ashamed of myself, I gave him another drink. For, after all, he probably had undergone a very arduous day's training. The eye of the Duchess was still cold on me.

3

Into the Vortex

Stoker may have enjoyed a bar room prank in Sydney, but he was still frustrated at missing out on the action in Europe. As *AE2* was winding up its Pacific mission news came through that HMAS *Sydney* had destroyed the German raider *Emden* off Cocos Island. Then, as *AE2* was berthed in Sydney for its refit, Spee's fleet was destroyed in the Battle of the Falkland Islands.

'The Pacific was now clear of enemy ships, and a submarine lying in Sydney Harbour could not claim to be of any useful purpose in the war,' said Stoker. Always one with a plan for action, Stoker wrote to the Australian Naval Board arguing that *AE2* should accompany the second Australian expeditionary force shortly to leave for the Middle East, and then serve with the Royal Navy in either Mediterranean or English waters. Stoker saw *AE2* replacing one of the lost Royal Navy E class subs. He reasoned that Australia was unlikely to buy any more of the E class as newer, improved submarines were arriving. Maintaining spares for one E class was wasteful.

Stoker somewhat loftily believed Britain in the future might help Australia replace its submarine fleet in return for *AE2*. (In fact, Britain did give Australia six J class submarines after the war, but these quickly became obsolete, and were scrapped in the early 1920s.)

With this line of argument Stoker gained permission to see the Minister for Defence, Senator George Pearce. In modern times it is inconceivable that a mere submarine captain should personally lobby the defence minister about orders for his ship. But this was 1914, the navy and the nation were new, and Australia was only a few months into its first war.

Stoker travelled to Melbourne, where the state parliamentarians had generously turned over their Parliament House to the fledgling federal government until it was relocated to the new federal capital of Canberra in 1927. Pearce, a former West Australian carpenter and trade unionist, was serving in his third stint as defence minister in early Labor governments under Andrew Fisher.

The two met behind the Speaker's chair in the House of Representatives, where Pearce, a Senator, was keeping an eye on the passage of one of his Bills. 'As I made my report and request to him, Sir John Forrest was speaking from the opposition front bench against the Bill, and I was greatly impressed with the manner in which Mr Pearce was able to pay perfect attention to me while he kept one ear for the criticising voice within,' said Stoker.

In retrospect, the scene painted by Stoker is amazing: a defence minister and a submarine captain meet behind the Speaker's chair in parliament to negotiate the future deployment of a navy ship. After pitching his case to Pearce to take *AE2* back to Europe, Stoker sat in the House of Representatives gallery to listen to the parliamentary debate. He noticed a 'small, lynx-eyed' man sitting on the government frontbench. 'I was a considerable distance away, yet his personality seemed the outstanding one of the House,' said Stoker.

The man with the cat-like movement of the head was Billy Hughes, then Attorney-General, soon to become Prime Minister before splitting the Labor Party on the issue of conscription.

Like Hughes, Pearce was also expelled from the Labor Party, but remained as defence minister in Hughes's new Nationalist government. Hughes later nominated Pearce Australia's representative at the postwar Disarmament Conference.

Stoker's pitch to Pearce obviously worked. The Australian Navy Board cabled the Admiralty offering *AE2*'s services in what Stoker believed would be British home waters. The Admiralty accepted 'the generous offer with many thanks'. *AE2* was ordered to sail as soon as her refit was completed.

AE2 left Sydney for the last time in late December 1914. 'Passing between Sydney Heads, one could not help thinking of the extraordinary chance of life it was which, seven months after our arrival, should see us starting to retrace our long journey from England,' said Stoker. 'But naturally all hands were delighted at the prospect of getting into the main scenes of naval activity.'

In Melbourne, *AE2* linked up with ships carrying 15 000 men and 5000 horses of the second contingent of the AIF sent to the Middle East. The convoy stopped in Albany, Western Australia, before the long voyage across the Indian Ocean. Stoker's bar room mate from Sydney was a soldier on board one of the transports, and Stoker often thought of him during the long voyage.

Amazingly, *AE2* was the only warship accompanying the convoy, though one of the transports was fitted with cannons. The Admiralty believed that with the destruction of the *Emden*, the Indian Ocean was clear of enemy ships. Fortunately that proved right, although *AE2* had all her torpedoes ready for action despite being towed throughout the voyage.

After seven months in Australia, the long Indian Ocean crossing proved an ideal opportunity for the half Australian, half British crew to engage in good-natured banter about the relative merits of life in the two countries. Stoker listened as, on dogwatches smoking the night's last pipe, small groups would cluster on the tiny bridge to wage a 'wordy war'. For many of the British seamen nearing completion of their service this was no idle banter; many were already considering moving to Australia after the war, and they did.

'Generally speaking, the young Australian seaman is a better educated man than his English brother; but no figures of demand, supply, present and future market value etc, which the former seemed to have at his fingertips, could exonerate in the latter's eyes one indisputable and damning fact: that in Australia beer was dear,' said Stoker.

The best parting shot Stoker heard in the argument was the night one British seaman appeared to let his Australian opponent down lightly. Disappearing down the conning tower, the British seaman muttered,

'Ah, well, Australia has one good thing about it—it's a h——l of a long way from my old woman!'

The convoy arrived in Suez on 27 January 1915 as Turkish forces were attacking the canal from the east across the Sinai Desert. It rushed through, fearing an attack would trap it at the Red Sea end. Allied troops lining the canal cheered as the *AE2* and the troopships passed through. Calls from troops of the different Empire countries intrigued Stoker. 'The hoarse cheers of the English regulars changed to lighter and shorter tones as the Territorials were passed; the Australians and New Zealanders rivalled each other in "Coo-ees" and weird cries; while the Indian troops, from a long-drawn-out roar, changed in some cases to simple clapping of hands, making one feel for all the world inclined to bow, like the lady on the circus horse after her act.'

In Egypt, where *AE2* was to leave the troops, the little submarine notched up 48 000 kilometres in less than a year, a new record. But instead of the expected order to move to 'home waters', the Admiralty ordered Stoker to join the force gathering off the Dardanelles. While this may have been surprising to Stoker, in reality *AE2* had been sailing into the Dardanelles vortex from about midway across the Indian Ocean. On 13 January, as *AE2* and the convoy were approaching Colombo, the British War Council made a crucial, if somewhat unclear, decision. 'The Admiralty should prepare for a naval expedition in February, to bombard and take the Gallipoli Peninsula, with Constantinople as its objective,' said the War Council.

The Gallipoli exercise may have been a grand strategic vision, but its genesis in the War Council decision demonstrated all the amateurism which was to mark it as one of the great military tragedies for Britain and its Empire. For Turkey, of course, Gallipoli represented a great boost to national pride, with its beleaguered army (albeit with German assistance) beating off an invasion from two of the world's greatest powers, Britain and France.

How could a navy, as the War Council seemingly ordered, capture a peninsula and a city? From the Dardanelles Commission in 1917 to current day historians, the question has pointed to the basic flaw in the original decision. The wording, however, drives home the fact that Gallipoli began as a naval show. Only when it stalled through indecision did it become the costly and tragic army campaign that was to figure so much in the formative history of the new Australian nation. Had the navy shown more initiative, Gallipoli may have been quite a different story. But that is one of the many 'ifs' that, as Churchill noted, bedevilled the whole exercise.

In any era the Turkish Dardanelles, the waterway separating Asia and Europe and the gateway to Russia's winter ports, is an incomparable strategic prize. Never more so than in 1915, when it was the key to whether Turkey would side with the Triple Entente (Britain, France and Russia) or the Central Powers (Germany and Austria-Hungary), as well as being the vital route for Britain and France to deliver aid to an ailing Russia and open a new flank of the Central Powers.

Turkey's final siding with Germany was close run. The Young Turks, led by the trio of Enver Pasha, Talaat and Jemai, who deposed the repressive Abdul Hamid in 1908 in a bid to restore the greatness of the Ottoman Empire, actually hastened its demise: Bulgaria declared its independence, Austria seized Bosnia, Greece took Crete and Italy pounced on Libya. The trio, headed by the egocentric Enver, played off both sides in the lead-up to the outbreak of war.

The Germans, however, were far more astute than the Entente powers in pandering to the vanities and prejudices of the Young Turks, gradually building up their military advisory role. A German military mission under Colonel Liman von Sanders, destined to become the defender of Gallipoli, had arrived in Constantinople in December 1913. The Triple Entente protested, but to no avail. The new German battleship *Goeben* became a powerful signal of German might to the Turks when it arrayed itself in the Golden Horn in early 1914, ablaze with lights at night.

Britain and Turkey even held secret negotiations in the months before the Gallipoli invasion to secure passage of a naval force up the heavily defended Dardanelles Strait, closed by Turkey since October 1914. Britain was to pay Turkey four million pounds, but the talks came to nothing.

The clincher that pushed Turkey into the German camp was the British appropriation of two new battleships being built in England for Turkey, already named *Sultan Osman* and *Reshadieh*. The British action was understandable. Turkey was acting as a German satellite, laying mines in the strait the very day the ships were appropriated. But it was also high-handed. Turkey had planned to use the new ships to regain the islands of Lemnos, Imbros and Mitylene lost to Greece. The battleships had been largely financed by popular appeals, and Britain's seizure deeply wounded Turkish pride.

At the declaration of war on 4 August, the German battleship *Goeben* and her accompanying cruiser *Breslau* were in the Mediterranean. The Royal Navy tracked them, but declined to fire in the crucial hours just before the midnight deadline given to Germany not to invade Belgium or face war. The German ships slipped away, but turned up a few days later outside the Dardanelles Strait.

Enver was in conference with a German military commander when Lieutenant Colonel von Kress of the German embassy was ushered in. He demanded permission for the ships to enter the partially mined strait. Enver reportedly hesitated, no doubt aware of the consequences of such a move. Kress also wanted the Turkish forts to fire on the Royal Navy ships should they try to follow. Enver again hesitated, but when the Germans demanded an immediate answer, he consented.

Turkey had effectively entered the war on Germany's side, but a charade ensued. The Germans 'sold' the *Goeben* and *Breslau* to Turkey, even dressing up the German crew in fezzes. This was trumpeted as 'compensation' for the British seizure of the two Turkish warships.

At the Admiralty, Churchill, the First Lord, was all in favour of a British fleet forcing the Dardanelles to attack *Goeben* and *Breslau*. Asquith, the prime minister, rejected the idea, although a swift British attack might have won through before the Turks with German aid improved the defences of the forts along the shores of the strait. 'Not to persevere, that was the crime,' said Churchill after a subsequent British bombardment of forts in the strait on 3 November also was not followed through.

Churchill was right. But many in the Admiralty had feared that the navy might be 'duckworthed' if it fought its way up into the Sea of Marmara. (In 1807 a British squadron under Admiral Duckworth had made an opposed passage up the strait, but suffered casualties fighting its way out.)

* * *

In the initial months of the war, Turkey and the Dardanelles took a back seat to the momentous events on the Western Front. The war quickly bogged down into trench fighting with enormous carnage—the Allies suffered a million casualties in the first three months. Churchill and Lord Hankey, secretary of the British War Council, still harboured hopes of a Dardanelles diversion, and even Greece proposed a major landing, but to no avail.

That all changed in early January 1915, when Russia's Grand Duke Nicholas asked for a British 'demonstration' against Turkey to relieve the Russian forces battling a Turkish army in the Caucasus. This coincided with a paper circulated by Hankey to the War Council arguing that a strike against Turkey was opportune for three reasons—opening sea routes to Russia, drawing wavering European states like Greece, Romania and Bulgaria in on the Triple Entente side, and removing Turkey as a German ally. But the formidable Lord Kitchener, Secretary of State for War, made it clear that despite the Russian request no troops could be spared from the embattled Western Front.

Churchill, however, promoted a plan to use old battleships fitted with mine bumpers to force the Dardanelles Strait. He fired off some cleverly phrased questions to Admiral Carden, then in command of the squadron off the Dardanelles. Carden's initial reply that the Dardanelles 'might be forced by extended operations with large numbers of ships' was exactly what Churchill needed to secure support for a naval attack.

Carden's more detailed plan called for 12 battleships, 3 battle cruisers, 3 light cruisers, 16 destroyers, 6 submarines, 4 seaplanes, 12 minesweepers and other craft. These would bombard the forts, both from the strait and over the Gallipoli Peninsula, clear the minefields, and then advance into the Sea of Marmara. Churchill took the plan to the War Council on 13 January. Hankey gives a dramatic sketch of the scene that created the eventual Gallipoli disaster.

> The War Council had been sitting all day. The blinds were drawn to shut out the winter evening. The air was heavy and the table presented the rather dishevelled appearance that results from a long session. I was looking forward to the release from the strain of following and noting the prolonged and intense discussion. I suppose the councillors were as weary as I was. At this point events took a dramatic turn, for Churchill suddenly revealed his well-kept secret of a naval attack on the Dardanelles! The idea caught on at once. The whole atmosphere changed. Fatigue was forgotten. The War Council eagerly turned from the vista of a 'slogging match' on the Western Front to brighter prospects, as they seemed, in the Mediterranean. The navy, in which everyone had implicit confidence and whose opportunities so far had been few and far between, was to come into the front line. Even French [chief of the British expeditionary force in France] with his enormous preoccupations caught some of the general enthusiasm.
>
> Churchill unfolded his plans with the skill that might have been expected of him, lucidly but quietly and without exaggerated optimism.

It is easy to see why Churchill's naval plan won instant support. Here was a way to outflank Germany without diverting valuable troops from the Western Front. The navy would just barge its way into Turkey. It would be better than troops 'chewing wire' in France, and could see the entire Ottoman Empire, which in those days swept down to Egypt and included modern-day Syria and Iraq, fall into Allied hands.

Carden got his ships, including the new battleship *Queen Elizabeth*, whose mighty 15-inch guns could hurl shells right across the Gallipoli Peninsula into the forts along the strait. The little *AE2*, the most modern submarine in the area had just arrived in Egypt, and was pressed into service to join the older B class submarines already on station.

Churchill, however, was not without opponents. His First Sea Lord, Fisher, who had been brought in to replace Battenberg, walked out in

May 1915 over the Dardanelles campaign. 'You are just simply eaten up with the Dardanelles and cannot think of anything else,' the elderly Fisher wrote to Churchill. 'Damn the Dardanelles! They will be our grave!' Fisher's prophecy went unheeded for months until the troops were finally withdrawn in December.

The navy campaign in February 1915 got off to a bad start. Turkish fire from forts and mobile howitzers along the strait frightened off the first British minesweepers, initially North Sea fishing trawlers pressed into service. As the navy campaign geared up, even the army caught some of Churchill's Gallipoli enthusiasm, with Kitchener agreeing to send a force, although this was seen as only to assist the navy to clear the Gallipoli penisula and advance on Constantinople. The British 29th Division as well as the Australia and New Zealand Army Corps training in Egypt would be sent to the Greek island of Lemnos. Kitchener appointed Sir Ian Hamilton, 62, a general with literary talents, but lacking the initiative and drive to lead what was then the world's largest amphibious invasion.

Hamilton left London in a rush, with little more than out-of-date details on Turkish defences. But his appointment provides an interesting glimpse into the military belief that the new submarines might be the key to the Dardanelles action.

'Suppose one submarine pops up opposite the town of Gallipoli [at the top of the strait as it opens into the Sea of Marmara] and waves a Union Jack three times, the whole Turkish garrison on the peninsula will take to their heels and make a beeline for Bulair,' Kitchener assured Hamilton. His formal orders stressed that land operations were only to be contemplated if the navy failed to force the Dardanelles.

Incidentally, Kitchener's comment provides a revealing insight into the widespread belief that 'Johnny Turk' was spineless. The fighting on Gallipoli was to prove that wrong.

Churchill, meanwhile, pressed for faster naval action. Carden continued shelling the outer forts of the strait. Marine parties landed, putting many guns out of action. On 2 March Carden optimistically told the Admiralty that, with fine weather, he could be in the Sea of Marmara and advancing on Constantinople in about a fortnight.

Hankey claimed that this period in early March was the most cheerful in the War Council's history. One blot, however, was Russia's opposition to Greek forces also invading Turkey. The Russians wished to be the power that would occupy Constantinople, once won, and control the strait. Britain acquiesced, and this pandering to Russian expansionist dreams would cost Britain—and Australia—dearly.

Any War Council optimism vanished after the dramatic naval events of 18 March 1915. Carden had collapsed under the strain of command, and been replaced by his deputy, Vice-Admiral John Michael de Robeck, who had a stern, authoritarian manner, but turned out to lack the determination to carry through a fight. (Carden's appointment was symptomatic of the 'muddle through' mentality that marked much of the British planning for the Dardanelles campaign. He had been plucked from relative obscurity as the superintendant of the Malta dockyard. The obvious candidate, Admiral Limpus, who had led the British naval mission to Turkey and knew the most about defences of the Dardanelles, had been overlooked on the grounds of not offending the Turks. Limpus had left Constantinople when Turkey was still a neutral state, although heavily leaning towards Germany.)

De Robeck stuck to Carden's grand plan to sail just about his entire fleet into the strait to blast the Turkish forts to smithereens. Minesweepers would then clear away the mines, allowing the fleet to sail into the Sea of Marmara to threaten Constantinople into submission.

Unbeknown to the British navy the defenders had secretly laid a single line of mines parallel to the shore of Eren Keui Bay, on the Asiatic shore at the opening of the strait. This new minefield had gone completely undetected by the Allies in the days before the fleet's attack.

De Robeck's fleet, led by 18 British and French battleships and surrounded by destroyers, steamed into the mouth of the strait on 18 March. All went well at first, although the ships took some hits from shore guns. The French *Gaulois* was damaged, forced to retire and eventually beached. The British *Inflexible* was also forced out of line, but returned.

But the French *Bouvet* strayed into Eren Keui Bay, was struck by a mine, and sank in minutes. Almost her entire crew of more than 600 were lost. At first it was believed *Bouvet* had suffered a direct hit. It was not until later that existence of the new minefield was discovered. *Inflexible* was also struck by a mine near where *Bouvet* had sunk and began to list. *Irresistible* signalled she had been hit by a torpedo, and began taking heavy Turkish fire as well. The *Ocean* was also sunk. Minesweepers fled in the face of heavy Turkish fire.

De Robeck, of the old naval school that dreaded losing capital ships, decided to retreat. He had lost three battleships, and three more were badly damaged. Some 700 sailors and officers had been killed. That night de Robeck told his chief of staff, Roger Keyes, that he expected to be relieved of his command.

Far from it. Churchill wanted him to press on. His First Sea Lord, Fisher, had calculated on losing possibly 12 battleships in forcing the strait. But de Robeck had lost his nerve. Much to the surprise of the Turks and their German allies he did not resume the battle in the following days.

The tragedy of this was later revealed by Henry Morgenthau, the American ambassador to Constantinople. What de Robeck did not know was that Turkish defenders in the forts along the strait were almost out of ammunition, with no hope of new supplies. If the armada had returned quickly and renewed its pounding could it have got through?

Morgenthau wrote later that the Young Turk leaders were in a funk and preparing to evacuate Constantinople in advance of the expected arrival of the British fleet. George Schreiner, the Associated Press correspondent spoke to General Mertens, the chief technical officer defending the strait on 18 March, and reported him as saying: 'We expect that the British will come back early tomorrow morning, and if they do, we may be able to hold out for a few hours ... I should advise you to get up at six o'clock tomorrow morning and take to the Anatolian hills. That's what we're going to do.'

According to Morgenthau, the Allied armada had sailed away on the point of victory. With ammunition of the forts running out, it could well have cleared a channel through the mines and then dealt with the 1835 vintage guns up the strait north of the Narrows at Chanak (Canakkale).

'Thus, once having silenced the outer straits, there was nothing to bar the passage to Constantinople except the German and Turkish warships,' wrote Morgenthau later. 'The *Goeben* was the only first-class fighting ship in either fleet, and it would not have lasted long against the *Queen Elizabeth*. The disproportion in the strength of the opposing fleets, indeed, was so enormous that it is doubtful whether there would ever have been an engagement. Thus the Allied fleet would have appeared before Constantinople on the morning of the twentieth.'

Morgenthau reckoned the Young Turk leaders would have fled, while the population at large, glad to be rid of them, would have welcomed the Allied fleet. 'The Turks themselves were praying that the British and French would take their city, for this would relieve them of the controlling gang, emancipate them from the hated Germans, bring about peace, and end their miseries,' Morgenthau reported.

The failure of nerve of the Allied fleet under de Robeck is another of the great 'ifs' of the Gallipoli disaster, as Churchill called them. Many historians doubt that if the fleet had ploughed on the history of Gallipoli and perhaps the Great War would have been much different. The battleship *Queen Elizabeth* was specifically ordered not to pass the Narrows.

Now, while Australians and Britons refer to the Battle of Gallipoli, Turks also celebrate what has become known as the Battle of Canakkale, named after the town at the Narrows in the Dardanelles Strait (now called Chanak). Turkey's annual celebration of its great naval victory, when the huge Allied fleet withdrew after suffering major losses, signals the importance in Turkish eyes of the straits in the Gallipoli campaign.

A few days after the 18 March losses, and without renewing the attack, de Robeck met with General Hamilton and agreed on a joint army-navy effort. That set in train the disastrous 25 April landings and the huge loss of life involved in the eight-month invasion of the Gallipoli Peninsula.

From 18 March the navy took a back seat. The looming army invasion, however, brought into sharp focus the issue of whether a submarine could get up the Narrows to attack the Turkish defenders of Gallipoli from the rear by cutting off their vital sea supply lines.

4

'It's Got To Be Tried, and You Shall Do It'

On 14 April 1915, as the huge Allied army gathered on scores of ships in crowded Mudros Bay on the island of Lemnos off the Gallipoli Peninsula, Commodore Roger Keyes, chief of staff to Vice-Admiral de Robeck, summoned a conference of his submarine commanders. His question was direct: could a submarine get underwater through the tricky Narrows of the Dardanelles Strait into the Sea of Marmara to attack Turkish supply lines to Gallipoli?

Keyes went round the table. The first four submarine captains, with early B class submarines and their limited batteries, answered with a 'no'. The last to be asked was T. S. Brodie, captain of the recently arrived *E15*.

'Yes, I think it could be done,' said the normally shy Brodie, whose navy nickname was 'Dummy Head' Brodie. His twin brother, C. G. Brodie, Keyes' aide and a friend of Stoker, was known as 'War Head'. The identical Brodie twins were impossible to tell apart. When both commanded submarines, ratings would often report to the wrong captain. The two shared the 'telepathic harmony' of close twins, apart from common tastes in everything from music to game.

On hearing T. S. Brodie's confident assertion, Keyes jumped to his feet. 'Well, it's got to be tried, and you shall do it.'

In his book *Submariners V. C.*, Rear Admiral Sir William Jameson neatly outlined the Allies' dilemma as they contemplated a frontal invasion of the Gallipoli Peninsula. 'The Turkish forces were almost entirely dependent on seaborne traffic through the Marmara for their supplies; the nearest railway was several days march away along rough and narrow roads. A submarine in the Marmara could attack the enemy at a vital point.'

Beyond attacking supply lines to Gallipoli, submarines could threaten Constantinople, the Turkish capital, at the other end of the Sea of Marmara. Stoker, who was kicking his heels in Malta, waiting for repairs to *AE2* while the 14 April meeting took place, says all the submariners dreamed of leading an attack on Constantinople.

Humour over allotted tasks in the capture of this exotic capital ran high. 'The captain of the submarine was immediately to proceed in search of rare and priceless gems,' Stoker joked, recalling the high spirits of the moment. 'The second officer was to inspect the ladies of the harem, during which process the third officer would engage the Chief Eunuch in polite conversation. That the fall of Constantinople did not take place may partly be attributed to the lack of patriotism of the third officers of submarines, who, it is regrettable to have to record, showed a great distaste for the duty allotted to them.'

Blocking such fantasies was a serious obstacle—the formidable Narrows of the Dardanelles Strait. The Narrows resemble the twisted neck of an hourglass. The Dardanelles Strait runs for some 75 kilometres, linking the ends of the hourglass: the Aegean Sea and the inland Sea of Marmara. On the European side is the Gallipoli Peninsula, stretching out into the Aegean almost in the shape of a foot. On the other side is Asia Minor.

The natural defences of the strait are strong—a surface freshwater outflow current of 1 to 4 knots, a little-known underwater inflowing current of salt water, and the twisting Narrows, the bane of invaders for centuries. Only 360 metres wide at the narrowest point between Chanak and Kilid Bahr, naval historians have compared the Narrows with its 4 knot outflow to a river rather than a strait.

A second strait, the Bosporus, links the Marmara with the landlocked Black Sea. The straits have strong countercurrents, as all the submariners were to find to their peril. The countercurrent in the Bosporus was discovered, it is said, when a sultan flung an unwanted wife into the water, only to see her body reappear opposite his palace the next day.

The ancients knew the Dardanelles as the Hellespont. Invading armies cursed the Narrows, the slender yet treacherous dividing line between Europe and Asia. Both Xerxes and Alexander battled to cross it. Xerxes led his army across into Greece in 480 BC, spanning the water with a boat bridge. But storms and currents blew away the first two attempts. Herodotus wrote that Xerxes publicly butchered the engineers responsible, gruesomely placed the two sections of one individual either side of the bridge his army finally crossed, and then gave the Hellespont 300 lashes for daring to thwart the great king. Later, in 334 BC, Alexander used a string of boats to cross in the other direction, although many ancients believed bridging the waters would bring damnation.

The perils of the waters were legendary. Leander swam the strait from the Asian side to meet his lover, the priestess Hero, on the European side. One night, a strong sea washed him away. A despairing Hero jumped from her tower into the waters, to be also swept away. Shakespeare knew of the treachery of the waterway. His Othello likened his bloody thoughts to the Pontic Sea:

> Never Iago, like to the Pontic Sea
> Whose icy current and compulsive course,
> Ne'er feels retiring ebb, but keeps due on
> To the Propontic and the Hellespont.

Over the years the Turks had added man-made defences to the natural barriers of the Narrows. Even in the early days of the fifteenth century the castles guarding the narrowest point at Chanak could shoot cannonballs from one side to the other. By 1915 forts with heavy guns and mobile howitzers were strung along both sides of the mouth near the Aegean. From Kephez Point, the first turn before the Narrows, rows of mines were laid. The single line of mines secretly laid parallel to the Asia Minor coast had cut the Allied fleet apart on 18 March when it first tried to force the strait. Sweeping searchlights were ready to pick out any night attacker.

T. S. Brodie was not the first to believe a submarine could crack the Narrows despite the currents, forts and mines. Brodie, in fact, was reacting to a Stoker-inspired scheme to attack the Narrows in stages when he volunteered on 14 April 1915.

* * *

Even before Stoker's audacious scheme came to light submarines had shown their potential in the Dardanelles campaign. Allied submarines had been stationed off the entrance to the Dardanelles Strait since the German battle cruiser *Goeben* and the cruiser *Breslau* had escaped into the Sea of Marmara. The British *B9*, *B10* and *B11* together with the French *Faraday*, *Le Verrier*, *Coulomb* and *Circe*, patrolled the entrance to the strait.

The British B class submarines were, as Jameson described them, 'primitive ... poor sea boats on the surface and not very easy to handle submerged'. Built in 1907, they were only a few years removed from the original Holland submarines which entered service with the Royal Navy in 1901. Petrol-driven, their fumes often caused a form of narcosis among the small crew of 13, forced to sleep amongst the pumps and motors in the cramped interior.

There was no chance of a B class submarine making it under the minefields of the Narrows and into the Sea of Marmara. They did not have the battery power for such a long underwater journey. The steam-driven French submarines had even slimmer prospects. But both the French and British captains longed to get into the strait to attack something rather than spending their time on boring patrol at the entrance.

In December 1914, 26-year-old Lieutenant Norman Holbrook of *B11* was given his chance, with orders to attack Turkish shipping at Chanak, the town right at the Narrows. To do this he would have to take the primitive *B11* under the minefield from Kephez Point, surfacing at Chanak.

Equipped with improvised mine guards and jumping wires—lessons learned from British submarine actions in the North Sea—*B11* set off at

3 am on 13 December. As the Turkish searchlights switched off, Holbrook crept along the European coast at the mouth of the strait. But as he tried to submerge, the *B11* was hit by vibrations. Surfacing, Holbrook found that part of the improvised mine guard around the hydroplane had come loose. It had to be jettisoned. Crew members jumped into the water and struggled to unscrew the guard as dawn broke and Holbrook watched from his tiny conning tower. Surely they would be spotted in the growing light and fired upon?

Without the guard the hydroplane would hook any mine it encountered, spelling disaster. But Holbrook decided to take the risk, moving up the strait submerged, rising every 45 minutes to fix his position. At 8.30 am, nearing Kephez Point, he took the *B11* down to 24 metres and spent the next hour feeling his way under the minefield. The submarine was obviously swept along by the deeper inward-flowing current. When he took a periscope sighting Holbrook was surprised to find himself off Chanak. And there, about 1.5 kilometres away, lay an old Turkish battleship, the *Messudieh*, carelessly left at anchor.

Holbrook manoeuvred several times in the fast flowing current to get into a firing position. Fire! Although hit, the *Messudieh* quickly returned fire, with shells splashing around the *B11*. As the great battleship sank by the stern and stopped firing, *B11*, swept by the currents, ran aground.

Forward or reverse? If Holbrook gave the wrong order he could force the *B11* up the sandbank and expose her to fire. 'Hard a-port' he ordered, guessing correctly as the submarine moved off into deeper waters. But *B11* quickly grounded again, and with his compass fogged up Holbrook desperately needed a fix to aim for the mouth of the strait. Coming up, Holbrook sighted the open mouth. But without a compass, the *B11* had to surface frequently to check its position as it moved down through the minefield.

The crew ate dinner (washed down with a tot of rum) in fading light as the batteries wound down. Holbrook polished off a lobster given to him by one of his French submariner colleagues. After two hours of bobbing through the minefield and then under Turkish fort guns, *B11* surfaced to find herself near a British destroyer. Home again! The air inside the *B11* was so foul that the submarine needed ventilation before the petrol engines would even fire.

Holbrook instantly became one of the early heroes of the war. Awarded the Victoria Cross on 22 December 1914, his fame was such that in Australia the little town of Germantown in southern NSW, then somewhat nervous about its image, changed its name to Holbrook. The town now boasts an excellent submarine museum.

B11 had made it to Chanak at the start of the Narrows, but its limited battery power for underwater running meant that the B class had no chance of running the entire length of the Dardanelles Strait into the Sea of Marmara. But the newer E class had more powerful batteries, and Stoker's *AE2* was due to arrive off Gallipoli shortly, after escorting Australian troops to Port Said.

In the meantime, the French were determined not to be left out. The *Saphir*, one of the new 'jewel' class of French submarines equipped with larger batteries, arrived at the island of Tenedos (between Lemnos and the coast, and the original fleet base for the Allied ships) in January 1915. Its captain, Lieutenant de Vaisseau Henri de Fournier, was bursting to win the glory of the submarine race for the Narrows. Despite being ordered to simply patrol off the mouth of the strait, he headed directly up it towards Kephez Point, the minefield and the goal of the Marmara.

De Fournier managed to get under the minefield despite water pouring into *Saphir* from ominous leaks in the hull. But near Chanak, *Saphir* ran aground, apparently pushed off course by the currents. Refloated but out of control, *Saphir* plunged. With water pouring in from leaks and acid spilling out of batteries, de Fournier hit bottom at 220 feet [66 metres]. *Saphir*'s hull started to buckle from the pressure. De Fournier managed to surface, only to be hit by Turkish fire. The crew abandoned ship as the *Saphir* was scuttled. De Fournier and thirteen of his crew of 26 were swept away in the swirling waters.

A few weeks later, *AE2* arrived at Tenedos. With its new diesel engines, external 'saddle bag' ballasts, torpedo strength double that of

Above: Map showing the location of the Turkish prison camps. (SIMON DANCE)

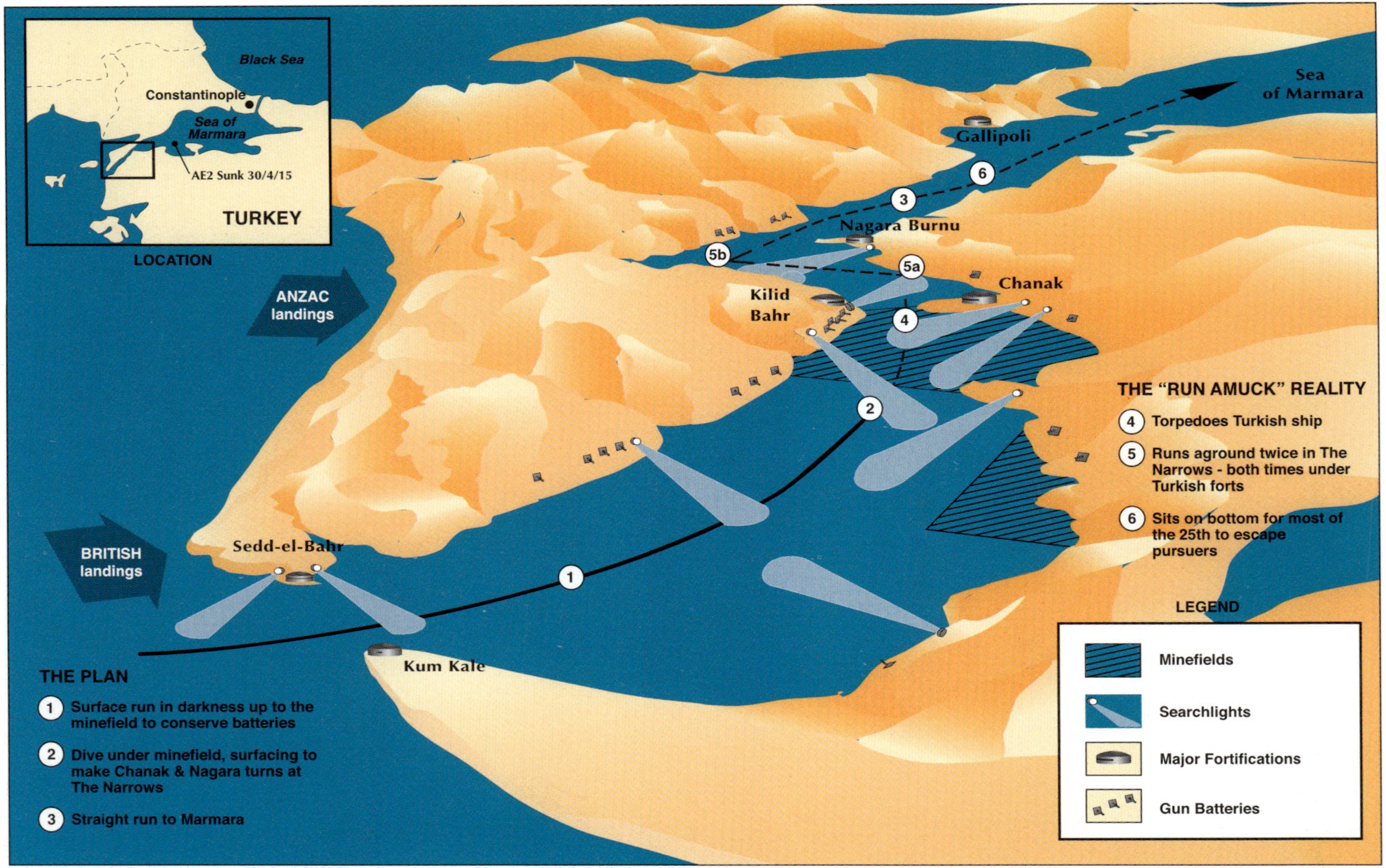

Above: Illustration of the Dardanelles offensive. (SIMON DANCE)

Above: Lieutenant Geoffrey Haggard, Captain Dacre Stoker and Lieutenant John Cary—growing beards in captivity.
(STOKER COLLECTION)

Above: AE2 in the Sea of Marmara. (CHARLES BRYANT; AUSTRALIAN WAR MEMORIAL, ART 09016)

Above: AE2 and the Turkish gunboat *Sultanhisar*.

(ARTIST UNKNOWN; NAVAL MUSEUM, ISTANBUL)

Above: Artist's impression of *AE2*'s Dardanelles journey. (ARTIST UNKNOWN; ROYAL NAVAL SUBMARINE MUSEUM, GOSPORT, UK)

ABOVE: *AE1* and *AE2* on arrival at Garden Island, Sydney NSW, 1914.
(RAN HISTORICAL COLLECTION, SYDNEY)

RIGHT: Selçuk Kolay admiring the *AE1* and *AE2* memorial window in the naval chapel at Garden Island, Sydney.
(DR MARK SPENCER)

RIGHT: Captain Stoker's niece Primrose Stoker, London, April 2000. (ELIZABETH BRENCHLEY)

LEFT: Selçuk Kolay, AO, the marine archaeologist who discovered *AE2*'s final resting place at the bottom of the Sea of Marmara. (ELIZABETH BRENCHLEY)

Above: October 1998: the discovery of the wreck of *AE2* on the floor of the Sea of Marmara. (DR MARK SPENCER)

Left: Touching the *AE2* for the first time in 83 years—the hatch left open by Captain Stoker. (DR MARK SPENCER)

the B class boats and larger batteries giving it a reach of about 80 kilometres underwater, the E class had a theoretical chance of running the Narrows.

With the fleet base moved to Mudros on Lemnos Island, Stoker and the *AE2* began routine patrols off the mouth of the strait. Stoker spent many hours contemplating the odds of a Narrows run. He came to the conclusion that there was sufficient chance of success to justify an attempt being made. It was not a popular view. 'The general opinion amongst officers present was that the feat was impossible; and a formal application to be allowed to make the attempt was not favourably received,' said Stoker.

The odds against success were high. Although the Es could dive for some 80 kilometres on battery power, theoretically enough to get through a 75-kilometre strait, the 1 to 5 knot outflowing current made an underwater journey doubtful. As well, the sets of the various bays along the strait made submarine navigation tricky, as the *B11* and *Saphir* had already found to their peril. Admiralty charts were hopelessly out of date. And then there were the mines and forts. Stoker also heard rumours that the Turks had brought an old bridge down from Constantinople and sunk it off Nagara Point, a few miles up from Chanak where the Narrows doglegs for the final straight run to the Sea of Marmara.

While on routine patrol watching the *Queen Elizabeth*, the newest and most powerful battleship in the Royal Navy, pound the Turkish forts with her 15-inch guns, Stoker refined his plan. The basic idea was to use darkness to run as far as possible on the surface up to the Kephez Point minefield to preserve battery power. *AE2* would then dive under the minefield, surface at Chanak to position itself through the Narrows, and run submerged to Nagara Point where another surface reading would be made to achieve that tricky turn before a final submerged run up the straight leg to Marmara. With luck, sufficient battery power would be conserved by the initial above-surface run to counter the effects of the outflow.

Stoker laid out his plan in a memo to G. C. 'War Head' Brodie of Admiral Keyes' staff. The letter concluded with Stoker's firm belief that 'the feat could be performed if one exercised the greatest possible care in navigation'. This was typical Stoker: nothing was impossible until it was shown to be so.

Stoker surveyed his completed memo with satisfaction. It really looked 'most convincing'. But, while Stoker was obviously pleased with himself, 'the gods were annoyed'. The night was unusually dark as *AE2* returned to Mudros. Thick, misty rain settled in. The *AE2* passed a French destroyer whose duty it was to flash that day's secret signal to enter the harbour, where the huge Allied fleet was gathering. Usually a light was positioned to show entering ships where to turn around Sangrada Point before entering the harbour. Unbeknown to Stoker it had been moved, and the French destroyer, for reasons unknown, failed to alert *AE2* as she passed.

'With no thought of disaster we held on our course, waiting the moment when the Sangrada light or its flare should be seen,' said Stoker. 'A glance at a watch showed that the time had nearly come, and we peered into the blackness. Does the darkness seem more dark there on the starboard bow? Let her come a point to port, Coxswain . . . is that the semblance of a filmy outline of land? By god! It is land—there are breakers! Hard s-starboard! Full speed astern! . . . CRASH!!!

'*AE2* was on the rocks. The Sangrada Point light was out.'

Stoker was in anguish. Waves lifted the little *AE2* and pounded it against the rocks. 'She seemed to cry out to her crew at the unfair cruelty of it,' he said. 'Was it for this she had carried us mile after mile roaming the world in record-breaking voyages? Was this the reward we offered? . . . To be the unwilling cause of great pain to a little child will produce very similar sensations.'

Careful navigation of the Narrows? 'And now look at the *AE2*,' lamented Stoker.

Help soon arrived, but attempts by a destroyer to pull *AE2* free failed. The submarine was taking water from leaks caused by crashing against rocks. 'The situation looked ugly,' reported C. G. Brodie, who was quickly on the scene.

Stoker ordered all but a few crew to jump to Brodie's nearby cutter.

It was risky, but it lightened the *AE2*. Then, as the wind subsided and the sea dropped away, the *AE2* with only Stoker and a few key crew aboard, was pulled free. Aboard the cutter, the rest of the crew cheered.

AE2 hobbled into Mudros for makeshift repairs. The damage, said Stoker, proved 'to be very serious', although the engine, propellers and rudder were all undamaged. Patchwork repairs would enable the *AE2* to get to fleet repair base at Malta.

Stoker was downcast. 'Hopes and ambitions [for a Dardanelles run] worked up slowly but surely through the weeks suddenly dashed,' he wrote. 'The imminence of the . . . main operations and landing of troops was known. Yet, we had to leave.'

It was little use, thought Stoker, to rail against the French destroyer for not warning *AE2* of the changed signals, or against the fickle goddess of fortune. 'She favour[s] the one who will come back smiling at her feet and woo her again,' he said.

In this Stoker was right. For in Malta the *AE2* acquired new equipment which was to stand her in good stead for the harrowing experience ahead.

* * *

It was while Stoker's *AE2* was in Malta that the great fleet off Gallipoli attacked the forts in the mouth of the Narrows on 18 March. Three battleships were sunk, the fleet limped away to lick its wounds, and Gallipoli became largely an army operation.

Missing the action was agonising enough, but Stoker and his crew were also caused much heartburn by the arrival in Malta en route to Gallipoli of three other E class submarines, all captained by submarine aces. Until then, Stoker had been king of the submarine castle off Gallipoli, the most senior captain with the most modern boat. The competition became intense with the arrival of *E11,* captained by Martin Nasmith, *E14,* captained by E. C. Boyle, and *E 15,* with T. S. 'Dummy Head' Brodie at the helm.

Of these three, Nasmith was unquestionably the top gun. A perfectionist, he tackled everything with seeming ease. The only criticism levelled at him was that he worked too hard. He had already devised instrumental aids to take some of the guesswork out of early submarine attack and had helped select the crews for the two Australian submarines before they sailed from England.

For Stoker, it was a case of the gods still appearing to be angry. With four E boats available, and three captains senior to him, the *AE2* was unlikely to be chosen 'when the long-awaited opportunity for work came'.

The arrival of the three new captains was not all bad news, however. They brought first-hand experience of North Sea submarine operations and called for new devices such as mine guards to be added to all the submarines, including *AE2*. 'It was a lucky chance we were able to receive this information before our own test came,' said Stoker.

Stoker shared a drink or two with his competitors in the officers mess, exchanging ideas on a Narrows run. Nasmith's *E11* was hit by mechanical problems, and was delayed in Malta with Stoker as Boyle and Brodie sailed for Gallipoli.

'Dangerous work ahead,' thought Stoker. 'It idly crossed my mind to wonder what fate had in store for the four commanding officers. Two months later I knew the answer. It was death for one; three and a half years of living death for another; and Victoria Crosses for the other two.'

Immediately *AE2* was repaired it set sail for Mudros. Stoker learned that Brodie in *E15* had failed in the first E class attempt on the Narrows. *AE2*'s crew were awarded a commendation and leave for their work in escorting troops to the Middle East, but the leave was postponed until the first opportunity—in this case several years.

* * *

In Mudros, the impending invasion meant pressure was mounting on the navy to get a submarine into the Marmara to disrupt Turkish supply lines to Gallipoli. Various tactics were canvassed. Destroyers might make a diversionary attack to help a submarine sneak through the Narrows. Aircraft could reach up the strait to Nagara Point, but their bombing capacity to create a diversion was doubtful.

Such were the pressures behind Commodore Keyes' summons to his submarine commanders, including the recently arrived Brodie and Boyle with their newer Es, to the fateful 14 April conference aboard *Queen Elizabeth*.

As his aide, G. C. Brodie, outlined what he later conceded was essentially Stoker's plan for the initial night surface run, Keyes posed the critical question to his captains: 'Do you think an E boat can make it?' T. S. Brodie's electrifying 'yes' set the scene for some serious planning.

T. S. received exceptional support in his preparation. A plane flew him over the Narrows so he could obtain a bird's-eye view of the 'jumps' along his planned course. *E15* was packed with food and gear for a three-week voyage. A former British vice-consul at Chanak was inducted into the navy and placed on board to act as an interpreter and to help identify marks on shore. As Brodie was about to depart on the morning of 16 April a personal message arrived from Winston Churchill, the First Lord of the Admiralty.

'I wish you God speed in your gallant enterprise,' Churchill wrote. 'Damn hot air,' said Brodie when he read it. 'We ought to be off,' he told his twin. Passing out of Mudros, *E15* was cheered by Australian troops crammed aboard an incoming liner.

While his twin brother battled the Narrows, C. G. Brodie spent a restless night. At daylight, shortly before he was due to fly in a Farman two-seater biplane to bomb Chanak as a distraction, C. G. Brodie claimed 'T. S.'s serenity passed to me'. Stoker believed this was a telepathic message at the moment of his twin's death.

As C. G. flew at 1800 metres he looked down on a beach near Kephez Point, spotting what looked like a grey straw at right angles to the line of the shore and a black straw at an acute angle beside it. 'I knew them for *E15* with thin oily smoke coming up from her conning tower, and a Turkish torpedo boat already investigating,' he said. 'I realised it was failure, and for *E15* final. I was conscious of disappointment, but, oddly, not surprise. It was as if I'd already known she could not succeed. Yet I had no anxiety for T. S. I knew beyond argument all was well with him.'

T. S. had stuck to the plan of going as far as possible in the darkness of early hours up to the Kephez minefield before diving. All seemed to be going well until *E15* tried to surface. The submarine was apparently caught in the changing layers of fresh and salt water and hit a bank. The current caught the bow, exposing the conning tower right under the guns of Fort Dardanos on the Asiatic shore below Kephez Point.

The Turks opened fire. A shell smashed into the conning tower, killing Brodie. Escaping clouds of chlorine gas suffocated six crew. *E15* was holed and unable to escape. But the Allies could not allow the submarine to fall into enemy hands. Destroying *E15* became a mission in itself. Destroyers and other submarines, one with G. C. Brodie aboard, made valiant efforts to sink her but were driven off by Turkish fire. The *B6* submarine was almost lost making another attempt before picket boats armed with torpedoes finally blew up the evacuated *E15*.

* * *

A few days later, on 21 April, *AE2* returned to Mudros after its refit. Stoker was amazed at the transformation of this once sleepy Greek port. 'There were a fair number of ships present when we had left, but now such a vast concourse were assembled as never before had met the eye,' he said. 'Battleships, cruisers, destroyers, submarines, aeroplane depot ships, and transports—multitudes of transports—filled every hole and corner of the huge harbour.'

Although the Allied landing was only four days away, the failure of *E15* cast grave doubts on any new bid to crack the Narrows underwater. With *E15* and *Saphir* lost, would the navy brass risk another submarine? Boyle's *E14* was ready, fully provisioned and stored awaiting orders. Stoker, recorded Rear Admiral Jameson in his book *Submariners V. C.* was 'burning with enthusiasm'. *AE2*, however, had had no opportunity for a shakedown after its refit, which had required three weeks in dock.

'Two days elapsed, days electric with anticipation for fleets and armies,' said Stoker as he also waited for a call. Admiral de Robeck faced a dilemma. Although he had lost two submarines already, the impending land invasion made it imperative to attack Turkish supply lines from any angle. He knew Stoker had worked up a plan to crack the Narrows, and summoned him to *Queen Elizabeth*, his flagship.

'An interesting psychological moment,' Stoker wrote. 'I should like to have a record of my thoughts as the steamboat carried me to the flagship. When one's heart is set on a thing it is not often that it comes within grasp . . .'

Keyes met him to take him to the admiral. The advance news was good. De Robeck and Keyes had two questions: did Stoker still believe it possible to dive through the Narrows, and, if so, was he still willing to make the attempt? 'Yes,' Stoker replied to both.

De Robeck quizzed Stoker on how he proposed to overcome the hazards of the passage. 'He found it difficult to believe the feat was possible, but its military value would be so great it must be tried,' said Stoker. 'If we got through, other boats would immediately be sent to follow.'

De Robeck then gave Stoker a farewell line that fairly lifted the Australian submarine captain's feet off the ground. Wishing him well, the fleet admiral said, 'If you succeed there is no calculating the result it will cause, and it may well be that you will have done more to finish the war than any other act accomplished.'

It was the remark of a man under pressure for the Gallipoli diversionary campaign to succeed. It showed his grandiose version of the stakes involved: if Russia could be relieved, Turkey removed from the war and Germany attacked on its flank, the stalemate in the trenches in France might be broken.

Two hours later, with no overhead surveillance flight and no personal farewell from Churchill, Stoker was piloting the hastily provisioned *AE2* out through the crowded Mudros harbour. De Robeck and Keyes waved *AE2* farewell from their quarterdeck on *Queen Elizabeth*.

The two hours had been packed with drama. Stoker spoke to the entire crew: they were volunteers on this mission; no man would be ill thought off if he decided not to go. None declined. All the crew wrote what might be their last letters to their families. Stoker packed an extra large white ensign to advertise the presence of a British sub should *AE2* make it through to the Marmara. Also into the provisions went a case of port—a sign of Stoker's optimism for the mission.

By comparison with the sophisticated planning of today's military ventures, *AE2*'s departure was breathtaking in its speed. For a submarine assignment that could last weeks, *there were only two hours from orders to departure*. *AE2* had no exit strategy, and no orders beyond harassing Turkish supply lines. What would it do if it succeeded in achieving its goal?

No such doubts entered the minds of the excited crew as they sheltered beside a destroyer near the mouth of the Dardanelles Strait, waiting for the moon to execute the plan of a surface run up to the minefields before diving.

Fortune this time seemed to favour Stoker's *AE2*. At 7 knots the submarine crept up the centre of the strait. Turkish searchlights swept across the water. 'As we drew nearer and yet nearer to the white cliffs it seemed as if progress on the surface must soon be stopped if we were to remain undiscovered,' Stoker worried. 'And then the goddess smiled. The light on White Cliffs sputtered and went out; we crept along with renewed sense of security.'

Another piece of luck—the Kephez Point searchlight was suddenly extinguished. 'What tremendous fortune,' exulted Stoker. 'We could now in safety follow our surface route right up to the main minefield.' The *AE2* crept on until Stoker sighted what he believed was the Suandere River on the southern shore. *AE2* had travelled further on the surface than he had dared to hope.

Suddenly an arc of light from the Kephez searchlight shot out again. 'To remain on the surface meant instant discovery,' thought Stoker, ordering the submarine to dive and closing the conning tower. But as Stoker clambered below, disaster struck. The shaft that worked the foremost diving rudder broke. It was impossible to repair without several hours work. Stoker had little choice but to return to base.

'Go back!' he cried. 'Ye gods! After all this; after all the working up to this moment; with a work before us that might have a bearing on the finish of the war; a chance of a lifetime—no, of centuries of lifetimes—

before us, and we must turn back! The hills and mountains of the Dardanelles echoed and re-echoed with the ironical laughter of that cursed goddess of fortune.'

But there was no alternative. The submarine had to be saved. Stoker turned it around and headed home, retracing his steps to the open sea. In the early light of dawn *AE2* passed the entrance of the strait and rejoined the patrolling destroyers.

It was only as they drew into Mudros that the anticlimax really set in for Stoker and the crew. 'To the feelings of disappointment you have ever felt, add those of which you have ever read or heard; again add all that your imagination can conjure—and perhaps you may arrive at a result approaching our feelings then,' he wrote. 'But I doubt it.'

To their credit, Stoker and his crew lost little time cursing their bad luck. They quickly repaired the broken shaft and that afternoon took a short dive to ensure it was working. Within a few hours they were again ready for the Narrows. But would they be given a second chance?

5

'Run Amuck!'

As he climbed the quarterdeck of the *Queen Elizabeth* to report his failed mission to Admiral de Robeck, an embarrassed Stoker felt that if he had a tail it most certainly would have tripped him up. His daring plan to crack the Narrows and cut Turkish sea supply lines to Gallipoli had failed at the first hurdle.

The Allied invasion of the beaches was only a few hours away. Was it too late for a second attempt?

'It was very bad luck,' de Robeck said, his kindness surprising Stoker. 'You did well to get so far. Try again tomorrow. If you succeed in getting through there is nothing you could possibly want that we won't do for you.'

Try again! Stoker's heart leapt.

But the orders for the second attempt suddenly changed. Dawn would bring waves of Allied soldiers landing on the Gallipoli Peninsula. British and French battleships would be in the entrance of the strait supporting the landings. With memories of the disastrous naval attack of 18 March still fresh, naval command was anxious to prevent the Turks launching mines that would float down into the fleet.

So, instead of just getting through the Narrows undetected and into the Marmara to attack supply lines, the *AE2* was ordered to attack any mine-dropping ships seen along the way.

'In fact,' said Commodore Roger Keyes, de Robeck's chief of staff, 'generally run amuck at the Narrows—if you get there.'

It was a foolish order that turned *AE2*'s assignment more into a suicide mission than a serious bid to get behind Turkish supply lines. But it was typical of Keyes. '"Offensive operations", not to say "stunts", interested him more than the routine work of a Chief of Staff,' said one staffer, who likened Keyes to Nelson in his love of danger and greed for glory. (Keyes went on to become Director of Combined Operations in World War II.)

Stoker at first burst out laughing at Keyes' doubtful 'if you get there'. But the sheer danger of the new order soon wiped the smile from his face. Cracking the Narrows submerged was a feat no submarine had yet managed. Now Keyes also wanted *AE2* to undertake combat duties in an extremely hazardous area.

'If you searched the whole world over I doubt you would find a much more unpleasant spot to carry out a submarine attack than this Narrows of Chanak,' Stoker wrote. 'Half a mile wide, with a current of 3 to 5 knots, it is certainly not an ideal place for manoeuvres in a comparatively slow-moving and difficultly turned submarine. Also, the thought that we ourselves might meet one of those floating mines hardly added to the entertainment the day was likely to provide for us.

'However, we were either going to get through or else we were not, and at this stage an extra difficulty or so did not make very much matter.'

It was another straw in the wind for Stoker. While he accepted it in his usual derring-do style, he admitted years later that 'this new order was going to have a far-reaching effect on our after life'.

Stoker repeated the previous night's routine: leaving Mudros about midnight and waiting outside the straits for the moon to set. His plan was the same—to go as far as possible on the surface while undetected to preserve battery power, before diving under the minefield.

About 2.30 am on 25 April 1915, as the Anzac troops were being shuffled from ships to landing barges to edge towards the coast, *AE2* entered the Dardanelles Strait. The sea was dead calm. *AE2* crept slowly along, trying to get as close as possible to the European shore without being spotted by the searchlights sweeping the waters. Several times an arc of light swept across the submarine but she sailed on undetected.

'Each time, as a beam of light touched the *AE2* with brighter and yet brighter finger, one held for the instant one's breath, lest the steady sweep, arrested for a moment, would show a suspicion of our shadowy presence,' said Stoker.

Then the shore battery of guns near the Suandere River picked up the submarine, and bang, a shell swished past Stoker's head on the tiny bridge. 'Mighty close,' commented Stoker, who immediately took the *AE2* down to periscope depth (6 metres) before diving to gain a passage under the main minefield.

Once under, the experience was chilling. 'The rappings and scrapings on the hull of the boat by the mooring wires of the mines, held taut by the buoyancy of the mines themselves overhead, seemed almost damnably continuous,' said Stoker. While the submarine should have been fairly safe below the minefield, there was always the chance that one of the wires would catch on the hull, bringing a mine crashing down.

Once completely under, with no periscope sighting to guide it, the *AE2* was blind. In 1915 sophisticated radar and sonar underwater guidance systems had not been invented. Submerged beneath a minefield in unknown swirling currents, the *AE2* was like a drunk staggering through a deadly obstacle course.

'Choose a wrong moment to rise for observation through the periscope and you choose a moment to hit a mine—so choose as few of these moments for observation as possible. Feel as safe as you care to when well submerged, and do not think of the result should one of the wires, catching a projection of the boat's side, drag its mine, with a bang, down on top of you.'

The *AE2* blundered along. Twice something harder than the wires hit the bows and bumped their way down *AE2*'s side. 'With extreme discomfort one presumed that they were mines failing to explode,' Stoker said.

Suddenly, an equally mysterious object seemed to catch up forward. It knocked insistently on the starboard side. 'For several minutes we all listened to it in uneasy silence before it broke away, tapped along the side, and followed the rest of our enemies astern.'

It was gut-wrenching for the crew. Seaman Charles Suckling later described it as 'an experience never to be forgotten'. Some of the crew started a card game to relieve the tension. But the players found it hard to concentrate with the constant scrapings of mine wires along the side of the hull. One crewman counted the 18 times that mine wires scraped *AE2*.

Twice Stoker risked surfacing for a periscope glance and was surprised to find how far the *AE2* had progressed. On his third rise at about 6 am Stoker found the *AE2* was through the minefield, abreast Chanak and only some 270 metres below the elbow of the Narrows. Clearly the deeper saltwater inflow was stronger than anticipated.

So as the Anzacs were trying to scale the cliffs of Gallipoli, and the Turks were beginning a desperate defence, Stoker's *AE2* found itself directly behind enemy lines.

To comply with Keyes's 'run amuck' command, Stoker had to mount a 'demonstration' off Chanak rather than moving directly up the Narrows. This meant keeping his periscope up, exposing the submarine's position in the flat oily calm. Shells rained in immediately.

'The shock of projectiles striking the water overhead caused subdued thuds in the submarine, whilst sounds as of hailstones were presumably caused by shrapnel bullets falling through the water on the boat's deck,' said Stoker. 'Around the top of the periscope, the water, lashed into white spray, caused a curiously pretty effect, but added little to the ease of taking observations.'

Further unease was caused by the appearance of Turkish craft trying to ram *AE2*'s periscope. Stoker sighted an old Turkish battleship hulk, perhaps used for laying mines, and decided to attack. Just then a smaller cruiser hurried out from behind the battleship. 'Now this was identically the kind of vessel that would be fitted as a mine-dropper, and from the course she was following it seemed most likely she was endeavouring to drop mines across our bows,' he said. 'Obviously a better quarry, and getting the sights on at a range of 300 yards [270 metres] I fired a bow torpedo at her.'

The cruiser was later identified as one of the '*Paik-e-Shevket*' class. With a destroyer closing in attempting to ram the *AE2* on the port side, Stoker ordered the *AE2* down to 21 metres at the moment of firing. 'A last glance as the periscope dipped showed the destroyer apparently right on top of us, and then, amidst the noise of her propeller whizzing overhead, was heard the big explosion as the torpedo struck.'

Stoker had another urgent concern—swerving to avoid hitting the sinking cruiser. At the same time he was acutely conscious of not straying off course in the narrow, fast-running channel. He tried to move back to the centre of the strait, rising to gain another observation.

But at 12 metres the *AE2* hit the bank of the eastern shore. It began sliding up to a depth of just 3 metres, clearly exposing the entire bridge and conning tower above water. The *AE2* had managed to land right under the guns of a Turkish fort!

Stoker looked in horror through the periscope. 'As I looked, one of the guns fired, apparently right into my eye, and seemingly so close that I involuntarily jumped back from the eyepiece of the periscope.'

The *AE2* was grounded—the very fate that had befallen Brodie's *E15* only a few weeks earlier. 'With the boat apparently fast aground and a continued din of falling shell, the situation looked as unpleasant as it well could be—suspiciously like the end of the story,' said Stoker.

It seems the *AE2* was only saved from being blasted out of the water by the fact that it was so close to the big guns they could not sufficiently depress to hit her!

For five minutes—an 'eternity of time' said Stoker—the crew worked frantically to refloat her. 'Surely the other forts and ship must have made very bad shooting to miss this standing target,' commented Stoker.

The frantic efforts worked as *AE2* began sliding down the bank, refloating to 21 metres underwater but pointing down the strait towards home. 'It would have been so comfortable to go,' said Stoker. With propellers of chasing craft whishing overhead, Stoker attempted to turn *AE2* around in the confined strait to point her back up towards the Narrows.

Crash! From 21 metres the *AE2* hit another bank and began sliding upwards to just 2.4 metres. 'Where on earth are we now,' groaned Stoker. In the attempt to reposition her, the *AE2* had slid right across the narrow Strait and amazingly run up the bank on the opposite side—

again right under a Turkish fort! Stoker wryly noted the *AE2*'s 'apparent liking for forts'.

The *AE2*'s new predicament was even worse than the first grounding. This time it was *stern* first up the bank under a Turkish fort, exposing the propeller to possible damage.

'A quick glance around showed a gunboat and some destroyers, little more than a hundred yards off, blazing hard with all their broadsides, a cluster of small boats which we guessed were picking up the survivors of the sunk cruiser, and then, best of all, a clear view up the strait showing that if we could only get off we were heading on the correct course,' said Stoker.

Able Seaman J. H. Wheat found the new predicament of the *AE2* 'indeed alarming'. 'We could hear the shells striking the water and bursting outside,' he said. Stoker told the crew to remain calm, although how anyone could do so in such a situation boggles the mind. 'During all this the captain remained cool, for all depended on him at this stage,' Wheat later wrote. 'It is due to his coolness that I am now writing this account. Nobody knows what a terrible strain it is on the nerves to undergo anything like this, especially the captain, as all depends on him.'

Full steam ahead, both motors, Stoker ordered. The submarine began to shake and move down the bank, although ominous aft noises sounded like the propeller was being mashed. As *AE2* slithered away, the crew heard two great bumps. But the sub then moved underwater to 9 metres, having been exposed, Stoker guessed, for about four minutes.

Reporting to the Admiralty after the war, Stoker heaped praise on his crew. 'In these two highly dangerous situations it was only their cool and intelligent performance of their duties which enabled the vessel to be refloated.'

Still, Stoker considered the second escape 'little short of miraculous'. The enemy had lost an easy chance of destroying the *AE2* by ramming it while it was aground, he said. 'But presumably they imagined they had us safe,' he concluded.

Not for the moment, at least. At 21 metres depth Stoker took aim for Nagara Point, which marks the turning and widening of the strait, and headed off. Stoker feared that the severe bumps might have caused leaks in the ballast tanks, which could cost him diving control. But all seemed well. If only he could see where he was going! After a spell, Stoker decided to rise to 6 metres to get his bearings.

Nagara Point, where Leander had swum to meet his lover, Hero, on the opposite shore, was dead ahead. This was the last navigational obstacle for the *AE2*, involving a sharp right turn before the straight run up to the Sea of Marmara.

With the posse of Turkish destroyers, a gunboat, tugs and smaller craft, closing in, Stoker snatched an accurate fix of his position and dived back to 21 metres just as a destroyer attempted to ram *AE2*.

How to round Nagara completely submerged? Stoker would have preferred another periscope sighting as he neared the bend. But the danger of a third grounding while nearing the surface, combined with the swirling currents at that point and the pursuing Turks, led Stoker to gamble on attempting the turn without another periscope fix.

The gamble paid off. When Stoker rose to 6 metres, Nagara Point was well aft and the *AE2* was heading into the wider reaches of the strait up to the Marmara. Even as Stoker looked, the periscope was sighted and the chase resumed, with shells again whistling by. 'The damnable calmness of the water did not permit of even the shortest spell of observation without the periscope being seen.'

Stoker kept *AE2* at 21 metres and aimed directly up the strait, rising after 45 minutes to see if he had shaken off the pursuers. 'But no such luck—the chasseurs were still in close attendance, so close indeed that the fear arose that we might have caught an observation net and be now towing a tell-tale buoy above our heads all the time we thought to be hidden by the friendly waters.'

Although Stoker could not see any such buoy through the periscope, he sighted something even more disturbing. Just ahead in the *AE2*'s path were two Turkish tugs with a wire stretched between them. *AE2* was headed directly into a trap!

Stoker immediately veered to starboard and dived deeper. This gave him time to consider the *AE2*'s situation. With 32 kilometres or so to go before the comparative safety of the Sea of Marmara, Stoker contemplated the *AE2*'s chances given the combination of pursuers and wire nets.

'The longer we remained in their unpleasant company the more chance was there of some ordinary diving accident forcing us to the surface and to instant destruction,' he concluded. 'Had we caught an observation net our end was certain in any case, and so it was delaying the inevitable to go on.'

With batteries running low, Stoker decided on the submariner's ploy of just lying on the bottom. He turned at right angles and headed for the Asiatic shore, where he believed the bank shoaled slightly.

Approaching at dead slow speed, the *AE2* grounded and rested at about 21 metres depth. Stoker and crew aimed to hide until night when the boat could surface to recharge its batteries. It was about 8.30 am, a few hours after the Anzac landing and the time of desperate fighting on the Gallipoli ridges.

But there was to be little rest for *AE2*'s crew. Stoker called this 'the most anxious period of the day', which after the trauma of minefields and two groundings, shows the extraordinary levels of stress that had built up.

The foul air on board was also thickening. The *AE2* had been submerged for many hours without a chance to rid the boat of its stifling diesel fumes. The crew was uncertain the *AE2* had not snagged a telltale net or buoy, and as Stoker noted, any intelligent sweeping operation would catch them as the bay they had chosen was one of the few places a submarine could hide.

Stoker ordered the crew to get some sleep. Wheat said they were all dead tired, having been up all the previous night preparing the *AE2* for its second run up the Narrows. One crewman was instructed to watch the diving gauge to ensure *AE2* did not slip to dangerous depth, and to report any outside noises.

Sleep, however, was difficult. After an hour a ship passed overhead with an accompanying knock on the *AE2*'s hull as something hit and jumped over it.

Other ships began passing at regular intervals, with the sound of their propellers echoing through the *AE2*. The watchman certainly did not need to make any 'reports' as all the crew were wide awake. They dubbed 'Percival' a single screw ship that regularly passed overhead, obviously searching for the *AE2*. 'Percival's repeated passages were trying on the nerves, and the fact that we were well out of the track of ships following their ordinary course up and down the strait proved that Percival and his friends were searching for us,' said Stoker.

After a few hours of nerve tingling, Stoker decided to move to another hiding spot. The crew was assembled and Stoker led the men in prayers. After all, it was a Sunday, and as Stoker noted, supposedly a day of peace.

After prayers, the crew went to their diving stations. But instead of lifting off, the *AE2* continued to slide down the bank to what Wheat called 'a great depth'. The *AE2*'s diving gauge was limited to 30 metres, supposedly the limit of water pressure that the hull could safely sustain. 'On this occasion our gauge was hard over and the needle of the gauge bending [beyond the 30-metre limit] so we did not know what depth we went to, but it was a very close call,' said Wheat.

The bumps from the second grounding had apparently so strained the *AE2* that two of the ballast tanks were leaking. Air pressure in the tanks was used to expel the water. Stoker decided that the only course remaining was to go astern, trying to shift the *AE2* back up the bank.

The *AE2* pulled itself up the mud to a depth of about 24 metres where Stoker decided to remain until darkness allowed a bid for the surface and a chance to recharge batteries and adjust the ballast tanks. 'To regain control without coming to the surface was most difficult,' said Stoker. 'We made several attempts unsuccessfully, and then, perforce, had to resign ourselves to remaining where we were, helpless, until darkness came.'

The next few hours were harrowing. The stricken *AE2* lay in mud as Percival and other pursuers passed overhead at regular intervals. 'We didn't need smelling salts to keep us awake,' said Wheat.

This is one of the few times that Stoker admitted to anything like fear. 'Have you ever known time move more slowly?' he recalled. 'Can you imagine the speed it had for us? Percival passed and repassed at steady intervals. Some of the crew—lucky creatures—succeeded in going to sleep. Attempted jokes as to Percival's appearance fell mighty flat. The few moments immediately after his passing were the bad ones. If any sweep he was dragging after him caught up, the side of our boat would be blown in on us very soon afterwards. As the day wore on, lying in my bunk, I will most unashamedly confess to a feeling of quivering funk each time he passed overhead.'

Percival's regular visits stopped about 6.45 pm. For some ten hours its regular passing had terrorised the *AE2*'s crew. Some two hours later Stoker decided to surface.

Twice the boat attempted to get underway but stopped when a loud swishing noise could be heard. Wheat said the crew suspected that a net or wires had been laid over the *AE2* during the day. After considering this for a while, another opinion was that the noise was made by the wash on the shingle on the bottom. Stoker ordered the *AE2* up, and on surfacing found that nothing was wrong.

Having been submerged for 16 hours, the crew was desperate to breathe some fresh air. It was a bright, moonlit night overhead. No enemy ships were in sight. As he prepared to open the hatch, Stoker warned the crew they would feel pressure on their ears, but not to take any notice of it. As the hatch opened and fresh air swelled in, a thick white mist caused by the bad air rose off everything inside the submarine.

'The crew swarmed on deck eager for the clean night air, after having passed the only twenty-four hours of their life without a sight of the light of God's day,' said Stoker. Wheat reported that it was delightful not only to breathe fresh air but to also have a smoke.

No smoking was allowed on the bridge as a light could give away *AE2*'s position. So men were forced to smoke inside the boat at the bottom of the conning tower. Wheat said it was 'not too bad' as in that location the diesel engines were drawing fresh air down and aft, so a match could be lit. But slightly forward of the conning tower the air was so bad that a match could not burn for more than a fraction of a second.

The *AE2* was about 800 metres from the Asiatic shore, off marshy swampland. This made it safe from a shore sighting. But Stoker needed about four hours on the surface with the motors running to recharge batteries.

As the submarine lay on guard against tracking Turkish ships, Stoker decided to signal fleet command that he had cracked the Narrows. This was crucial information. If the *AE2* could make it, others would follow to destroy Turkey's sea supply lines to Gallipoli and threaten Constantinople.

Telegrapher William Falconer flashed the signal out in the longs and shorts of Morse code. But there was no answering call. 'Obviously there was something the matter with our receiving instruments, and possibly with the send too,' lamented Stoker. Falconer checked and rechecked his Marconi wireless set. All he could do was send out the signal again in the hope that some Allied ship would pick it up.

With the sounds of the big naval guns off the Allied landing beaches echoing up the strait to where the *AE2* lay, this was a very frustrating moment for Stoker and the crew. Knowledge of *AE2*'s feat could prove crucial to the success of the invasion. If *AE2* had not succeeded it would have been the third submarine loss in attempts to penetrate the Dardanelles Strait. After three losses, it was doubtful that any further submarines would be risked.

As Sunday turned to Monday, rain began to fall. A thick, heavy fog formed around the charging *AE2*. But the rain and dark hid it from a passing ship, and Stoker decided not to stop recharging. Sighting of three small torpedo boats, however, caused him to pause, but they passed without incident.

About 3.30 am on 26 April, with the weather cleared and the moon well down behind the hills of the Gallipoli Peninsula, Stoker ordered readjustment of the *AE2*'s lost diving trim. The submarine moved slowly along the surface up the strait towards its final goal of the Sea of Marmara. As dawn began to render *AE2* visible, Stoker dived.

Through the periscope and dawn's greyness, Stoker sighted two men-of-war approaching. 'The leader, as far as I could see in the bad light, was the smaller; both had two funnels,' said Stoker.

As the white wash of the periscope made it easy to spot in the morning calm, Stoker took the submarine completely under. He steered what he calculated was a parallel and opposite course to the enemy ships, and judging the *AE2* to be in torpedo range, hoisted the periscope.

'Right abeam was a ship, looking mighty big at a range of 500 yards [457 metres], and I jumped to the conclusion that she was the second, or rearmost ship,' said Stoker. 'The bearing for firing the port torpedo was on, and we fired. The ship dodged, the torpedo passed ahead of her; and then, looking around I found to my disgust I had fired at the smaller of the two ships, a cruiser. The other, a battleship—either the *Barbarossa* or *Turgood Reis*—was following, but it was now too late to bring any of the other tubes to bear with good chance of the torpedo hitting.'

Stoker was hard on himself. In a subsequent report to the Admiralty, he attributed the failure not just to the state of the sea, but to 'my personal error in overdoing an unseen attack'. In his memoirs, Stoker rapped himself again. 'We had lost a glorious chance, and through my fault alone. Of little use to think that two sleepless nights and the experiences of the previous day hardly tended to produce the even, balanced mind necessary to successful submarine attacks in these unsuitable conditions of bad light and smooth sea . . . Sick at heart, we dived on along our course, forming the resolve to find a quiet spot for rest before carrying out another attack.'

About 7 am on 26 April *AE2* passed the little township of Gallipoli, situated where the Dardanelles Strait opens into the Sea of Marmara. But there was nothing there worth attacking except a row of small fishing boats. These were strung out from shore to shore in a way that Stoker felt was designed to hinder the submarine. He dived to 21 metres under the boats.

Coming up to surface again, the forts outside Gallipoli opened fire on the *AE2*'s periscope. As Wheat said, it was lucky they did. If the Turks had waited a few minutes they would have had a good shot at the *AE2* lying on the surface. Stoker dived out of range and into the Sea of Marmara.

'Our great wish was realised,' he said. 'The submarine passage of the Dardanelles was not only possible but made.'

It also 'made' the *AE2*. Despite later imprisonment and lack of recognition, even in Australia, the *AE2* crew could always hold their heads high that they had pulled off one of the most remarkable feats in submarine history.

Stoker, said C. G. Brodie in his revealing book of the Dardanelles naval campaign, *Forlorn Hope 1915: The Submarine Passage of the Dardanelles*, published some forty years later, was 'the gifted amateur who stole the show from the professionals'. Maybe this was a factor in *AE2*'s lack of recognition.

6

'It's Done the Trick!'

Purple blue sparks had flashed off the damp aerial of *AE2*'s new Marconi wireless set as Stoker tried several times to signal Allied high command that he had breached the Narrows. When there was no answering signal, Stoker and his crew were disconsolate. Admiral de Robeck had told Stoker that, if he succeeded, others would be ordered to follow. Without the news of *AE2*'s success, such orders would be unlikely. High command's approval for *AE2*'s bid had probably been a last-ditch effort on the eve of the Gallipoli landings.

'It was of the utmost importance that we should get into communication with the admiral and tell him that the most difficult part of our task was accomplished,' said Stoker as he recalled signalman Falconer's desperate attempts to get through. 'Whether any other submarine should be risked would depend on the success or failure of our attempt, so he must know as quickly as possible that we had practically succeeded. This wireless failure was a very great disappointment.'

But the message had in fact made it through. Moreover, it was to figure in one of the most crucial decisions of the invasion, forever weaving the *AE2* into Gallipoli's ill-starred history.

Sunday 25 April, the landing day, was a day of horror for the Allied invaders. Sir Ian Hamilton's plan was simple: 'to get a good run at the peninsula and jump plumb on—both feet together'.

Sir Ian planned that his main force, the British 29th Division, would land on the beaches of Cape Helles at the foot of the peninsula, quickly capturing the crest of Achi Baba. The combined Australian and New Zealand forces would land slightly up the peninsula between Gaba Tepe and Hell Spit, moving inland to capture the heights of Chunuk Bair and the Sari Bair ranges, overlooking the Narrows. The Anzacs would then move across to Mal Teppe, the mountain where the Persian invader Xerxes reportedly sat to watch his forces crossing the Narrows. The Anzacs at the top and the British at the bottom would have the Turkish defenders of the Narrows at Kilid Bahr in a pincer, wiping them out so that the navy would sail triumphantly up the Narrows, clearing mines along the way. Meanwhile, the French, with their colourful Foreign Legion and Senegalese soldiers, would mount a diversionary attack at Kum Kale on the Asiatic shore of the Dardanelles, while another feint would be made up at Bulair at the European neck of the Gallipoli Peninsula.

A simple plan, but flawed. Historians have flayed the Gallipoli campaign for poor leadership, inaccurate maps, lack of co-ordination between the army and navy, the somewhat cavalier approach to planning and underestimation of the Turkish defences.

Few of Churchill's famous 'ifs' went the way of the Allies on 25 April. The British 29th Division, landing at beaches along Helles Point, found some virtually uncontested while others were death traps. At Y Beach on the western seaboard of the peninsula some 3000 troops waded ashore and by late afternoon had consolidated their positions. At X and S beaches British troops dug in after little resistance.

But at W and V Beaches Turkish defenders cut down the landing troops. At V Beach, the idea that 2000 troops could run ashore from a grounded freighter, the *River Clyde*, has been likened to setting up a shooting gallery for the Turks. Some 1000 men were trapped on board as shots pinged off the hull.

While there was great heroism amongst the troops they were let down by indecisiveness at the top. From his *Queen Elizabeth* flagship off the coast, Hamilton and his staff could clearly see what was happening at V Beach, and how a diversion of men from Y Beach could turn the situation. Troops on Y Beach could hear the noise of battle but did not know that a quick movement by them might have won the day. Hamilton and his staff were loath to intervene, but eventually signalled the ground commander, Major General Sir A. G. Hunter-Weston. Rather than giving Hunter-Weston a command, Hamilton merely asked if he would like to switch some men to Y Beach. Hunter-Weston did not reply to the first message, and declined the second.

Hamilton already had a reputation as a soldier-poet, and was now also gaining one as a ditherer. He had used inspirational words to exhort his troops before the landing, reminding them of Lord Kitchener's advice to 'fight the thing through to the finish'. But Hamilton did not instruct Hunter-Weston to move quickly inland once ashore.

Up the Gallipoli Peninsula, towships mistakenly put the Anzacs ashore north of their planned landing spot. Instead of sandbanks, the Australians found themselves facing steep cliffs and ravines. Military historian John Laffin in *Damn The Dardanelles* says the landing error was a 'disastrous mistake'. 'Had it not been made, the 4000 Australians who disembarked before 5 am, and the 4000 who followed them between 6 and 8 am, could have pushed back the Turkish outposts and established themselves on the vital Gun Ridge and dominating Chunuk Bair before the arrival of enemy reinforcements.' Others claim the Anzacs may have faced even stiffer resistance.

The Australians nevertheless fought their way up the cliffs and onto the first ridges. The landing spot, (now Anzac Cove), presented another problem. It was a small beach, making the landing of troops and stores and evacuation of the wounded a nightmare.

As the Anzacs fought their way inland, the young Mustafa Kemal, the able Turkish commander who, as Ataturk, was later to lead the Turkish nation in the transition to a modern secular state, organised fierce resistance. Kemal's fighting spirit was epitomised by his command to Turkish defenders: 'I do not order you to attack, I order you to die.'

Kemal came onto the scene just as the Anzacs were pushing the Turks back over the first ridges. Kemal, says his biographer Patrick Kinross, stopped his retreating troops and asked, 'What's up? Why are you running away?'

> 'They come, they come,' was the reply.
>
> 'Who comes?'
>
> 'Sir, the enemy. Ingiliz, Ingiliz.'

'Where?' he asked.

They pointed down the slope to a patch of scrub, from which a line of Australians was freely advancing. They were closer to Kemal than his own troops, whom he had left behind to rest. 'Whether by logic or instinct' as he afterwards put it, he said to the retreating soldiers, 'You cannot run away from the enemy.'

They protested, 'Our ammunition is finished.'

'You have your bayonets,' he said. He commanded them to fix bayonets and to lie down on the ground. He sent an officer back to instruct his own infantrymen to come up at the double, together with any available gunners from the mountain battery. Then, as he observed, 'When our men lay down, the enemy lay down. This was the moment of time that we gained.'

It was a moment of hesitation by the Anzacs which may well have decided the fate of the peninsula, says Kinross. It was Turkey's good fortune and Australia's bad luck that Kemal was on the scene. His inspirational leadership, in marked contrast to that of some British commanders, turned the tide on that fateful day.

Throughout the day fighting on the ridges above Anzac Cove was fierce and bloody. Hill Baby 700 changed hands several times. The bravery of the fighting on both sides was extraordinary. Robert Rhodes James in *Gallipoli*, records some of the events of the afternoon in fighting around Monash Valley and The Nek.

A thin drizzle began to fall. The Turks came on again and again, with their patchwork uniforms, old-fashioned rifles and screams of 'Alah!'. Cut down in swathes, the second and third waves would come on over the bodies of the dead and dying. Units were cut off and killed to a man; neither side was taking prisoners, and the fighting was frenzied and savage.

By nightfall the Anzacs were clinging to a small patch of land about 2.4 kilometres long and 750 metres inland. The scene was utter chaos as the wounded and stores were lined up along the beach. Units clung to exposed positions, with officers fearful that a renewed Turkish attack would sweep the force into the ocean.

> The confidence of the dawn and early morning had gone [said Rhodes James]. On the beach the confusion was growing; men were coming down from the firing-lines, no one knew what was happening. 'There was no rest, no lull, while the rotting dead lay all around us, never a pause in the whole of that long day that started at the crack of dawn,' an Australian soldier has recorded. 'How we longed for nightfall! How we prayed for this ghastly day to end! How we yearned for the sight of the first dark shadow!'

As darkness fell, Anzac Cove was a shambles. The two divisional commanders, Major General W. T. Bridges and Major General Sir A. Godley, asked General Sir William Birdwood, the British commander of the Anzac forces, to come ashore to assess the situation. Huddled under a tarpaulin with two candles, Birdwood was stunned to hear the two commanders arguing the case of their fellow officers that an evacuation should be contemplated.

'Outside, the rumble of the firing could be plainly heard above the shouts of the beach personnel, the cries of the wounded, the crash of the waves, and the uproar of an army in apparent confusion and disorder,' says Rhodes James. 'All were dead tired, although Birdwood was the freshest.' Reluctantly, Birdwood agreed, and dictated the following message to Hamilton.

> Both my divisional generals and brigadiers have represented to me that they fear their men are thoroughly demoralised by shrapnel fire to which they have been subjected all day after exhaustion and gallant work in the morning. Numbers have dribbled back from firing line and cannot be collected in this difficult country. Even New Zealand brigade which has only recently been engaged has lost heavily and is to some extent demoralised. If troops are subject to

shellfire again tomorrow there is likely to be a fiasco as I have no fresh troops with which to replace those in firing line. I know my representation is most serious but if we are to re-embark it must be done at once.

The message found its way out to the *Queen Elizabeth*, which had just arrived offshore after sailing up from the Helles landings. Hamilton had retired to bed. His last diary entry for 25 April showed a somewhat naïve 'lady luck' approach to a major military operation and his lack of any real grasp of the desperate situation ashore.

No word yet about the losses except that they must have been heavy. If the Turks get hold of a lot of fresh men and throw them back upon us during the night—perhaps they may knock us into the sea. No general knows his luck, that's the beauty of the business. But I feel sanguine in the spirit of the men; sanguine in my own spirit; sanguine in the soundness of my scheme. What with the landing at Gaba Tepe and at Kum Kale, and the feints at Bulair and Besika Bay, the Turkish troops here will get no help tonight. And our fellows are steadily pouring ashore.

Just after midnight Hamilton was roused from a dead sleep by his chief of staff, Major General Walter Braithwaite, shouting, 'Sir Ian! Sir Ian!' As Hamilton struggled to consciousness, Braithwaite explained, 'You've got to come right along—a question of life and death—you must settle it!'

Braithwaite had the reputation of being a cool hand, and Hamilton said the tone of voice had him 'awake in a second'. Hamilton pulled on his 'British warms' over his pyjamas and followed Braithwaite from his cabin into the dining saloon. There he found a council of war of his senior officers, including Admiral de Robeck; Rear Admiral Thursby, who was in charge of the landing of the Anzac forces; Roger Keyes; Brigadier-General Carruthers, the deputy adjutant and quartermaster general of the Anzacs; and General Cunliffe, commander of the Anzac artillery.

'A cold hand clutched my heart,' said Hamilton as he scanned their faces and read aloud the message from Birdwood. The scene bears contemplation. Only 19 or so hours before, Hamilton had flung a massive force onto the Gallipoli coast, carrying with it British hopes to relieve Russia and perhaps break the stalemate in France with a bold attack against a seemingly weak ally of the Central Powers. Yet late the same day Hamilton, dressed in pyjamas, was confronted with a humiliating evacuation.

Hamilton tried to gain time by asking questions about the tactical situation ashore. 'The faces around that table took on a look—when I close my eyes there they sit—a look like nothing on earth unless it be the guests when their host flings salt upon the burning raisins,' he later wrote in *Gallipoli Diary*. Hamilton turned to Rear Admiral Thursby and asked him what he thought about evacuation.

'It will take the best part of three days to get that crowd off the beaches,' Thursby replied.

'And where are the Turks?' asked Hamilton

'On top of 'em.'

'Well, then,' Hamilton persisted, 'tell me Admiral, what do you think?'

'What do I think? Well, I think myself they will stick it out if only it is put to them that they must.'

Hamilton contemplated his reply to Birdwood. Keyes, de Robeck's somewhat swashbuckling aide, was in a state of denial. 'It was difficult to believe that those splendid people we had watched training for their ordeal, who had justified all that had been expected of them in the assault of the morning, could have been reduced to such a state,' he later wrote.

Outside the dining room, C. G. Brodie, Keyes' aide, had been assigned the task of looking after the lesser fry and stopping the conference being interrupted. *AE2* was probably the last thing on Brodie's mind. Indeed, the navy had picked up a Turkish message earlier in the day that a British submarine had been sunk, which could only have been *AE2*.

Suddenly, the yeoman of signals handed Brodie a signal marked 'from *AE2* for C-in-C [Commander in Chief]', telling of Stoker's success in making it underneath the minefields and up the Narrows. The yeoman, said Brodie, 'had a glint in his eye that told me he knew something of what it meant'.

Defying orders, Brodie burst into the dining saloon and sought out Keyes. 'Keyes was furious at my intrusion, but I refused to be shooed out until he came with me and read it,' said Brodie.

Keyes quickly grasped the significance of Stoker's message. He rushed back into the dining saloon as Hamilton, pen in hand, was beginning his reply to Birdwood. Such was the drama of the moment that Keyes took it upon himself to read out Stoker's message. In somewhat dramatic tones, he added, 'Tell them [the troops on shore] this. It is an omen. An Australian submarine has done the finest feat in submarine history and is going to torpedo all the ships bringing reinforcements, supplies and ammunition into Gallipoli.'

Keyes wrote later that he may have gilded the lily somewhat. 'It is true that *AE2* was commanded and officered by our submarine officers, and only about half her crew were Australians, but she belonged to the Australian government.'

Hamilton looked up and nodded as Keyes read out Stoker's message. He had just begun to write. He read out his reply to the assembled officers:

> *Your news is indeed serious. But there is nothing for it but to dig yourselves right in and stick it out. It would take at least two days to re-embark you, as Admiral Thursby will explain to you. Meanwhile the Australian submarine has got through the Narrows and has torpedoed a gunboat off Chanak. Hunter-Weston, despite his heavy losses, will be advancing tomorrow, which should divert pressure from you. Make a personal appeal to your men and Godley's to make a supreme effort to hold their ground.*
>
> *PS—You have got through the difficult business; now you have only to dig, dig, dig until you are safe.*

De Robeck and Keyes patted Hamilton on the back as he finished his message. 'I hope they will go on doing so if things go horribly wrong,' thought Hamilton. Keyes said that in the drama of the moment he remembered thinking Hamilton a 'stouthearted fellow with the warrior spirit', although he could never understand why Hamilton had not taken control of the battle in the southern landing areas.

Keyes darted back out to where Brodie and others were waiting. 'It's done the trick,' he said of Stoker's message. Keyes later wrote that *AE2*'s message 'could not have been received at a more opportune moment'.

Keyes may have believed Stoker's message was the turning point, but some historians say Thursby's sobering view on the problems of re-embarkation was the real influence. Interestingly, this was the only order Hamilton gave on the days of the landings.

Stoker himself wrote that years later he learned that his message had been received at a 'critical moment' during the council of war onboard the *Queen Elizabeth*. It had 'altered the whole tide of discussion, and it was decided to hold on,' he believed.

Many historians disagree. Their argument is that nobody at the time set much store by *AE2*'s chances of achieving any significant blow behind enemy lines to alter the balance in the Anzac sector. While *AE2*'s voyage was indeed epic in early submarine warfare, it would be wrong, they argue, to credit it with having any significant influence on Hamilton's decision to keep the Anzacs at Gallipoli.

Some participants, however, take a different view. Brodie, the officer who brought the message to Keyes, wrote: 'On the night of April 25, the signal from *AE2* seemed to Keyes and myself the turning point, certainly for Anzac, perhaps for our campaign, and thus, in our soaring fancy, possibly even for the war.' Brodie says Hamilton reckoned his mind was made up before he heard of *AE2*'s breakthrough. 'No doubt it was, but *AE2* at least saved him any argument with his advisers,' said Brodie.

E. Keble Chatterton in *Dardanelles Dilemma: The Story of Naval Operations* offers another insight. He says that Stoker's message had the psychological effect of enlivening drooping spirits, giving the discussion a new turn. 'The Council decided to hold on,' he says. 'Submarines might yet be the controlling influence.'

Onshore, the news of *AE2*'s feat was perhaps the only bright spot for the beleaguered Anzacs. One notice stuck to a stump read: 'Australian sub *AE2* just through the Dardanelles. Advance Australia!' Australia's official war historian C. E. W. Bean later wrote of Hamilton's firm order:

> The effect of this resolute and definite order, quickly taken ashore by Admiral Thursby, was electrical. All the vague doubts which spread around the beach were settled. From that moment there was no further talk of evacuation at Anzac, and all the ranks were soon filled with the same determination as the men in the front line, none of whom had any idea that a retirement was under discussion. By the morning of the 26th they had achieved what most thought unachievable—the successful invasion of a heavily fortified enemy coastline.

Brodie again disagreed. 'As we learned during the following days from all at Anzac, high and low, everyone on the beach had recovered their nerve before the deputation got back. All concerned only wished that the gloomy message had never been sent, and any orders to evacuate would have been met with protest, not to say derision.' Brodie says the unhappy incident of the message to Hamilton was soon cast into oblivion—which may have contributed to *AE2*'s feat being practically unknown.

It was not until 259 days later that the Anzacs were evacuated, without loss. In those eight months the Australians mounted heroic efforts to break through, suffering 26 094 casualties, with 7594 men killed.

Did Stoker's crucial message delay the eventual evacuation, prolonging the fighting and dreadful loss of life? In 1965, the fiftieth anniversary of Gallipoli, Tudor Jenkins, himself a veteran of the fighting, wrote in the *London Evening Standard* of the pivotal role of Stoker.

Now a spry 80, he lives in Chelsea. I asked him whether he sometimes wondered whether it would not have been better if his message to de Robeck had not got through.

'Maybe an immediate evacuation would have saved those terrible casualties,' Stoker replied.

In a letter to Australian crew member Cecil Bray in the mid 1960s Stoker reaffirmed his belief that the *AE2* had been pivotal in keeping the troops on Gallipoli. 'The receipt of our signal stopped the Anzacs being withdrawn that night,' he told Bray. 'What a tragedy that campaign failed. It would have altered all history. No Russian revolution and possibly no communism.'

7

'E14, By All the Gods!'

Oblivious of their role in the Gallipoli evacuation drama, Stoker and his crew in their battered and bruised submarine enjoyed a rare sense of achievement in reaching their elusive goal—the Sea of Marmara. It was short-lived.

'Something accomplished, something done, is much vaunted as a source of satisfaction,' Stoker reflected after the war on the *AE2* proving that a submarine could burst the heavily defended and treacherous Narrows. 'I doubt if its vaunting is justified. Often and often we cry: "Ah! If only I could accomplish that; if only I could gain that position, or win to that goal, how happy I would be then!" Yet there is always a trap in it. Happiness and contentment are elusive things, with a nasty, elusive habit of slipping on ahead of us. We attain to the new and longed-for position only to find that new responsibilities face us. I often think that happiness can only lie in striving, never in winning. Yet while we strive we have no leisure to realise and enjoy our happiness.'

On 26 April 1915, however, Stoker did not have much time for such philosophising. First, there was the utter frustration of apparently not being able to get a wireless message out. Wireless, of course, was a new addition to the submarine fit-out.

Signalman Falconer tried several more times, but apparently to no avail. It was not until years later that Stoker learned of the dramatic timing of his signal.

More pressing was the problem of what to do next. The *AE2*'s primary mission—'all our thoughts and endeavours', as Stoker put it—had been to prove the submarine passage of the Marmara. The duty beyond that, as Stoker saw it, was to prevent the passage of enemy troops and supplies to the Gallipoli Peninsula.

But *AE2* carried no gun to harass Turkish shipping lanes. Indeed at that time, no British subs were fitted with guns. As well, *AE2* had only a few torpedoes, and even those, Stoker lamented, 'were not of the most modern type'. Stoker agonised over the *AE2*'s parlous position—behind enemy lines while a huge battle raged, seemingly unable to communicate and likely to be isolated.

'The failure of the wireless receiving instruments left us in doubt as to whether any other submarine would be sent to join us,' he said. 'How, then, could we best fulfil our duty? It seemed that we must endeavour to utilise moral effect to its utmost. Great care must be exercised in the expenditure of torpedoes, and all ships not fired at must be frightened as much as possible.'

Stoker's musing over the *AE2*'s plight was quickly put aside when, through the periscope on their first day in the Marmara he sighted several columns of smoke ahead, indicating approaching ships. He ordered a new course to put the *AE2* right at the centre of them.

The *AE2* found itself amidst four fairly small Turkish ships. All were steering zigzag courses. A small motorboat from shore was obviously warning each ship that came along that a submarine was about. Stoker was already winning on the 'moral effect'.

Stoker steered for the largest of the ships, no more than about 1500 tonnes. It was flying no colours—nor were any of the others—and there was nothing to suggest it was a transport. 'I decided that only if troops could be discerned on board would we be justified in firing a torpedo,' said Stoker.

As the *AE2* moved to within 180 metres, no troops could be seen. There was nothing to distinguish the ship from the general run of merchant shipping. 'A perfect target, well nigh unmissable, she made, and the temptation to fire was immense,' said Stoker.

He resisted the temptation. Suddenly, as *AE2* was passing away astern, the ship hoisted a Turkish flag and opened fire on the submarine's periscope from an aft gun that had been hidden from Stoker's sight.

'The impertinence of the thing was damnably irritating—had she fired one minute sooner we would have had the greatest pleasure in blowing her sky high!' said a fuming Stoker. 'Now it was too late.'

AE2 moved to the next target. This was a smaller ship, but again with no sign of troops. Stoker's sense of irritation was such that he felt 'we must fire'. He did, but the torpedo missed. With the periscope down, Stoker could not see what happened, but believed the ship dodged to avoid the shot. Crewman Wheat thought the ship's shallow draught might have saved her.

Two shots since the successful hit in the Narrows, and two misses.

Stoker dived away. Resurfacing some distance away, he took up a popular pastime for the *AE2* and future Allied submarines—scaring Turkish fishermen. Stoker hoisted his big white ensign and steamed up close to a group of fishing boats.

'The excitement caused was amusingly intense,' he said. 'With frantic gesticulations and calls to Allah, the fishermen endeavoured to impress us with their harmlessness, some even holding both hands palm upwards above their heads with piteous "don't shoot" looks on their faces. But it was well to frighten them, and let them return to their villages with tales of the immediate coming of the British fleet; the moral effect would all help. And so, in this pleasantly interesting manner, we passed the afternoon.'

Nightfall, however, brought renewed anxiety. As *AE2* was again trying to signal the fleet, a small Turkish patrol boat came into sight, immediately opening fire. The *AE2* dived before the chasing craft could find the range. But the rest of the night was spent under constant attack.

'Dived we this way, or dived we that, we had barely returned to the surface for five minutes before we were forced to dive again,' said Stoker. 'The waters seemed stiff with pursuing craft.'

Stoker later found out that from the moment of the *AE2*'s passing the Narrows, six Turkish craft had been detailed with the sole duty of harassing the submarine. 'Had they been six hundred they could not have worried us more than they did that night,' he said. 'We longed for a gun to enable us to remain on the surface and give them fight.'

One incident was uncomfortably close. A Turkish warship, painted white and difficult to spot in the moonlight and mist, moved in very close as the *AE2* was on the surface. As Stoker attempted a quick dive, the watertight lid on the conning tower jammed and would not shut. To find the fault it was necessary to show a light, making the conning tower an easy target.

'The coxswain [chief petty officer Harry Abbott] who was attempting to close the lid—in all other things of life a truthful man—will assure you that the flash from the white vessel's gun scorched his eyebrows,' said Stoker. 'But we were never hit.'

It was a restless night for the crew. Stoker, however, could always spin a lighter side to adversity. In heaven, he said, he would apply for the billet of the Man in the Moon. 'To sit on high and watch a number of craft creeping about in the darkness chasing one poor submarine must be an exciting amusement. But I shall have a mighty fund of sympathy for the submarine!'

The next day brought calm waters to the Marmara, a curse for the *AE2* trying to hit small ships, which the Turks were clearly using to resupply Gallipoli. In 1915 technology dictated that a submarine had to keep its periscope down from the time it was about 2700 metres away from a small target. At about 270 metres, the periscope could be hoisted and the torpedo fired. Calm seas meant a target could readily spot the periscope and the fired torpedo. Small ships can more easily swerve to avoid being hit.

A transport came into view, headed for Gallipoli. Her two guarding destroyers immediately proved to Stoker that she was worthy of attack. Stoker carefully manoeuvred the *AE2* between the transport and the destroyer on her starboard beam. With her presence undetected, the *AE2* edged up to about 270 metres. As Stoker angled for the right bearing for his bow tube, the range shorted to about 180 metres. A perfect target.

'Bow tube, stand by! Fire!' he ordered.

With a rush of escaping air, the torpedo left the tube. Then it rose quietly to the surface and lay motionless, the compressed air of its motive power 'puffing furtively' out of its stern. The torpedo's engine had failed to start.

Stoker was mortified. 'Words cannot describe my feelings at the sight,' he said. 'Never has ship had more fortunate escape. Nothing on earth could have saved her had the torpedo run'.

Other E class submariners following Stoker experienced similar problems. One of the most enterprising, Martin Nasmith, even devised a daring scheme to recycle failed torpedoes. Nasmith would dive overboard to disarm the moustache trigger on the torpedo before sucking it back into its tube. While Stoker, characteristically, would often blame the periscope operator (himself), C. G. Brodie in *Forlorn Hope* claimed most torpedo failures were due to faulty running. 'No one who knew the troubles all our submarines had in 1915 with the depth-keeping of their torpedoes, and the difficulty of maintenance when without a parent ship, will wonder at these failures,' he wrote.

As Stoker stared in disbelief at his failed shot, one of the destroyers charged down on the diving *AE2*. It swished overhead, missing, says Stoker, by inches.

Three firings. Three failures. 'Everyone was getting very disheartened about so many failures with the torpedoes,' said Wheat. Later, says Wheat, *AE2* sighted three lighters being towed by a tug. 'We proceeded to within about 1000 yards [914 metres] of them and saw that they were full of soldiers. We could do nothing but watch them. How we were longing to have a three-pounder gun mounted. We should have had some good sport.'

That night, Stoker headed for a quiet spot on the northern side of the Marmara so that the crew could get some rest. He wanted no repeat of the previous night's 'entertainment'. After trying again unsuccessfully to signal fleet command, the *AE2* sank to the bottom at 18 metres to hide for the night. Everyone turned in, except for the watch-keeper delegated to keep an eye on the depth gauge.

Stoker ruminated in his jocular style about this task. 'The only man awake in the boat, practically his sole duty is to watch the diving gauge to see that the submarine does not unexpectedly rise to the surface.

Or slip along the bottom to a greater depth. What sort of fancies, do you think, he indulges in as he gazes at the big round gauge in front of him, with its needle pointing firmly to the fact that 60 or 70 feet of water lie between him and the world of men above? Curious thoughts they ought surely to be.' But don't ask him, advised Stoker, for fear that he might be thinking about the bad beer they sell in Port Said!

The next day was a busy and fateful one for the *AE2*. Stoker took the submarine up to the centre of the Sea of Marmara to get a closer look at the entrance to Constantinople. His plan was to launch an attack in the harbour the next day.

Returning towards Gallipoli, Stoker sighted a Turkish gunboat, too small to waste a torpedo. But not too small to play a trick upon to convince the Turks that more Allied subs were in the Marmara.

Stoker dived underneath the gunboat, steering down towards the strait, and then turning to rise to 6 metres, upped periscope to sail back into the Marmara. The joke proved great fun.

'Nearer and nearer we drew to the gunboat—indeed, we began to wonder if she was ever going to see us,' he said. 'So close did we get that I could plainly see two stout and elderly gentlemen languidly up against the compass on the bridge. Suddenly one of them gave a marvellous leap perpendicularly in the air, and with a sweep of his arm which knocked the other gentleman's fez off, pointed to the periscope, now not 200 yards off. Then such hurryings and scurryings and waving of arms! Men rushed in all directions, and the two stout gentlemen looked as if any moment they might fall off their bridge into the water!'

With the gunboat firing and the two stout gentlemen preparing to ram the *AE2*, Stoker plunged away to safety at 21 metres.

Crewman Wheat wrote of another firing that day which is unable to be confirmed as a hit or a miss. After checking the harbour at Gallipoli township and failing to gain an accurate bead on a gunship moored there, the *AE2* was moving away back into the Marmara when a transport approached, accompanied by two destroyers.

'We fired our starboard torpedo but missed,' said Wheat. 'We immediately turned a little and fired our stern torpedo. On firing this torpedo we immediately had to go down out of sight, as the destroyers were attempting to ram us. We showed our periscope five minutes later but there was no transport to be seen, only the destroyers.'

Had the *AE2* finally made a hit? Stoker does not record the event. Indeed, there are several differences in the various diaries of *AE2*'s crew about the days on patrol in the Marmara, and torpedo firings. As all records were lost, and the crew's accounts written later—in some cases several years later—this is not surprising.

On the possible transport hit, crewman Albert Knaggs wrote that the *AE2* 'sank one transport' that day while it was being 'chased and worried' by destroyers. Similarly, Able Seaman Charles Suckling records that he was later told by Turks that a transport had been hit and sunk, although Suckling's account appears to refer to an earlier attack.

Stoker, however, records an attack on a gunboat after leaving the Gallipoli area. The *AE2* fired, but again the torpedo missed. 'Gunboat dodged and torpedo passed one yard ahead (this I afterwards learned),' Stoker said in his official report to the Admiralty after the war.

Later, on the surface and heading back towards Constantinople, the *AE2*'s watchman spotted something approaching. 'There's something ahead there, sir, looks like a periscope,' he reported to Stoker.

'It *is* a submarine, and she's coming up!'

Stoker watched as 180 metres off there rose, slowly and gracefully, first the periscope and then the conning tower, and then the grey, dripping hull of a submarine.

'Yes! No ! Yes! *E14*, by all the gods!'

Stoker and his crew were bowled over. Although there had been a telltale sign the previous evening when another ship attempted to make the *AE2*'s number in Morse code, the crew thought they were entirely alone, except for the pursuing Turks, of course.

While the clock dictated that *AE2* had been sailing solo around the Marmara for five days, Stoker said it felt more like five years. Yet here was the *E14*, commanded by Lieutenant Commander E. Courtney Boyle right in front of them. Boyle had been ordered to sail immediately Stoker's news of the *AE2*'s success had reached the fleet. Like the *AE2*,

E14 had undergone six gut-wrenching hours through the minefields of the Narrows. But unlike the *AE2*, it had no orders to attack enemy ships in that confined and treacherous space.

'The pleasure of a stranger in a strange land when he sights one of his own kith and kin is proverbial,' Stoker said. The two submarines sidled up to each other. Boyle and Stoker exchanged greetings and news through megaphones as the crews stood on full alert for an instant dive should enemy ships appear.

The two captains swapped torpedo stories. Stoker told Boyle *AE2* had had bad luck with many of its shots. As it happened, Boyle had just missed on his first shot, apparently damaging another transport with his second.

As the *E14*'s captain was senior to Stoker, Boyle had the power to direct future operations of the two subs. What's your plan for tomorrow? inquired Boyle. Go to Constantinople and possibly launch an attack, replied Stoker, although *AE2* was now down to its last torpedo. Stoker reportedly asked Boyle to let him have one or two torpedoes. But Boyle, who had six of his ten 'fish' left but still facing a long patrol, could not comply.

Boyle counselled against attacking Constantinople the next day. Wait until he had received Admiral de Robeck's orders by wireless that night, he advised. He ordered Stoker to rendezvous with him at the same spot at 10 am the next day. The two subs parted.

This chance meeting, which ultimately doomed *AE2*, remains one of the mysteries of the Marmara submarine campaign. Why did Boyle pull rank on Stoker? Boyle may have been senior, but in the context of the Marmara Stoker was clearly the more experienced. There is a slight hint in Brodie's *Forlorn Hope* that Boyle may have been a bit peeved at playing first reserve to two of his juniors in leading the submarine attack on the Marmara. Although Boyle was the senior captain who would have been given the task if it had been ordered, both T. S. Brodie and Stoker had volunteered, while Boyle and others suggested it was not possible to crack the Narrows.

'Life, I suppose must be ever thus,' Stoker said philosophically of the meeting with Boyle and the *E14*. 'This, seemingly one of the most pleasant and happiest moments of *AE2*'s life, was in reality to be an indirect cause of her greatest calamity—no less than her death.

'Had the chance meeting with *E14* not occurred, we would have been on the morrow a hundred miles away from the spot where *AE2* was to find her fate.'

8

'How I Sank the *AE2*'

After a night on the bottom of the Marmara, Stoker was back at the rendezvous point at 10 am. There is some confusion in the various accounts of whether *E14* was sighted. Stoker said *AE2* saw what 'it believed' was *E14* some 8 kilometres ahead, but then lost it. Albert Knaggs aboard the *AE2* says *E14* was sighted being chased by Turkish torpedo boats.

But all accounts agree there was smoke on the horizon. Paradoxically, it turned out to be British smoke from a Turkish ship. The Turkish torpedo boat *Sultanhisar*, under the command of Captain Riza, had sighted what it thought was the marauding submarine. Riza said he ordered his 'good British coal' to be used to gain full speed for an attack. Just how a Turkish torpedo boat came to be fuelled by British coal some months into a conflict between the two countries is one of the ironies of war.

Sultanhisar's very presence at the rendezvous point is another irony—the torpedo boat was under orders to return to Constantinople and only the determination of Riza to have another look for the invading submarine took it to the area.

Riza later told his story, *How I Sank the* AE2, in a small book published in Turkey in 1947. The little-known book has never been quoted in any Australian account of the *AE2*'s loss. Riza and current-day Turks refer to the incident as the Battle of the *AE2*, although the fight has never been accorded this status in Australian accounts.

Riza's book is a highly colourful and idiosyncratic account. The captain rarely loses an opportunity to blow up the significance of the battle and his own role in it. Nevertheless, it is the only eye-witness account of events from the Turkish side.

Riza's *Sultanhisar* was one of the few warships in the Turkish navy without a German supervisory officer. *Sultanhisar*'s main task was to patrol a set area of the Marmara for submarines as well as escorting transport vessels from Constantinople taking military reinforcements to the Gallipoli front. 'A foreign submarine had penetrated into Marmara and caused some incidents,' says Riza in an acknowledgement that the *AE2*'s arrival had made an impact on the Turks in the days after the Gallipoli invasion.

But Riza also had another job. Liman von Sanders, the German general placed in charge of Turkish defences on the Gallipoli Peninsula, had made his headquarters in the little Marmara seaside port of Gallipoli. But every day he sailed down to Maydos in the Narrows to be closer to the action. After transporting Sanders, *Sultanhisar* would go hunting for the submarine that was attacking Turkish shipping.

Riza's account of 27 April states: 'We sighted the ferry numbered 38, which was transporting soldiers to the front with a lot of fanfare, singing, dancing etc. Suddenly I noticed a torpedo directed at 38 and I alerted them so that 38 quickly changed direction. The torpedo missed and blew up at the shore.' This was one of *AE2*'s several torpedo misses.

For Captain Riza, the next day was a disaster. Maydos was under shellfire when he arrived to pick up Sanders to return him to Gallipoli. The German general was nowhere in sight, and Riza was ordered by Turkish officers to help ferry wounded to hospitals. When Sanders returned and found *Sultanhisar* on other duties, 'he got even more agitated and reprimanded me,' said Riza. Sanders, according to the Turkish captain, 'was not inclined to be understanding ... That made me feel indignant because I thought he had treated me unduly harshly.'

Later the same day Riza received orders to return to Constantinople as another boat would replace the *Sultanhisar*. 'I was relieved, as this removed the need for me to patch up relationships with General von Sanders again,' commented Riza.

Heading back to Constantinople on 30 April, Riza decided to divert to the area around Karaburun Point at the southern end of Marmara just near the opening of the Dardanelles Strait to have another look for the marauding submarine. He sighted a vessel afar and ordered 'the good quality British coal' to be used to gain maximum speed. But Stoker in the *AE2*, as indeed it was, had seen the smoke of the approaching torpedo boat and dived to avoid it.

'The submarine was diving easily and comfortably; not a suspicion of impending disaster lay in our minds,' said Stoker. Suddenly, all hell broke loose. For no apparent reason, the *AE2* instead of diving, pointed sharply upwards and started rising in the water. Frantically Stoker juggled the diving rudders, increased power and shifted water ballast. But nothing could change the *AE2*'s strange upward thrust.

As *AE2* broke the surface, Stoker saw the *Sultanhisar* only 90 metres off, firing hard. 'We must get under again at once,' said Stoker, ordering the forward tanks to be flooded.

Riza had sighted the periscope and started firing. 'The periscope was damaged, but the submarine disappeared,' he said.

As the *AE2* dived again, Stoker tried to level off at 15 metres. But now the diving rudders seemed powerless and the *AE2* continued a downward plunge. Stoker expelled water ballast as quickly as possible to halt the descent, but the *AE2* simply kept plunging, quickly descending beyond 30 metres, the limit of its gauges.

'When that depth was passed she was still sinking rapidly,' said Stoker. 'We could not tell to what depths she was reaching. I ordered full speed astern on the motors ... In a few moments—moments in which death seemed close to every man—there came a cry from the coxswain: "She's coming up, sir!" and the needle seemed to jerk itself reluctantly away from the 100-feet [30–metre] mark, and then rise rapidly.'

With all her ballast expelled, the *AE2* literally jumped to the surface. Stoker and his crew had lost control of their boat. As Stoker was ordering reflooding of the tanks to regain the ability to dive, another officer looked through the periscope and reported that the *Sultanhisar* was firing as it circled, and a second Turkish gunboat was approaching.

Riza claims that as *AE2* dived again it fired a torpedo at *Sultanhisar*. 'With a quick turn, we avoided the torpedo,' he said. 'Now a ferocious fight had started between the submarine and us. We had two torpedoes and I ordered them to be prepared to be fired. The submarine had submerged again.'

No account from the *AE2* reports that it fired a torpedo. Indeed, the submarine's yoyoing left it in no position to fire anything. At the time Riza says a torpedo was fired, *AE2* was desperately trying to dive to avoid being hit by Turkish fire. And as the *AE2* started to submerge, Stoker had a new crisis on his hands that would have quickly obliterated any thought of attacking the Turkish ships.

The *AE2* started a new and even steeper downward plunge, once again out of control. Stoker gives a spine-tingling account of the next few minutes.

> Down and down she went, faster than before, 60, 80 and 100 feet [18, 24 and 30 metres]. The inclination down by the bows became more and more pronounced—she seemed to be trying to stand on her nose. Eggs, bread, food of all sorts, knives, forks, plates, came tumbling forward from the petty officers' mess. Everything that could fall over fell; men, slipping and struggling, grasped hold of valves, gauges, rods, anything to hold them up in position to their posts.
>
> Full speed astern again ... a thousand years passed—well, this time we were gone for ever.
>
> In heaven's name, what depth were we at?... Why did not the sides of the boat cave in under the pressure and finish it?

The nosedive to dangerous depths and the chaos aboard must have been terrifying. Able Seaman Charles Suckling reported that everyone's eyes 'were on the sides of the boat waiting for it to cave in'.

AE2's needle suddenly began to jump back from its 30-metre limit mark. The submarine began to shoot back up again, quickly rising to the surface where *Sultanhisar* was firing.

'BANG!... a cloud of smoke in the engine-room,' said Stoker. 'We were hit and holed! And again in quick succession two more holes.'

Riza's account aboard *Sultanhisar* again differs markedly. Riza says that as the submarine resurfaced he saw another torpedo coming towards *Sultanhisar*. 'If we were hit, there was no hope of any of us surviving,' he wrote. 'I ordered full speed ahead to try and avoid the torpedo as much as possible and minimise the damage. *Sultanhisar* suddenly turned and the torpedo barely missed us.'

Stoker reports no such firing. Indeed, he was in dire straits simply trying to control the *AE2* without positioning it for a torpedo attack. Riza, meanwhile, tried to ready his own torpedoes for firing. The first failed to ignite and fell overboard. Riza fired a second, which missed the *AE2*.

By now, the two craft were quite close. 'The 93 ton *Sultanhisar* paled by comparison to the 800 plus ton *AE2*,' said Riza. 'I decided to attack the submarine at its weakest point, its tail rudder, and started going towards it full speed'. Riza says that as *AE2* was again submerging *Sultanhisar* hit the sub headfirst.

'This could almost have cost us our lives,' he said. 'Suddenly *AE2* started resurfacing very close to our vessel. The waves it created while resurfacing were splashing onto our deck. If its head had been in the direction of our deck, it would certainly have pushed us up from underneath and caused us to capsize. We quickly started to pull away. While we pulled away, the submarine fully resurfaced. The British flag was pulled up the mast.'

While Riza was grappling with his version of the monster from the deep, aboard *AE2* things looked bleak. Holed three times the submarine could no longer dive. 'Finished! We were caught!' thought Stoker. 'It but remained to avoid useless sacrifice of life. All hands were ordered on deck and overboard.'

Lieutenant Haggard apparently disagreed. 'My father was not in favour of scuttling the boat and thought they should at least have tried to fight on,' relates Jenny Smyth, Lieutenant Haggard's daughter.

But the hard reality of their predicament quickly overruled any foolhardy actions. The *AE2* could not submerge. And what could the *AE2* have done to attack *Sultanhisar* or the approaching Turkish warships? It did not have a deck gun, and was in no position to fire its last torpedo. Short of waving his revolver, Stoker and *AE2* had run out of options.

Stoker does not mention this difference with Haggard. Quite the contrary. In his official report to the British Admiralty he lists Haggard's assistance in flooding the tanks to scuttle the *AE2*. Stoker was very concerned not to allow *AE2* to fall into enemy hands. The submarine, little more than a year old, was state-of-the-art military technology. The Royal Navy had risked further losses to destroy Brodie's *E15* after it had run aground in the Narrows only a fortnight before.

As the crew clambered out, led by Stoker's batman, Thomas Cheater, the third officer, Lieutenant John Cary stood on the tiny bridge watching the water rise. His job was to tell Stoker and Haggard, then flooding the tanks, when they had to get out. Petty Officer Harry Kinder was one of the last crew to leave. He retrieved some of the *AE2*'s papers, a feat for which he was later mentioned in dispatches.

Cary shouted for them to hurry, but Stoker looked up through the conning tower and saw from the water level that there was still a minute or so to spare.

> I jumped down again and had a last look round—for, you see, I was fond of the *AE2* [he wrote later]. What a sight! Pandemonium—I cannot attempt to describe it—food, clothing, flotsam and jetsam of the weirdest sorts floated up on the fast-entering water in the place which we had been so proud to keep neat and clean . . .
>
> An anxious shout from above, 'Hurry, sir, she's going down!'
>
> In the wardroom my eye was caught by my private dispatch case, which contained, I remembered, some money. That was bound to be useful—I ran and picked it up, and darted up the conning tower. As I reached the bridge the water was about two feet from the top of the conning tower; besides this only a small portion of the stern was out of the water. On it were clustered the last half dozen of the crew, the remainder were overboard.
>
> Curious incidents impress one at such times. As those last six men took the water the neat dive of one of the engine-room ratings will remain pictured in my mind for ever.

Other incidents impressed crew members. One recounted Stoker on the deck as the sub was sinking telling him, 'Come on then, it is no use stopping here.'

Riza had another view of these last moments of the *AE2*. He watched as the *AE2* crew jumped into the water. 'Finally, there was only the captain left,' he said. 'He was refusing to leave his ship and was saluting the British flag. This demonstration of patriotism moved us immensely. We all saluted the British flag which was by now floating in the water.'

As Stoker struggled in the water with his dispatch case, and together with his crew was hauled aboard *Sultanhisar*, the *AE2* slipped beneath the surface.

Stoker was quite emotional about the loss of his submarine. Sentiment is something to which Englishmen never admit, he said. But not so the Irish. Stoker listed the achievements of the short life of the *AE2* as it 'slid away to her last and longest dive'.

> *AE2* was in commission as a unit of his Majesty's Australian fleet for exactly 14 months. During that time she traversed 35 000 miles, of which the great portion was under war conditions. The first submarine to travel halfway round the world, she all but completed the return journey. The first submarine to pass the Dardanelles, to her fell the honour of proving the aforethought impossibility possible.
>
> From west to east, and east to west; now at an English manufacturing town, now at a tropical cannibal island; now in a vast ocean, now in a narrow coral sea; now midst the cheers of little children, now midst the roar of enemy guns; now in success, now in failure; now in hope, now in disappointment—a life of adventure and, at last, death at the hands of her own officers.
>
> And of the men who served her; no captain has ever been more proud of the men under his command that I was whilst commanding, in my good fortune, that Australian submarine. In the writing of this record of their work I have risked the charge of ingratitude through, in many places, belittling the difficulties they had to overcome; in places I have deliberately omitted problems of

> a technical nature which involved hard work and dangers in their solution. Here I have written, in describing perchance a two-thousand mile run, 'no incident occurred'; here you read ,'Orders were received and next day we sailed'—for Europe from Australia! The statements are true, but in the periods of time covered by such simple words the crew were worked like slaves. Hard work, privation, discomfort, dangers, were their companions during practically the whole of the *AE2*'s short life. And, if that were not enough, they entered, at her death, on a new life which was not a life, but a sorry existence. Good comrades, loyal servants, and brave men; the straws in the wind led them to captivity.

* * *

What had caused the *AE2* to behave so erratically? Stoker was puzzled by the submarine's original loss of trim, the submariner's expression for the right amount of ballast water necessary to manoeuvre a submarine safely underwater. He did not believe that water leaks from the many bumps the *AE2* had received hitting the shores in its zigzag up the Narrows was a satisfactory answer.

Wheat reported a variation on the water leak theory. He said a main ballast tank had been found to be full of water. 'The valves on this tank had not been touched,' he said. 'How it came to be full was a mystery. The only thing we could put this incident down to was that the water had leaked into this tank during the time we were lying on the bottom, for we had a hurried refit in Malta.'

Michael White, in *Australian Submarines* joins others in discounting the water leak. He points the blame to the submarine entering a markedly denser layer of water. 'Such layers of markedly denser water were a common phenomenon in the Sea of Marmara, where the fresh and sea water were not fully mixed,' he says. 'Denser water would have made the bows light and could have led to it commencing to rise.' C. G. Brodie agrees. 'It seems certain that an upset of trim, due to the unexpected passage from fresh to salt water, was the cause of *AE2*'s loss,' he says.

The British 'ace' submarine captains who followed Stoker—Boyle and Nasmith—worked out how to use this denser layer of salt water around the Marmara as a cushion. They would 'sit' on it overnight at a depth of 18 to 27 metres while the crew slept.

* * *

Back on the *Sultanhisar*, Captain Riza, according to his account, was proving himself a Turk of the old school. He called his crew onto the deck and told them they had seen the fruits of their labour in the sinking of the *AE2*. Now they had to remember their duty to humankind by picking up all the survivors and making sure no one was treated badly. Riza sent a boat to pick up Stoker.

The two captains shook hands. Riza said he felt the urge to console Stoker by telling him, 'These things happen in wars, I wasn't really expecting to fight with and capture a British submarine.' Stoker, he says, asked him where he got the idea to attack the *AE2* in the way he had. 'In fact, from you, the British,' Riza replied. 'I had read about the various manoeuvres that could be used against a submarine in a book titled *Danger* by a British naval officer.'

Instructing his crew to show the three officers to the captain's quarters while the *AE2* crew shed their wet clothes to dry on deck, Riza dealt with the other two Turkish warships arriving on the scene. Both wanted to share in the glory of *AE2*'s sinking by taking off some of the prisoners. Riza fended them off.

Riza went down to his lounge to talk to Stoker and his two officers. Haggard and Cary saluted as he entered, while Stoker apparently remained seated. Riza pulled up a chair and sat across from the submarine captain. 'Captain Stoker was a fair, bony man of around 35,' he said. 'He had dark green-brown eyes which looked very tired. He introduced his officers to me, who were barely 25 and looked tired as well.' Riza says that Stoker confirmed that he had taken a pot shot at the transport ferry which Riza had witnessed. Stoker, said Riza, then started talking very rapidly and excitedly, saying:

> Today's outcome is a quirk of chance. I was around the Marmara Island last night and I saw you travelling towards Istanbul [Constantinople] in the morning as the fog cleared. I did not think your small vessel could pose any danger to us, but I still decided to submerge to be on the cautious side. We proceeded underwater for a while and then had the periscope up on the direction of Istanbul. There was nothing on the horizon, so I realised you must have changed your direction. As I was turning the periscope around, one of your shots hit the periscope and made the controls inoperative. I could neither submerge the submarine nor observe you. This made it almost impossible for me to judge the distance between us.
>
> I fired the two torpedoes, but these did not hit their targets so I decided to fire the cannon. However, your last move had made that impossible as well, so I had no option but to surrender.

There are elements of pure fiction in these words Riza put into Stoker's mouth. *AE2* did not have a deck cannon. Neither Stoker nor any of his crew mention firing a torpedo. And two torpedoes? By all accounts, the *AE2* was down to its last torpedo in the 'battle' with *Sultanhisar*.

Riza was clearly determined to grab the maximum glory from the episode. *AE2*'s arrival in the Marmara posed a huge threat not just to Turkey's Gallipoli defences but to Constantinople itself. Sinking this marauding submarine was a feather in his cap, particularly as he captained a Turkish ship with no German officer on board. Riza's grandstanding is understandable. The Turkish navy was dominated by Germans, and Riza himself was already offside with one of the most powerful, Sanders, the Gallipoli defender.

Riza says Stoker quickly changed the subject after this outburst. He asked whether Riza knew Captain Mehmet from Tekirdag. Stoker and Mehmet had apparently met on an artillery course. Riza told him that Mehmet was captain of the *Barbados*, an identical vessel to *Sultanhisar*. 'Captain Stoker then said he would have been very sad if he had come across the *Barbados* and had attacked and destroyed it,' said Riza.

Whatever Riza's romancing about the event, he behaved in a civilised fashion towards his prisoners. He agonised about whom he should take them to. 'I firmly decided to deliver the prisoners of war to a Turkish commodore rather than my immediate commodore, who was German,' Riza said. 'There were numerous reasons for this. One was the general arrogance of the German officers, another was the unseemly treatment by German soldiers of the prisoners of war on previous occasions. I believed these [sailors] deserved being treated as honourable people and should not be subject to ridicule.'

Riza's decision not to hand the *AE2* crew to the Germans may have cost him dearly in a career sense. While Riza was later promoted, contemporary Turks believe German hostility stopped any further advance.

Riza's first port of call with his prisoners was the little fishing port of Gallipoli, then a major base for the Turkish Dardanelles defence. The *AE2* crew was driven to a garrison amid cheers from crowds delighted at the *Sultanhisar*'s victory. As Riza was recounting the 'battle' to the Turkish commandant Kazim Bey, General Liman von Sanders entered the room. Kazim Bey related the events to Sanders, who shook Riza's hand and congratulated him. 'I said I hoped this would serve to alleviate his displeasure with me from the night before,' Riza wrote. 'General Sanders replied that I was a very sensitive officer!'

Sanders then inspected the *AE2* crew. He was certainly living up to his reputation as a 'calm and steady hand', as Alan Moorehead, author of *Gallipoli* described him. With the Allied landing less than a week old and the Turks scrambling to defend their country, he nevertheless found time for a quick look at the captured submariners. But Sanders would have appreciated that this was no ordinary prize. The *AE2* had blazed a submarine path behind his lines. It had started the process—soon to be backed up by some of the British E class aces—of cutting off his vital sea supply routes, forcing him to use the slower land routes.

Curiously, Sanders wanted the *AE2* prisoners kept in the Gallipoli garrison. Riza said Sanders did not believe it prudent for Riza to try to deliver them himself to Constantinople. But Riza insisted, and Sanders backed off, even giving him two more prisoners to take to Constantinople.

Arriving in Constantinople, Riza was still puzzling over which Turkish authority to hand the prisoners to. He decided to go to the top—Commander-in-Chief Enver Pasha. Riza was trying to exploit his coup to the hilt. He rang Enver Pasha's office, and believing he was talking to a junior officer explained the situation. He also asked for coats and fresh clothing to be sent to the wharf as the prisoners had only damp shirts and trousers to wear. 'Don't worry, my son,' said the person on the other end of the line. 'I will ensure that it is taken care of.' Riza realised he was talking to Enver Pasha himself.

A group of Turkish officers quickly arrived at the dock, complete with coats. Enver Pasha also sent a carriage for Stoker and his officers. As the *AE2* crew was about to be marched away, Riza says Stoker gave him a silver tobacco case as a memento. 'I did not want to take it,' said Riza. 'Captain Stoker insisted, saying his admiral had given it to him at the dinner organised on the night when he gave orders for Captain Stoker to proceed to Marmara and he wished me to have it. I accepted. I still keep it to this day.'

* * *

For the Admiralty and the Australian navy, the *AE2* had simply disappeared. Submarines were racking up heavy losses. On 31 May Turkish radio had announced the destruction of the French submarine *Joule* in the Narrows, with all hands lost. That brought submarine losses in the Narrows to three. Now the *AE2* was missing. Turkish radio accounts of captured crew from the *AE2* were at first ignored. But on 2 May a wireless message in English from the *Goeben* was intercepted, claiming that *AE2* had been sunk by a Turkish torpedo boat, and the crew taken prisoner.

Newspaper reports started to appear in Britain. In Australia, the navy office sent an urgent telegram to the Admiralty: 'Press cable states *AE2* sunk in Sea of Marmara and crew taken prisoners. Have stopped publication, please inform if true.'

The Admiralty cabled back on 19 May. 'No communications having been received from Submarine *AE2* since 26 April, her loss must be presumed. From a report received through diplomatic channels at Athens it would appear that 3 officers and 17 men were taken prisoners out of a total 3 officers and 29 men. Every effort is being made to ascertain further particulars of the survivors.' Fortunately the Admiralty was wrong—all 32 were alive.

It was not until May 1916, when Sub-Lieutenant Geoffrey Fitzgerald, Stoker's companion in a Constantinople cell was released after intervention by the Vatican, that the story of the *AE2* started to flesh out. Fitzgerald gave the Admiralty a brief outline of Stoker's daring voyage up the Narrows. But, like the press cables arriving in Australia, many sections of this were marked by Australian navy authorities as 'confidential'.

With the troops by then evacuated from Gallipoli, the exploits of the submarine well known to the Turks, and *AE2*'s crew languishing in Turkish POW camps, it is difficult to understand exactly what the censoring authorities were trying to hide about the *AE2*. Stoker himself was disappointed by this secrecy. In a letter to his mother dated 5 May 1915—only a few days after the *AE2* was sunk—Stoker said: 'I am very sorry if they have not published the doings of my ship in home papers . . . [censored] . . . but I am very glad that all my crew are safe, as they have behaved themselves like really brave men and never once complained of the dangers they have been led into although they might all this time have been enjoying themselves in Australia.'

Stoker must have been in a Constantinople prison when this was written. Censors on both sides obviously were at work. 'Of course [I] can put nothing in,' said Stoker, assuring his mother that he was well and that there was no need to worry.

'It was sheer bad luck the way the boat was sunk,' he said. 'But even so your mascot did his work right nobly, saved us all from what seemed certain death at least three times . . . [censored] . . . the enemy guns hitting the boat.'

The mascot Mrs Stoker had given her son remains a mystery. As does the reason Australian and British authorities were so keen to hide the exploits of the *AE2*. The secrecy was to cost Stoker and his crew much of the recognition they deserved for their historic submarine penetration of the Narrows.

9

Tales of the Trade

Stoker and *AE2* had blazed the trail. But it was the gun British submariners, Nasmith and Boyle, in their E class boats who really turned the shipping supply route across the Marmara from Constantinople to Gallipoli into a submariner's happy hunting ground.

While Stoker and his crew were imprisoned for three and a half years, Nasmith and Boyle returned to tell their tales. Their daring adventures were lapped up by a public anxious for some good news as a relief from the tragic butchery in the trench warfare on the Western Front and on the Gallipoli Peninsula. Both were awarded Victoria Crosses.

Such were Nasmith's exploits that as late as the 1960s he was still being lionised in British children's comic books as 'The Scourge of the Marmara'. Rudyard Kipling, the great wordsmith and author of ripping adventure stories, was given access to the operational reports of Boyle and Nasmith. In his *Sea Warfare: Tales of 'The Trade'*, he turned both into wartime folk heroes. Their Dardanelles exploits helped make submarines a more acknowledged part of naval warfare.

Early submarine officers had been belittled by their naval colleagues as being in a 'trade' because they worked side by side with their men, learning engineering trades unheard of by gentlemen. Submariners were derided as dressing like North Sea fishermen. The 'Trade' later became a term of pride for submariners, who got some of their own back with sayings such as, 'There are only two kind of ships—submarines and targets.'

The outbreak of war had changed all perceptions about submarines. In 1914, shortly after the outbreak of war, the German *U9* had torpedoed and sunk three British cruisers within an hour off the Dutch coast. So much for the submarine as merely a defensive weapon!

After the British *E9* sank the German light cruiser *Hela* in September 1914, British subs had been sent into the Baltic. Initially limited to attacks on warships, they were later ordered to hit enemy trade routes, particularly the crucial iron ore traffic.

It was there that Lieutenant Commander N. M. Nasmith of *E11* and E. C. Boyle, of *E14*, cut their teeth. Nasmith, although only in his early thirties, was a submarine veteran, reputed to have the best periscope eye in the Trade. He was the consummate professional who, with his tricks, somehow seemed to make it all look simple. After missing one shot on a German battleship in the Baltic he swore he would never drink again. It was only after sinking a Turkish battleship (directed by the Germans) that his crew presented him with a ceremonial beer.

Boyle's *E14* was immediately ordered to follow Stoker's path after the *AE2*'s message late on the night of 25 April showed that submarine passage of the Narrows was possible. Although he had expressed doubts at the Keyes meeting a fortnight earlier that it could be done, Boyle was ready for immediate action.

E14's experiences were similar to *AE2*'s with mine cables scraping down the side of the submarine as it slid under the Narrows minefields. Kipling called these minefield crossings 'six hours of blind death'. Boyle sank the Turkish gunboat *Berki-Satvet* on his way through the Narrows. Just as he was watching a column of smoke and water shoot from the sinking torpedo boat, an extraordinary incident occurred. It helped create the folklore of the submarine campaign in the Marmara.

Boyle's periscope view suddenly went black. *E14* was very close to one of the Turkish steamboats on picket duty, and Boyle was astonished to realise that a man from the steamboat was leaning out and clutching the *E14*'s periscope in his hand!

Just what did the Turkish defender imagine he would do with the periscope—pluck a 720-tonne submarine out of the sea by brute force? While the incident contributed to the legend that grew up around the British submarines in the Marmara it had a serious side. If the Turkish hand had been equipped with a hammer or weapon, *E14*'s periscope—

and its attack capacity—could have been damaged. Boyle quickly dived to safety.

'Nobody loves the Trade, although *E14* did several things which made her popular,' wrote Kipling. 'She let off a string of very surprised dhows [they were empty] in charge of a tug which promptly fled back to Constantinople; stopped a couple of steamers full of refugees, also bound for Constantinople, who were "very pleased at being allowed to proceed" instead of being Lusitaniaed as they expected.' (The liner *Lusitania* was sunk by a U-boat in May 1915 off the Irish coast, with a large American civilian loss of life, helping turn the tide of US opinion against Germany.)

The *E14* sailed right into the harbour at Rodosto, but refrained, before being driven off by rifle fire, from torpedoing a steamer full of refugees from Gallipoli. The brazen attack unnerved Turkish defenders, although one turned it to his advantage. According to a US diplomat, the keeper of government stores in Rodosto reported to Constantinople that a submarine flying the Turkish flag had entered the harbour and been supplied with petrol and other provisions before the truth was discovered. Surely he deserved an award for disguising 'shrinkage' of government stores.

Like Stoker, Boyle experienced problems with torpedoes. But he sank a big transport crowded with Turkish troops and harassed Turkish supply lines. After 20 days on his first mission, and with only a defective torpedo remaining, Boyle was ordered to return, perhaps still wondering what had happened to Stoker and *AE2* after their failed rendezvous.

After allowing his crew time for a swim, Boyle passed easily down the Narrows, seeing no sign of the nets he had been warned the Turks were putting in place. Taking full advantage of the outflowing current, Boyle remained at periscope depth, even tailing a Turkish patrol boat, which obviously knew a safe route, through parts of the minefield. Boyle noted positions of Turkish guns as he floated along behind the patrol boat.

Back amongst the Allied ships, *E14* was escorted around the entire fleet to great cheering. 'The Marmara is practically closed by English submarines,' wrote the US consul in Constantinople, Mr Einstein.

General Sir Ian Hamilton, doubtless keen for something to cheer about, declared that the small *E14* with a crew of not many more than 30 had been worth an army of 50 000.

That night at the admiral's table, Boyle recounted his Marmara experiences. 'We were all thrilled,' wrote Keyes. Later that night Boyle was awoken from sleep to be informed by a signalman that he had been awarded the Victoria Cross. His officers and crew were all decorated.

Coming right on Boyle's heels was Lieutenant Commander Martin Nasmith. Showing his professional approach, Nasmith made an aerial survey of the Narrows. A few hours after dinner with Boyle and the admiral he was heading into the strait.

'There was perhaps a touch of the fanatic in Nasmith,' suggested Rear Admiral Sir William Jameson in *Submariners V.C.* 'But his judgement was excellent, his grasp of his profession absolute and his courage of that entirely unflinching kind which is very rarely met with.'

Finding that *E14* and *AE2* had scared off much of the Marmara traffic, Nasmith devised a scheme to lash his *E11* to a captured small sailing ship, effectively hiding his conning tower behind the sail. He abandoned this after it didn't work.

After sinking a gunboat (the *E11*'s periscope was damaged by shellfire from the sinking Turkish craft) Nasmith bailed up a steamer at rifle point in order to conserve torpedoes. As the Turkish crew jumped overboard to escape in small boats, Nasmith's log records the following:

'An American gentleman then appeared on the upper deck who informed us his name was Silas Q. Swing of the *Chicago Sun*, and that he was pleased to make our acquaintance. He then informed us that the steamer was proceeding to Chanak, and he wasn't sure if there were any weapons on board.'

Rudyard Kipling said that if anything could astonish the Trade, the appearance of Silas Q. Swing should have 'started a rivet or two on *E11*'s placid skin'. Brushing Swing aside, Lieutenant D'Oyly-Hughes, a demolition expert, boarded the steamer and found two six-inch guns, pedestals for twelve-pounder guns and a store of shells. The steamer was promptly dispatched to the bottom. No doubt the crew of *E11* was left wondering about the reporting skills of Silas Q. Swing, who was sent packing with the Turkish crew in their lifeboats.

After sinking another steamer at her mooring in Rodosto, Nasmith upped the tempo by stealing into Constantinople Harbour, right into the Golden Horn. This, of course, had been Stoker's aim. Nasmith fired two torpedoes, one sinking a gunboat and the other exploding a wharf, sending the local population into a panic.

'The Turks, utterly dumbfounded, were at a loss to know what could have happened,' said Jameson, as *E11*'s brazen entry had been undetected. 'Orders and counter-orders added to the general confusion as troops were hurriedly disembarked from transports waiting to sail. Rumours flashed through the streets of an invasion, shopkeepers put up their shutters; for several hours the normal life of the great city was brought to a standstill.'

Trying to manoeuvre for an exit, Nasmith grounded *E11*. But was he on the European or Asian shore? An incorrect action to get off the bank in the currents could drive *E11* even harder aground. As the helmsman reported that *E11* was pivoting anticlockwise, Nasmith correctly deduced that the boat must be on the Asian side, and ordered full port rudder. *E11* rumbled off the bank and headed south out of the harbour, stopping out of sight of land to hold prayers.

Nasmith returned to Constantinople the next day, but after the previous day's attack the Turks had cancelled all sailings and closed the Golden Horn. *E11* must have had a devastating effect on local morale: no foreign invader had penetrated the Golden Horn for centuries. Unable to re-enter, Nasmith calmly photographed Constantinople's minarets and mosques through his periscope.

Nasmith's return to the fleet was a testimonial to his professionalism. He had saved one 'fish' (torpedo) for the Turkish targets Boyle had reported on his exit, but Nasmith was disappointed to find no such targets as he slipped below Nagara Point into the Narrows. Turning *E11* in a strong current and a minefield, he calmly returned above Nagara Point and sank a transport he had earlier passed by in the hope of larger game.

The excitement was not yet over. After turning for home, Nasmith took a peep through his periscope to investigate an odd noise. The sight would have been petrifying: a mine cable had caught on *E11*'s forward hydroplane and the attached mine was floating ahead of the submarine in the current.

Keeping this to himself in order not to unduly frighten the crew, Nasmith calmly proceed down the strait, with the mine bumping in front of the submarine. Then he gave some baffling orders: reverse engines and blow the aft ballast tanks. The result was that *E11* rose to the surface with the stern up and bow down. Nasmith watched through his periscope as the mine floated away, pushed by both the current and the rush of water from the reversing screws, its cable slowly unravelling.

An awed Kipling wrote: 'Now a fool, said Dr Johnson, would have tried to describe that.'

Nasmith was awarded a Victoria Cross for this patrol. But it wasn't the one which really earned him the reputation as 'the Scourge of the Marmara'.

Returning to the Marmara, Nasmith had to burst through a net which the Turks had finally strung across the Narrows. Although the steel wire slid down the hull with a loud crack, Nasmith was unfazed. In the next few days he sank both a transport and the battleship *Harridin Barbarossa*, which the Turks had dispatched to Gallipoli so that its big guns could support the army's artillery. Nasmith's accurate torpedo hit the battleship amidships. When the ship's magazine exploded, *Harridin Barbarossa* rolled bottom up and sank.

E11's next exploit, however, was the real show stopper of the Marmara campaign. With the Turks forced to send most reinforcements to Gallipoli by rail and road, Nasmith and D'Oyly-Hughes devised a plan to block the rail line running down to the coast on the Asia Minor side.

Using material stolen from Turkish ships, the crew built a raft. That night in the Gulf of Ismid, Nasmith ran *E11* up to a beach near a viaduct on the railway line. D'Oyly-Hughes was floated to shore with a demolition charge. Armed with a revolver and bayonet, and carrying a torch as well as the explosive device, D'Oyly-Hughes set off for the viaduct.

He found his path was blocked by a Turkish patrol. Undaunted, he headed inland, stumbling through a fowl yard along the way. He found the viaduct, but it was under guard; damage from an earlier shot from *E11*'s gun was being repaired. (After the *AE2* breached the Narrows, Marmara-bound subs were equipped with guns to attack ships. Stoker's crew had cursed their lack of a gun.)

D'Oyly-Hughes stumbled back along the railway with his heavy package until he found a suitable spot in a culvert for the explosive charge. But firing the fuse-pistol gave away his position. He was chased to the beach by a Turkish patrol. D'Oyly-Hughes exchanged shots on the run. The demolition charge exploded just as he re-entered the water to swim out to where he thought the *E11* would be.

But the submarine was not there. D'Oyly-Hughes returned to the shore where he threw away his pistol, bayonet and torch, deciding to swim along the coast in search of his submarine. He was pretty much exhausted when he sighted what appeared to be a Turkish rowing boat. He turned for the beach, but on looking back saw that what he had thought was a rowing boat was actually the conning tower of *E11*. Nasmith picked him up just as pursuing Turks on the cliff opened fire with rifles.

With adventures like that it was no wonder that Nasmith, Boyle and D'Oyly-Hughes captured the public imagination.

The Narrows, however, retained its perils for intruding British and French submarines. The *Mariotte* became the third French submarine to come to grief. It struck an obstacle near Chanak, was abandoned and its crew all taken prisoner.

The British *E7*, after a successful raid in July when it emulated the *E11* by getting into the Golden Horn and shelling the Zeitun powder mills, had no luck on its second attempt in September. Captained by Lieutenant Commander Archibald Cochrane, *E7* was caught fast on the net the Turks had strung across the Narrows at Nagara. A 3-metre mesh of 7.5-centimetre wire, crossed and joined, it trapped Cochrane when he charged it. For three hours *E7* twisted and turned in the current. After a vain attempt at lying still before another charge at freedom, an explosive charge apparently dropped by the Turks rocked the boat. Cochrane brought the enmeshed *E7* to the surface to allow the crew to evacuate before scuttling the submarine.

Later, in a Turkish POW camp, Cochrane teamed up with Stoker in a failed escape bid. Cochrane eventually made it to freedom in a famous escape documented in Johnston and Yearsley's *Four-Fifty Miles to Freedom*.

One incident, however, marred the heroism of the Allied submarine campaign in the Marmara. In October 1915, the French submarine *Turquoise* under Captain Ravenel joined the fleet. Commodore Keyes gave Ravenel an extensive briefing to enable him to work with the British submarines already in the Marmara. This included precise details of a rendezvous he was expected to make with *E20*.

Ravenel took *Turquoise* safely under the mines and through the nets, followed the next day by *E20*. One British submarine reported him on the surface in the Marmara flying an enormous tricolour. But after eight days Ravenel unexpectedly headed for home. Moving down the strait *Turquoise* grounded in a shallow area before the Nagara net. Shore batteries opened fire. Ravenel's periscope was damaged, and he brought *Turquoise* to the surface, showed a white flag and surrendered.

The Turks captured *Turquoise* intact. One German report said the crew left in such a hurry that all the lights were left burning and an alarm bell ringing. *Turquoise* was towed to Constantinople, renamed *Mustejab Onbashy* (Worthy of Acceptance) and put to work as a charging station for German U-boats.

In Ravenel's cabin the Turks found his confidential papers, including details of his planned rendezvous with *E20* on 6 November. In Constantinople, the *U14* under Lieutenant von Heimburg hurriedly put to sea to make the meeting with an unsuspecting *E20*. A month before in the Mediterranean *U14* had sunk the troopship *Southland* with some 1400 Australians on board. Most were saved.

Heimburg recorded in his diary how he spotted *E20* waiting for its

Above: *Sultanhisar*, the Turkish torpedo boat that sent *AE2* to the bottom of the Dardanelles Strait.
(SELÇUK KOLAY—TURKISH ARCHIVES)

Above: *AE2* arriving at Portsmouth in 1914, before its voyage to Australia.

(S. CRIBB; SMYTH-HAGGARD COLLECTION)

Above: Detail of *AE2* and crew at Portsmouth, 1914.

(S. CRIBB; SMYTH-HAGGARD COLLECTION)

ABOVE: *AE2* crew at Malta, 1915. *Top, l-r:* Jenkins, Johnson, Walker, Broughton, Harding, Kerin, Knaggs, Suckling, Mitchell, Wilson. *Second row, l-r:* Gwynne, Talbot, Williams, Cullen, McCready, Nichols, Norris, Falconer, Wheat, Wishart, Cheater. *Third row, l-r:* Robinson, Fawns, Gibson, Vaughan, Abbott, Haggard, Stoker, Cary, Broomhead, Bell, Smith, Varcoe. *Front, l-r:* McGregor, Nash, Gilbert, Brown, Churcher, Bray, Kinder, Holderness, Thomson. (STOKER COLLECTION)

Above: *AE2* alongside HMAS *Sydney* in Trinity Inlet, Cairns, North Queensland, August 1914.

(CAIRNS HISTORICAL SOCIETY)

Right: *AE2* at Cairns, August 1914, en route to Kabaul.

(SELÇUK KOLAY—NAVAL MUSEUM, ISTANBUL, TURKEY)

Above: E class submarine's control room, including bunks, and washing and cooking facilities. (ROYAL NAVAL SUBMARINE MUSEUM, GOSPORT, UK)

Above: E class engine room—heat, noise and fumes.
(ROYAL NAVAL SUBMARINE MUSEUM, GOSPORT, UK)

Above: German propaganda postcard of the March 1915 Dardanelles action. (BRAY COLLECTION)

Above: Captain Stoker takes a bath at sea. (STOKER COLLECTION)

Above: *AE2* loading a torpedo warhead. (SMYTH-HAGGARD COLLECTION)

ABOVE: *AE2* passing a ship in the Suez Canal en route to Australia, showing how small it really was. (STOKER COLLECTION)

meeting with *Turquoise*. 'Very nice of her,' he commented. *U14* scored a direct hit. Picking up survivors, Heimburg told *E20*'s captain, Lieutenant-Commander Clyfford Warren, how he had learned of the rendezvous. 'The information left him speechless,' Heimburg said. 'Later I heard him discussing the situation with his officers. They were cursing their French allies as I had hoped.'

U14's hit showed that submarine success was not all on the Allied side. U-boats harassed the Allied fleet off Gallipoli, with the *U21* sinking two British battleships, *Triumph* and *Majestic*. The U-boat threat drove the big Allied battleships into harbour, disheartening the troops on Gallipoli. Commodore Roger Keyes, exasperated at the navy's failure, said these losses to German submarines were probably more than the fleet would have suffered had it made a direct charge at the Sea of Marmara through the Narrows. Keyes continued to push for a frontal attack on the Narrows by the navy, but de Robeck's dithering won the day.

Before the Allies evacuated Gallipoli eight months and many hectic battles after landing, nine British and one French submarine had passed through the Narrows into the Marmara. Nasmith and Boyle did it three times each, *E2* and *E12* twice. Jameson records that four British (including *AE2*) and three French submarines were sunk, either in the strait or the Marmara.

The last British submarine was recalled from the Marmara on 2 January 1916. The Turkish navy had all but ceased to operate in the area, while merchant shipping was drastically reduced. The tally of marauding submarines was one battleship, a destroyer, 5 gunboats, 11 transports, 44 steamers, several ammunition and supply ships and 148 other smaller craft sunk. In addition, they shelled troop concentrations and railway lines. 'Seaborne traffic through the Marmara was reduced to a trickle,' says Jameson in *Submariners V.C.* 'The enemy was forced to divert much of his limited resources to retaliation, using U-boats, guns, mines and personnel which were badly needed elsewhere.'

The official German naval historian, Admiral Eberhard von Mantey, commented: 'The activity of hostile submarines was a constant and heavy anxiety. They dislocated very seriously the conveyance of reinforcements to the Dardanelles and caused many disagreeable losses. If communication by sea had been completely severed, the Turkish army would have been faced with catastrophe.'

Winston Churchill said, 'The naval history of Britain contains no page more wonderful than that which describes the prowess of her submarines at the Dardanelles. Their exploits constitute the finest example of submarine warfare in the whole of the Great War.'

Dacre Stoker and the Australian *AE2* wrote the introduction to those Churchillian pages.

10

Noble Is As Noble Does

Constantinople turned on a stunning spring day on 1 May 1915 to greet the dishevelled crew of the *AE2*. The domes and minarets of mosques and palaces of the old Ottoman Empire glimmered in the sun as the *Sultanhisar* with its prisoners entered the Golden Horn.

On the streets, however, it was far from a warm welcome. Little boys ominously drew their fingers across their throats as the *AE2* crew was marched along through small crowds to the military barracks.

The crew had already spent an uncomfortable night. Captain Riza initially took the captured crew to the town of Gallipoli at the western end of the Marmara, immediately behind the fighting. That night, after what crewman Wheat described as 'a good meal for Turkey'—bread, garlic stew and some salad—the crew was crammed into a small cabin on the *Sultanhisar* for the voyage to Constantinople. Fleas and bugs in the confined space kept them awake. 'Nearly eaten alive with bugs and lice,' Knaggs noted in his diary.

At the dockside in Constantinople, a military guard came on board and issued the crew with the overcoat and trousers of a Turkish soldier's uniform that Captain Riza had requested. They were also issued slippers and a red fez. 'There was great laughter and joking amongst us while we were shifting into these clothes,' said Wheat.

The three officers refused to wear the fez, donning the navy caps they had kept despite losing the rest of their uniforms. The officers were put into a carriage sent by Enver Pasha. Guards with fixed bayonets surrounded the crew for the march to the main military barracks.

'A dismal proceeding, but marked by little incident,' noted Stoker. 'People gathered on the pathway, shopkeepers and their assistants crowded to the shop doors, trams and cabs stopped, and here and there behind heavily curtained windows a slight movement showed that even in the harem an interest in our passing was taking place.'

After moving through the big archway of the barracks with its two clocks—one for Turkish time and the other British time—the crew was ordered to a large room in what appeared to be the barrack prison. Guards brought tea and cigarettes.

Stoker was escorted to the office of the Commandant of Constantinople, 'a fine, tall, good-looking man with a cigarette holder about a foot long'. Stoker asked for food and a bath for his crew, and these were granted. The captured Australian crew must not look on themselves as prisoners, but more as honoured guests of Turkey, said the commandant. 'It sounded very nice,' said Stoker. 'But we were very young in the ways of the Turk.'

That afternoon, 'a most affable and polite gentleman' visited Stoker. He presented himself as the envoy of Enver Pasha and asked if he could do anything to assist the captured crew. Stoker was charmed. Enver Pasha, leader of the Young Turk rulers and the man who styled himself on Napoleon, was inquiring after the welfare of the *AE2* crew.

'Of course you know you have caused a great deal of trouble to everyone here, but in spite of that I think you will find your treatment will be very good,' the English-speaking envoy said. There were just a few questions that Enver Pasha would like answered. Stoker assured him that, if possible, he was quite ready to answer.

> 'How many torpedoes did *AE2* fire?' he asked.
>
> I regretted this could not be answered.
>
> It did not matter, he assured me; of course Enver Pasha knew.
>
> 'What day did you enter the Marmara?'
>
> I again regretted. It did not matter, of course they knew that too.

Further questions flowed in the same vein. Stoker refused to answer. Departing, the visitor held out his hand and smiled.

'Oh, well. Perhaps you will change your mind. It might be to your advantage to do so. Think it over. Goodbye.'

The smile had died from his face, said Stoker. 'Into the last two sentences he placed such inflections on the simple words that converted them into the most ominous threat I had ever heard. I turned at the door and looked at him, but his face was now an expressionless mask.'

Food for the crew quickly deteriorated. 'Not fit for pigs,' was Knaggs' description of an evening meal of boiled peas with what Wheat called a 'nauseous grease floating over the top of the water'.

Some ten crew were questioned on similar lines to Stoker. All either refused to answer or gave absurd answers. The three officers were separated from the men, but all suffered from nightly attacks of bugs and lice.

Stoker quickly found the sting to the threat from his well-spoken visitor. He was brought before three Turkish naval officers, who quizzed him intently on the same issues; of the number of torpedoes on the *AE2*, how the submarine had got through the Dardanelles, and how many had followed. Stoker refused to answer.

Led away, he was taken down a long, damp passage and escorted into a small, dark room. Though a cloud of tobacco smoke he could see a group of six or seven Turks crammed on two bench bunks along the walls. 'There must be some mistake,' Stoker protested in a rage as the guards cleared a bunk space for him amid the 'evil looking men' and disappeared.

'*Bonjour, m'sieur*!' said one of the powerfully-built inmates, offering Stoker a cigarette. Asked who he was, Stoker replied that he was the commander of the submarine *AE2*.

'And a brave commandant, too,' said his Turkish cellmate. Why was that, inquired Stoker. 'Because you passed the Dardanelles.' Stoker was instantly on guard against these obvious plants, who admitted that they were officers but would not say why they were in the cell.

As the hours wore away, Stoker's sniffly cold turned to fever. The heavy cigarette smoke in the small room brought on an acute headache as well. Cries for a doctor were ignored, as Stoker's 'evil-looking friend' pummelled him for information about the *AE2*.

'Answers he wants, so let him have them—and such gloriously beautiful lies came to my tired and fevered brain,' said Stoker. 'I more than doubled the number of torpedoes *AE2* carried. She had cut her way through the minefield with marvellous wire-cutters fitted in the bows. Oh yes, men could get out of the submarine and walk along the bottom. There were heaven knows how many submarines in the Marmara at the present moment ... and while he was yet talking I dozed off into unconsciousness.'

When Stoker woke the room was empty of smoke and his evil-looking friend, one of only three Turks left, was asleep. Piecing the incident together later, Stoker believed the men were Turkish officers arrested in a victualling scandal who were later executed. 'But on that night I am certain they were promised some reward if the required information had been got out of me. Or was it all a dream?'

Next day, Stoker was cross-examined by Enver Pasha himself. The threats, said Stoker, 'were now less thinly veiled'. Refusing to answer, Stoker was hustled off to solitary confinement 'until I should show some sign of sense'.

The small cell had a window onto the barrack square, where soldiers spent the day drilling. Left alone to watch the stomp of training, Stoker somehow acquired a pencil and paper to indulge his 'distressing habit of perpetrating bad verse'.

They locked me up alone here
Because their 'Third Degree'
Hadn't gained the information
They wished to force from me,
Concerning how the submarines
Had reached their private sea
To stop the Turkish soldier
Do the Goose-step.
It isn't very pleasant
In my solitary cell,
But fancy them believin'
This can ever make me tell
The way to catch the other boats!

I'd rather go to—well,
Where Turks and Germans both
Perform the Goose-step.
Goose-step, Goose-step,
The Kultured soldiers' Goose-step,
With toe a-pointed fling your leg in loose step.
But if I was out there learnin'
I'd get close behind some German
And fling my foot up higher
Than the Goose-step.

Stoker obviously had strong inner resources. These would be sorely needed in the years ahead. Several days later, after being taken into a courtyard for a photograph with his men, the entire *AE2* crew was moved out by ship and then train to Afion Kara Hissar (modern Afyon) in the centre of Asia Minor.

The name Afion Kara Hissar means black opium fortress. In ancient times the town had been the centre of the pre-Hellenic Phrygian culture. While the old ruin on the town's summit of a sheer rock looks impressive, the *AE2* crew found it a mercilessly cold and dirty place.

Stoker was appalled by the 'indescribable filth', and the 'absolute lack' of sanitary arrangements. 'Houses simply cast their rubbish out of the front or from a window; the only scavenging is done by the numerous mongrels.' The three officers and the crew were again separated, with the crew finding their room so cold they could not sleep.

'That night, we shall never forget,' said Wheat. 'First of all we stowed ourselves together to try and keep warm but it was no good, so most of us spent the night marching up and down the room singing to try and keep life in us, for the cold made it impossible to sleep.' Appeals to the guards brought cries of 'Did England send all invalids to fight for her?'

Two days later they were moved to another building, where the 29 crew had to eat, sleep and sit on the floor of a small room close to the obnoxious smell of what passed for toilets. But there was company. Survivors of Brodie's *E15*, lost in the Dardanelles Strait only a fortnight before the *AE2*'s successful passage, were next door. So were about 200 Russian seamen captured in Constantinople, and several French sailors. A few Australian soldiers captured in the Gallipoli fighting also straggled in.

Some of the crew were put to work on local roads. They were allowed to buy small necessities, and Stoker somehow found £6 which he sent to them. The American embassy in Constantinople also sent money, which the camp commandant eked out to the prisoners. But the prisoners felt they were overcharged for food, and at two piastres a bath the view set in, as Wheat said, that 'we were robbed'.

The months of 1915 wore on. Stoker called the camp 'living death'. The *AE2* prisoners heard nothing of the failed August offensive, in which the Allies tried to break out of their Gallipoli stalemate. Gallipoli then became synonymous with failure, and it was only a matter of months before all the troops were evacuated.

Then along came one of Stoker's straws in the wind. One day the camp commandant summoned the officers together. 'Well, gentlemen, I want to find out which among you are of the highest and most distinguished families in England,' he said.

This was indeed a strange request. Stoker, as the senior officer was quick to point out that it was not an easy one to answer. Surely, said the commandant, there were degrees. 'Some must be higher than others, and some of you may have relatives who are ministers or holding high military or public posts in England at present,' he said.

Stoker said they would discuss it. 'I turned to admire the row of noblemen seated around the room,' he said. 'With their nondescript clothing, their various stages of grown and growing prisoners' beards, and their general air of dejection, they were not—if the truth be known—showing many outward signs of the very blue blood which was doubtless coursing through their several veins. One Australian military officer, two Australian volunteer officers, four English RN officers, one RNR [Reserve] officer, one RNVR [Volunteer Reserve] officer—and the greatest of these . . .?'

As the commandant had omitted to disclose his purpose, the suspicion arose that the two selected would be somehow rewarded.

A great game ensued. Claims of family connections up through the peerage, politics, judiciary—even to possible succession to the late Queen Victoria—were aired. The commandant, says Stoker, looked pleased, noting 'weird Turkish hieroglyphics against our names'.

Eventually, Lieutenant Geoffrey Fitzgerald of the *E15* was awarded top spot. 'Fitz', as Stoker put it, was 'a shining, if minor, light of a famous Irish family boasting a reigning Duke as its head'. Stoker himself, although not nobility, could claim his affluent family of Dublin doctors, not to mention his relationship with Bram Stoker, the famous author of *Dracula*.

The commandant then revealed his hand. Enver Pasha had written him a letter saying that Turkish prisoners of war in Egypt were being very badly treated by the British. 'Was it imagination, or did Fitz's blue-blooded face take a slightly blue-greyish tinge?' quipped Stoker.

The prisoners protested that the information was wrong. Stoker offered to immediately write to the British government for assurances of fair treatment of Turkish prisoners. But he demanded permission to write more than four lines, the maximum allowed for each letter by a prisoner.

'I shall do better than that,' the commandant replied quickly—a bit too quickly for Stoker—'I shall send you and Monsieur Fitz to Constantinople and there you can explain to Enver Pasha and the American ambassador everything you have said to me.'

A trip to Constantinople! After five months of Afion Kara Hissar, Stoker and Fitzgerald found the prospect overwhelming. 'Well, I'll be damned,' exclaimed one of their colleagues. 'If I'd known there was a trip to Constantinople in it, I'd have been a viscount at least!'

Stoker was suspicious. It all seemed too sudden. Months of captivity and experience with the Turks had taught him that things were not always as they seemed. 'One wondered . . .', he wrote.

He turned to the commandant. 'I should like your assurance that we are not going to be shot immediately we arrive.' The commandant laughed. 'I will give you my parole that you will not be shot immediately you arrive,' he responded. 'I cannot say exactly what you will do. The position is that unless this matter is adjusted reprisals will have to be commenced against the prisoners here to force the English government to behave in a humane manner. Therefore all prisoners should write about it in their next letters, and you two will go to Constantinople and explain all you know to Enver Pasha and the American ambassador, from whom I believe this information comes. You will start tomorrow.'

Tomorrow! Stoker and Fitzgerald were dumbfounded. 'Can you imagine being dead—having been dead for five months—and then being awaked to be told that tomorrow you will enter upon life again?' Stoker said. 'The result, to put it mildly, is bewildering.'

The Russian, French, English and Australian prisoners buzzed with excitement. They quickly divided into two camps. The Optimists wished Stoker and Fitzgerald luck; they were going to ride on a train, see a city again and speak to a known friend, the American ambassador. The Pessimists doubted the whole thing: would Stoker and Fitzgerald ever be seen again?

For their part, Stoker and Fitzgerald sided with the Optimists. In the heady atmosphere of imminent freedom, they pictured themselves as representatives of the British aristocracy going to do the noble work of righting wrong, returning to Afion Kara Hissar with glorious news about the imminent end of the war.

'Go to, Pessimists, go to!' Stoker philosophised in his inevitable erring on the bright side of life. 'We will have none of you! Ye would destroy all that makes life worth living. Yesterday—what is it? Dead and gone; it holds no interest. Today? A hard and unpleasant reality. But tomorrow. Ah! Tomorrow will be different. Tomorrow will be glorious. Tomorrow will be splendid. Our hopes and dreams of wonderful Tomorrow make life. Go to, Pessimists. Ye do not live!'

The next morning guards came to escort the two to Constantinople. Colleagues shouted farewells. But at the railway station, said Stoker, mocking himself, their aristocratic tastes were offended: the guards escorted them into a second-class carriage for the journey to Constantinople. The disappearing hovels of Afion Kara Hissar as the train pulled away relieved any mock distress. Stoker and Fitzgerald revelled in their first private discussion outside prisoner of war camp.

'We were going to have a most amusing experience; we were having a glorious break in the cruel monotony of a prisoner's life,' Stoker parodied. 'We were representing British Nobility, and were going to act to it for all we were worth. Noble is as Noble does. Just a touch of a swagger as one entered the room; a hint of drawl in the voice when talking; a subtle conveying to Enver Pasha that, though he might be a deuce of a fellow to the Turks, some of his attributes did not commend themselves to a British gentleman's ideas. In short, we were going to be rather devils of fellows ourselves.'

Then came the first excitement of the trip. As the train stopped at a station Fitzgerald jumped up and flung himself at a window. The guards leapt to attention, thinking he was trying to escape. But Stoker quickly discovered the cause of Fitzgerald's excitement. He had seen an unveiled woman!

''Twas indeed a wondrous sight!' said Stoker. She may have been a Greek or an Armenian; unless she were a goddess she can have had little idea of the most unaristocratic excitement she raised in two feigning aristocratic breasts.'

11

'What About Me?'

The dreams of the two 'noble' submariners were quickly shattered. On arrival at the office of the Commandant of Constantinople there was nobody to greet them. Even the commandant was out. The two were marched straight into a prison cell. 'Bang went Optimism,' Stoker said, recalling the divided views of his colleagues left in Afion Kara Hissar.

For a week the two shared a cell, swearing and telling themselves that all would be right as soon as the commandant or the American ambassador discovered what had happened to them. Stoker later indulged his acute sense of irony. 'The Nobility have been known to display a very fair command of the stronger forms of language as spoken in moments of stress, in the hunting field, for example, so we considered this form of cheap relief quite permissible.'

As the days dwindled by, their optimism diminished. But a little remained, and each day they shaved, cleaned their shoes and brushed their clothes. They had been allowed to bring books from Afion. Each day they penned letters to the commandant.

Fitzgerald, a merchant seaman in civilian life, proved a great companion for Stoker. His natural humour and strong sense of confidence made people around him, as Stoker noted, feel that life, after all, must be a good thing. Stoker relished Fitzgerald's stories of supposed hardship. 'His tales of these were just the things to beguile the monotonous days away, and take one's fancy roaming far from our bestial surroundings to scenes of merry life, fashionable restaurants, night clubs, shaded lights, lovely ladies, soft music, bathing picnics in semi-tropical sunshine—or by moonlight—with beauteous American heiresses, etc, etc,' Stoker reminisced. 'Oh, but indeed he had led a sorry life! Poor old Fitz!'

A week later, after an uncomfortable bath with Turkish soldiers, the two were returned to their cell to find their bags and small possessions had been searched. 'Now you will be moved to another room,' a guard told them.

The two were bundled into a courtyard where their bags were stripped of most articles, including safety razors, insect powder, medicines, books and letters. Both were searched, with guards removing their pocketknives and letters.

Stoker was marched off alone, down corridors and dark passages until an officer, with mock ceremony, ushered him into his new 'room'. Inside, Stoker could not see anything as it seemed completely dark. 'Then, as my sight became more adjusted, I saw that the details would not require much taking in,' said Stoker. 'A prison bed and a small round table stood in sorry occupation of a cell of the precise dimensions of ten square feet. High up one of the walls a tiny hole of a window opened, not to the air, but into an adjoining and gloomy room, this being the only means by which the tiny amount of light entered the cell. The floor was swimming in water, having apparently just been sluiced down. And this was my new home!'

Then, another shock. The food that arrived with a small, rickety oil lamp was a plate of three small potatoes soaked in greasy oil, and a small portion of dark bread. 'It was, indeed, a fitting repast for a representative of the noblesse,' said Stoker. 'But that amusing idea did not occur to me at the time—I fear my sense of humour had totally and completely disappeared by then.'

Stoker tried unsuccessfully to eat, and then to sleep. But the bed was crawling with bugs. Stoker 'slaughtered' several hundred. The stench of dead insects combined with the lack of ventilation and wet floor was dreadful. He tried to sleep, but within minutes he felt a bug on his face. 'I jumped up and held the lamp over to search,' he said. 'The bed was swarming with the filthy brutes.'

After another failed attempt to kill them off, Stoker took to pacing the floor. He could manage just four paces each way. He spent the night until dawn in bouts of trying to sleep, killing bugs and walking the floor before exhaustion took over.

About 10.30 am guards roused him. 'There did not seem to be a single portion of my body that the bugs had not visited,' Stoker said. Breakfast, a *chaubar* of grain immersed in broth, was eaten in darkness as his lamp had been removed. With the floor still wet, Stoker was in a grim mood as he was taken to see the commandant.

In an overfurnished office, and surrounded by officers all heel-clicking and saluting, the commandant addressed Stoker through an interpreter. 'First of all I should like you clearly to understand that everything that follows is an entirely impersonal matter,' he said. 'This is an affair between governments, and in no sense are you personally concerned. I hope you understand that point.'

Stoker forced himself to smile as the commandant continued. It was, thought Stoker, much the same tale as he had heard at Afion Kara Hissar with a few adornments. The Turkish government was horrified to learn of 'indignities and sufferings' handed out to Turkish officers in prison camps in Egypt. Stoker suppressed a smile at the thought of Enver Pasha and Talaat Bey—the Young Turks then had something of a gangster reputation—weeping in each other's arms at the sorrows of their countrymen.

And where had this information come from? It had been reported officially to the War Office by the Turkish Foreign Minister. Stoker protested that it was completely wrong, but the commandant would hear none of it. Reluctantly, he said, it had been decided that as a reprisal to force the British government into action, two British officers would be given the same treatment as that endured by the Turkish POWs. It was, repeated the commandant nothing personal, merely a misfortune. Stoker and Fitzgerald should consider it an honour that they should suffer for the sins of their government.

A remarkably doubtful honour, thought Stoker.

The Young Turks were fond of reprisals. American ambassador Henry Morgenthau later recounted that after the Gallipoli invasion he had to dissuade Enver Pasha from a madcap scheme of rounding up British and French expatriates in Constantinople and putting them on the front line.

Stoker and Fitzgerald, said the commandant, would be confined to their new cells and receive the food of a Turkish soldier until a 'satisfactory report' was received of the state of Turkish officers in Egypt. They would also write to all their influential friends asking them to help relieve the plight of the Turkish POWs.

Nothing would dissuade the commandant. He clearly had orders. Stoker asked that Fitzgerald be sent for to have the situation explained to him. Stoker was sitting to one side as Fitzgerald entered the commandant's office.

'I could not help laughing,' Stoker said. 'Game to the last, he rolled from the door up to the commandant's table with superb swagger and a gloriously aristocratic, supercilious look—despite the fact that his toilet had obviously not been performed in the careful manner of the past week.' When he spotted Stoker, the two shared their experiences of the darkness, bugs and horrible food of their new cells.

Stoker had to explain the situation to Fitzgerald, who at first became agitated and uttered some 'quite unaristocratic language'. Stoker tried to calm him. Later, Fitzgerald attributed to Stoker some remarks which proved quite prophetic.

'There is no good our getting excited over this business,' Fitzgerald claimed Stoker told him. 'The only thing to do is to go through with it like good little boys, and if we do that in all probability we will gain a lump of chocolate in the end.'

Stoker, of course, had no idea of the lump of chocolate that Fitzgerald would eventually receive, but his words turned Fitzgerald to consider the more practical aspects of their situation. What about extra food, could they buy it? 'No,' responded the commandant.

'Will we be allowed to smoke?' The commandant hesitated before answering 'yes' with a smile. ''Twas a little straw, but little straws often lead to great differences—the difference between sanity and insanity, for example,' said Stoker.

Fitzgerald and Stoker then asked the commandant to note their formal protest, and to grant four requests: an officer should visit their cells every day; a doctor should visit them once a week; arrangements should be made that letters of request or demand would be immediately delivered to the commandant; and insect powder should be provided.

The commandant assented to all these requests, writing down an order immediately for the insect powder to be delivered.

The two were marched back to their cells, dawdling in the barracks square to gain some of 'God's fresh air'. 'The last time we would taste it, for how long?' Stoker wondered. 'The brain reeled at the thought of how long it might be.' Fitzgerald thought a week of solitary confinement in a dark hole on bread and water would be enough to send any man mad.

Stoker feared, however, that there was little hope of them being freed in a week. British officials might react quickly, but the Turkish style meant 'there was sure to be much delay'. The two decided, as they lingered in the square, to write to as many people as possible. Fitzgerald had an uncle in the War Office who, he thought, 'may be honoured with a letter'.

As Stoker turned towards his cell, he was arrested by a cry from Fitzgerald: '"Goodbye," he said, stretching out his hand. I have heard many goodbyes spoken—they play a large part in a sailor's life—but few I have heard could compare in depth of feeling to Fitz's effort then!'

Back in his cell, Stoker paced the wet floor and was surprised to find himself remarkably cheery. 'It is, I am told, a characteristic of Irishmen that they always dwell either in the heights of lightheartedness, or the depths of depression, little moving them to either extreme.' The reason for his lightheartedness, Stoker theorised, was that at least he knew what was ahead of him. 'Unknown is the thing above all others which we poor mortals tend to funk.'

And then there was the added impersonality of it all. How grateful the British government must be at their incarceration! As a 'fitting partner' to his mental picture of the Young Turk leaders weeping over their ill-treated compatriots, Stoker conjured up a picture of Asquith and Sir Edward Grey (the British Prime Minister and the Foreign Secretary) pouring profuse thanks on the two prisoners at cabinet meetings.

The small black airless cells the two had to endure over the following days and weeks sorely tested such humour. The first night the promised insect powder failed to arrive. Stoker waited most of the night for it, using a box of matches to try to burn out the insect holes. In between times, he wrote letters by the feeble light of his lamp. The most important, as it later transpired, was to the American ambassador, Henry Morgenthau.

The days and nights dragged on, although for Stoker and Fitzgerald it was hard to tell the difference. With no exercise and poor food, the treatment was close to torture. Stoker liked to make jokes about it in his later writings, but in his first reports immediately after the war he was clearly angry at the treatment.

Stoker, in fact, wrote out a charge sheet against the commandant, Djevad Bey, in 1918. Amongst the many cruelties, he listed the fact that while in solitary confinement he had often to wait hours before a corporal would escort him to the toilet.

Insect powder finally arrived, although there were no regular inspections by an officer or doctor as promised. Stoker started a calendar on his wall to tick off the days. How many would he have to cross off?

'Lying in darkness, in utter idleness all day, no exercise, no proper nourishment—what must be the natural result? A diseased body or a diseased mind ... oh, come, come! I was making rather heavy weather of it. It wasn't going to last as long as all that. Ten days or a fortnight should see the end. But, ye gods, even a fortnight would take some sticking!'

Stoker tried to set himself a regime. He began a journal and performed daily exercises in his cramped room. The journal, he said, proved a godsend, and he would endlessly conjure up entries as he paced the floor. What, he speculated, would Mr Pepys have written in the circumstances? Then Oscar Wilde came to mind. But he would even have lacked the company of those men in Reading gaol who 'looked so wistfully at the sky', and would have longed for a tiny glimpse of the 'fleecy little clouds that went a-scurrying by', said Stoker, parodying his situation while desperately trying to retain a vein of humour.

Once Stoker spent an entire day trying to recollect as many stories as he possibly could from *Punch*, the popular British weekly. It ended with him composing a letter to the editor.

Dear Mr Punch

It has often been my custom in moments of depression to rouse my drooping spirits by recalling to mind the words of wit and wisdom I have seen in your pages. In particular I have found much amusement and instruction in the cartoons you published some years ago on the subject of 'The Unspeakable Turk'. But as I write, from solitary confinement in a darkened cell where I am the prisoner of the aforesaid Turks, I somehow find that the memory of these very cartoons fails to stir my soul to such paroxysms of mirth as formerly, whilst the lesson I should take from their instructiveness is now far from plain to me!

This, you will realise, is a most sad state of affairs. Must I consider that my sense of humour is vanishing?

In my anxiety I hasten to ask your advice. For if it be really true that my sense of humour is already going I can but subscribe myself, in deepest sorrow,

Yours, etc

Too Old at Thirty

The letter was not dispatched for fear that the Turkish censor might lack a sense of humour.

Stoker soon discovered that he was not completely alone. His cell was also inhabited by a very large rat, which Stoker estimated at half the size of a grown rabbit. Christened 'Archibald', the rat appeared to reside inside the walls around the cell, and paid Stoker many visits.

Although Stoker made light of Archibald, saying he should have tamed him and sent him out with a note to the American embassy, he was quite alarmed by his presence. A friend had been bitten in bed by a rat while staying in a country hotel years before, and suffered acute blood poisoning. He developed into a 'pitiable sight', and doctors could give him no promise of a permanent cure.

Apart from Archibald's excessively noisy eating, Stoker also endured the nightly noise of a Turkish military band playing in the square outside the adjoining Ministry of War. 'Their selection was not a very vast one—appearing to consist of only five numbers, of which they gave three each night, so that one got to know them all intimately,' he recalled. 'One also got to know the places where the brassy gentlemen invariably seemed to get short of wind, where the piccolo insisted on inserting two false notes, where the gentleman with the big drum always came in too late with his thump. There is a supreme agony in these things when your nerves are already on edge from over-solitude and gloomy darkness. It was a very real torture—a fiendish, devilish torture to me.'

Stoker, however, tried to laugh it away, claiming it quite proper that a nobleman's dinner should be accompanied by music. But the darkness, the discordant music and the solitude conjured up vivid dreams and imaginative flights in which Stoker pictured himself and Fitzgerald being executed. If that happened, the commandant would surely explain that it was impersonal! 'One could occasionally defeat the depression caused by the band,' Stoker joked.

A week dragged by. Fortunately, Stoker found that he could work his way into a daily sleeping routine. After dinner, he would pace and write until the early hours, sleeping until breakfast, when he would smoke to produce drowsiness until the midday meal, after which he would sleep until dinner. 'So the days passed.'

Surprisingly, letters from his sister were delivered. Then, after daily written complaints to the commandant, a parcel arrived. Apparently from the American embassy, it contained two excellent rugs, a pillow, sponge, toothbrush and tooth powder, socks, slippers, handkerchiefs and — 'wondrous links to civilisation'—pyjamas.

After about a fortnight, Stoker began to hallucinate. He later recalled details of long conversations with Archibald and various pieces of furniture. One day he was taken out for a bath before being brought in front of the commandant. Stoker was amazed to see in a mirror how much weight he had lost. 'There did not seem to be an ounce of flesh left on me,' he said. 'Every rib was sticking out in most startling manner.'

In the commandant's office, with a lamp shining directly on his face, Stoker was informed that 'negotiations between the two governments were in progress, a few days should see them finished'. The commandant handed Stoker an overcoat that had been received from the American embassy.

Back in his cell, the days passed with no sign of release. As he lay in the dark, Stoker began to worry about events outside his prison walls. The entry of Bulgaria into the war on Germany's side gave him cause for concern.

Earlier the POWs at Afion Kara Hissar had discovered a secret conduit to the American embassy. An Austrian woman allowed to live in the town with her interned Bulgarian husband had offered to transmit messages to the embassy on her periodic visits to Constantinople. She proved a reliable emissary, and an emboldened Stoker had written a long message on the appalling conditions of POWs. This message was still in the woman's hands, and now her husband's country had joined the war on the other side.

There was nothing Stoker could do except ponder secrecy and women, coming up with a gallant piece of poetry.

Constant you are
But yet a woman; and for secrecy
No lady closer.

Stoker later learned that the message was delivered safely. But life in his cell—particularly after a brush with a second rat that had jumped onto his bed—was becoming unbearable.

Just as he was contemplating how the utter abhorrence of life can crush one's soul, his circumstances changed dramatically. 'The gods are kind—something always happens.'

On 4 November, 32 days after the pair had arrived in Constantinople and 25 days since his entry to the black hole, Stoker was awakened from a doze to find the commandant in his cell. Was there anything he needed, the commandant inquired? 'I smiled, and replied there were a great many.'

After the commandant had issued orders for food to be delivered, an interpreter told Stoker he would be allowed out for air. 'For good?' inquired Stoker. No, just for an hour or so. Stoker dressed and was escorted into the garden.

'Hullo, old chap.'

'I looked up,' said Stoker, 'and there, with outstretched hand, was the one and only blue-blooded, ginger-bearded, aristocratic impersonal reprisalist, Fitz! His face, as ever, was covered by a glorious grin; but its colour was ghastly—a light canary yellow, with greyish streaks, well matched by some of the dead autumn leaves lying in the little railed-in patch of garden where we sat.'

Fitzgerald and Stoker stumbled out their experiences of 25 days in solitary confinement, to find they had been remarkably similar. Fitzgerald told Stoker how he had fallen into the habit of holding imaginary conversations, his favourite being a train station meeting with his sister followed by a restaurant meal—with Fitzgerald doing the ordering. Fitzgerald also had rats, but, said Stoker, 'had not met Archibald'.

The two were allowed to chat for a while before being returned to their cells. Then, about an hour later as Stoker began to contemplate how solitary confinement could become tolerable if he were only allowed more such outings, he heard Fitzgerald calling and shouting his name in the passageway before bursting into his cell. He brought exciting news: 'We are to be released!'

The two were taken to a large, airy room in the prison. Stoker and Fitzgerald savoured the atmosphere. 'Hundreds of windows it seemed to have, and they could be opened, and were opened, on to the outside world,' said Stoker. 'Through them came the clean sweet evening breeze. We could see the lights of houses on the banks of the Bosporus more than two miles off, and the very lights of God's heaven millions of miles off—think of it, millions of miles we could see instead of a view bounded by four walls ten feet apart! And tomorrow we would be awakened by the light of day and be able to look on the sparkling waters of the Golden Horn and the Bosporus, on houses which contained living and free people, on ships moving and ships at anchor, on the sun in the sky, on those "fleecy little clouds" ... Oh, it was good to be alive!'

The next day the pair were taken before the commandant who told them that their part in the game between the British and Turkish governments was over. He wished them a speedy return to health, and told them they would be sent out to a hotel to recuperate. Provided the two gave their word not to attempt escape, they would be free to move around, although accompanied by a Turkish guardian. They were to look on the guardian as a mentor and friend. Had they any money? No. Sign for £5 each, please. The commandant wished them goodbye, and asked them when they returned to England to speak well of the Commandant of Constantinople.

'We gasped, and continued to gasp,' said Stoker. 'Gaspingly, later in the day, we were led by our guide, mentor and friend without the precincts of the prison and to the hotel. Gaspingly we ordered a colossal dinner and ate it. Gaspingly we asked for a bottle of whisky, and got it! Gaspingly I tried to write in my journal, and gaspingly we went to bed. And I'd have you to know that our bed had clean white sheets and SPRINGS!'

The person behind this incredible transformation from 25 days in solitary confinement to white sheets in a leading Constantinople hotel was Henry Morgenthau, the US ambassador to Constantinople from 1913 to 1916. Morgenthau's various books provide a rare insider's view of Constantinople's machinations during the Gallipoli campaign. His report of the widespread Turkish belief that the mighty British navy had been on the brink of victory in its 18 March attack on the Dardanelles Strait, despite huge losses, illustrates the cost of indecision on the Gallipoli exercise.

Morgenthau also reported a fascinating conversation between Baron von Wangenheim, the powerful German ambassador to Turkey and Field Marshal von der Goltz Pasha, who was then governor of Belgium. Over coffee in Wagenheim's office, both Germans pondered deeply on why Britain had been so public about the naval losses it suffered in the 18 March attack. Unheard of, extraordinary, the German master diplomats muttered. Their only rationale for Britain's failure to resume the attack was that, in the event of success, it did not want to hand Constantinople over to Russia, as agreed by the War Council. By publishing its losses, Britain demonstrated to Moscow the impossibility of the task. 'After such losses, England intended Russia to understand that she had made a sincere effort to gain this great prize of war and expected her not to insist on further sacrifices,' Morgenthau reported. While this involves only the naval exercise, it provides a revealing insight into German thinking about Gallipoli.

Morgenthau had received the letters Stoker and Fitzgerald had sent him from prison. Interestingly, he believed both were Australians. He suggested to Enver Pasha that a neutral doctor be appointed to examine the truth of reports that Turkish prisoners in Egypt were being mistreated by the British. Word was promptly received that the reports were false.

'You see how shamefully you treated these young men?' Morgenthau told Enver Pasha in typically frank American style. 'You should do something to make amends.'

As prisoners of war, Stoker and Fitzgerald normally would have been sent back to prison camp. But Morgenthau urged Enver to give them a 'vacation' of eight days.

Enver 'entered into the spirit of the occasion', and agreed to their release. 'They certainly presented a sorry sight; they had spent twenty-five days in the dungeon, with no chance to bath or shave, with no change of linen or any of the decencies of life,' said Morgenthau. 'But Mr Hoffman Philip [a counsellor at the US embassy] took charge, furnished them the necessities, and in a brief period we had before us two young and handsome British naval officers.'

Stoker's record of these few days of freedom reads like a dream sequence. Cars at their disposal, complete new outfits at the best shops, moved to one of the best hotels, swank lunches and American Red Cross Hospital treatment for the deafness the two contracted in prison.

During the 'vacation', Stoker developed a great fondness for the Reverend Dr Robert Frew, an expatriate Britisher, and Hoffman Philip, the American diplomat who had worked hard for British prisoners in Turkey. Frew was a Scot, and Stoker relished the yarn that after Philip had recovered from a life-threatening illness, Frew had visited him. 'Ah, Philip,' he said, 'ye're better, are ye? Mon, I'd arranged the finest funeral for ye that there'd ever been in Constantinople!' Later Dr Frew arranged for a bolt of English suit cloth to be delivered to the officers at Afion. They had very strange garments made up by a Turkish tailor unused to western styling.

The following Sunday the two were taken for a drive in the 'million-horse-powered ambassadorial car' along the shores of the Bosporus to the American Girls College for a church service. Morgenthau, giving the reading, noted the attendance of the two who had come 'from out of the world'.

Stoker and Fitzgerald were entranced by the 'groups of pig-tailed faeries' who gazed at them in wide-eyed wonder. It must have been an enchanting day for the men after their traumatic experience. Stoker said Morgenthau spoke of the different nationalities and religions mixing in peace at the school. 'The girl on the extreme left of the front row of the choir had an extremely pretty profile,' commented Stoker, demonstrating that 25 days in solitary confinement may have temporarily robbed him of his hearing, but not his eye for a pretty face.

Then it all disappeared as quickly as it happened. Five days into their 'vacation', not eight as Enver had promised, the two awoke to find military police in their hotel room. 'Without a handshake or goodbye to any of our new-found friends, we were bundled into a train, and returned to Afion Kara Hissar,' said Stoker.

But the adventures of the two 'nobles' had one final bizarre twist.

About the time Morgenthau had found out about the two languishing in solitary confinement as a reprisal, he had an audience with Monsignor Dolci, the Catholic Apostolic Delegate to Turkey. Monsignor Dolci told him he was very interested in finding a certain Lieutenant Fitzgerald, a prisoner at Afion Kara Hissar who was engaged to the daughter of the British Minister to the Vatican. Dolci had taken up Fitzgerald's case with Enver, who had promised he would receive special treatment.

12

The Fourth Man

The sudden Allied withdrawal from the Gallipoli stalemate in December 1915 caused consternation amongst the prisoners of war in Turkey. While the fighting continued there was always the hope of an end to the war and release from prison. When the troops were evacuated and the armada sailed away, those hopes were dashed. 'To me personally the event marked the fixing of my determination to attempt escape at the first possible moment,' said Stoker.

But how? Afion Kara Hissar was some 208 kilometres from the Mediterranean coast of Turkey, not counting the perils of the mountainous country in between. There was no chance of support from the locals. The consensus in the camp was that escape was impossible.

Stoker, however, had the same view about impossible escapes as he had about impossible submarine penetration of the Narrows—nothing was impossible until it was proven so. He sent a secret message home via the departing Fitzgerald that he would attempt an escape in a few months, as soon as the snow melted.

Stoker believed his plan was simplicity itself. The sleepy guards presented no problem. Once past them he would travel by night over the mountains to reach the coast, 'dodge the coastguard, steal a boat, and make for an island—hoping in the meantime to fall in with a friendly patrol ship'.

Stoker was careful not to tell his fellow *AE2* officers, Haggard and Cary of his plans. 'I knew [they] would have insisted on starting with me no matter how hopeless the chances seemed to them.'

The arrival in Afion Kara Hissar of the captured crew of the *E7*, and its captain, Archibald Cochrane, presented Stoker with an opportunity. A conversation with Cochrane revealed that the two had similar ideas

'What's his first name?' asked Morgenthau.

'Geoffrey.'

'He's receiving special treatment indeed. Do you know that he is in a dungeon in Constantinople at this very moment?'

Morgenthau took up the case with Enver. 'Don't you think he's been punished enough?' he asked. 'Why don't you let the boy go home and marry his sweetheart?'

The proposition immediately appealed to Enver's sentimental side. 'I'll do it,' he replied, 'if he will give me his word of honour not to fight against Turkey any more.'

Back in Afion Kara Hissar, Stoker and Fitzgerald were unaware of this bizarre twist. But about a month after their return, two priests arrived at the camp by special arrangement of the Pope and Turkish authorities. They brought astounding news from Monsignor Dolci. Owing to the intervention of the Pope, Fitzgerald would be released to go back to England on account that he had suffered unjust imprisonment.

'But what of me?' Stoker cried. 'I, too, you know, underwent the unpleasantness of this unjust imprisonment!' Be patient, the priests counselled. Monsignor Dolci would work for his release as well as soon as that of Fitzgerald was assured.

If Fitzgerald was bewildered by this turn of events, Stoker found himself mulling over the potential injustice if only one was released. He started to question his religious values. Stoker, although Irish born, was a Protestant of Huguenot origins.

'The only reason put forward for the invidious distinction was that Fitz was a Catholic and the Pope had intervened for him,' he said. 'But surely His Holiness himself would not care to have such an injustice done in his name? Was a difference of creed to condemn me to months—great heavens, perhaps years!—of captivity with all its attendant suffering?'

If he was not to be released, Stoker rationalised it as due to his rank as captain of an invading submarine. 'The Turks were flattering enough to think I had done them a bad service when *AE2* proved that the passage of the Dardanelles could be made.' If only Fitzgerald was released, he must just grin and bear it.

The days dragged by in agonising suspense. Weeks later, the Turkish commandant sent for both men. Stoker was beside himself with anticipation: would his name also be on the release order?

The commandant obviously had a cruel streak, for he wanted to play a game. 'What do you think is the best possible news I could bring?' he asked. As the visiting priests who had just left the commandant had delivered their news in secret, Stoker and Fitzgerald had to guess their way up the ladder from a visit to Constantinople to returning home.

'And that it is,' replied the commandant to the final guess of returning home.

'But who?' begged Stoker.

'Why, Monsieur Fitz, of course,' he replied. 'You didn't think you were going, did you?' the commandant said, laughing at his little joke. Stoker stood by his determination to grin and bear it as the two read a telegram addressed to Fitzgerald from Monsignor Dolci.

> *In compliance with the request of His Holiness the Pope, His Excellency Enver Pasha has agreed to grant your release on condition that you sign a written parole stating that you will take no further part in the war on any front against the forces of Turkey or those of her allies.*

Fitzgerald doubted he could agree to these parole terms. Stoker argued strongly for him to sign. Everyone agreed escape was impossible, and even if he worked back home in the countryside he would be helping the war effort. More importantly, Stoker told Fitzgerald, he could tell British authorities of the appalling conditions of the prisoners. 'At this time the men were suffering terrible hardships—underfed, ill-clothed, bootless, and with no bed covering to protect them against the twenty or more degrees of frost which was a common temperature.' The chance of being able to do something to alleviate this, Stoker argued, could not be allowed to pass.

Finally, with Stoker as senior officer taking the
Fitzgerald signed, adding on the parole that if British auth
approve he would voluntarily return.

Fitzgerald's departure was not without irony. Stoker, reac
story of Fitzgerald's engagement to the daughter of
ambassador to the Vatican, was intrigued. Morgenthau, he
been misinformed. Fitzgerald had no romantic attachment at t

The Vatican's lobbying apparently had wider repercussions
prisoners. The Turks agreed to separate the Catholic and Protesta
the Protestants allocated the worst tasks and poorer accommodat
favouritism amongst Christians in a Muslim country is strange.
the Young Turks were trying to curry favour with the Vatican
attempt to keep Italy from joining the Allies. If so, they were unsucc
Or Monsignor Dolci may have been a particularly persuasive envoy.

Stoker had to swallow hard to suppress his jealousy of Fitzge
favourable treatment. 'Fitz, led by straws in the wind, returne
London three years (as it afterwards proved) ahead of me; whi
resumed the ordinary, and purely personal, existence of a priso
of war.'

Morgenthau, however, had the best line. Still clinging to h
engagement story, he wrote: 'As poor Stoker had formed no romanti
attachments that would have justified a similar plea in his case, he had to go back to the prison in Asia Minor. He did this, however, in a genuinely sporting spirit that was worthy of the best traditions of the British navy.'

about escape, and Stoker confided his plans. They decided they needed a third man to enable them to push a boat down a beach into the sea. 'There were three officers we thought might have cared to come, so we told them of our intention,' said Stoker. 'Two, being wise, refused the offer; the third, Price, accepted.' Lieutenant Price, also from *E7*, was a good friend of Stoker.

The three refined their plans through early 1916, as the seemingly pointless battle of Verdun on the Western Front began to take a horrific toll. The escape plan was concealed from the other prisoners to save them from reprisals by the Turks. As the snow melted in the European spring of 1916, Stoker hoped to escape on St Patrick's Day, 17 March—'an obvious day for an Irishman to start off on a desperate sort of enterprise'—but preparations were not completed by that date.

Only a few days before the date finally set for the escape, the senior Russian officer, Bykoff, visited Stoker. He was worried that any escape would create trouble for the other prisoners. And that escapees recaptured would be shot. Escapes must be prevented, he said. 'I managed to answer him without directly lying, but wondered if he would remember my exact words a few days hence,' said Stoker.

The shooting threat, however, concentrated Stoker's mind. He wrote one letter for Haggard to send on via the secret channel to the American embassy outlining the escape plan, saying the three planned no civil crime, except of course stealing a boat, and would offer no resistance to recapture if found. If facing starvation, they would head for the nearest village. 'So the ambassador will then know that the Turkish authorities can have no right to order or condone our execution, and that if they say we were found dead or not found at all, it will not be true.'

Stoker wrote another note to the camp commandant. In this he tried to turn the commandant's own words back on him. When the commandant sent Stoker and Fitzgerald off to solitary confinement in Constantinople he had asked them to remember that he had always had a great friendship for them. Now, said Stoker, he wanted to employ the same words to the commandant, and he wanted him to understand that in escaping he was only performing his duty.

In his writings, Stoker only touches lightly on the details of the escape. It seems the three officers simply climbed out a window while an accomplice distracted the guards. Stoker's reticence is at odds with his usual eye for the drama of an occasion. *AE2* crewman John Wheat in his account of imprisonment says the three 'left in disguise', fuelling a persistent rumour that Stoker was dressed as a woman. Certainly Stoker dressed as a woman for some of the plays later staged in the camp. Thomas Cheater, Stoker's batman, told relatives after the war that he had purchased female clothing for Stoker in the village, and was punished for his part. If Stoker did escape as a woman he was too coy to mention it in his memoirs.

The three fought their way through the hills all night. At daybreak they had made only about 13 kilometres. The town was still in sight. The first week continued much the same, with the three struggling through rough mountains but making little progress. 'As we were often above or near the snowline the cold was intense, and sleep impossible when further progress was barred,' Stoker said. 'Ever present was that ghastly hunted feeling; and hunger, thirst, footsoreness, and physical strain.'

Strange events started to occur. Clearly exhausted and probably poisoned by contaminated water, Stoker became obsessed with the idea that his two companions were officers from *AE1*, which had disappeared without trace off Rabaul some 18 months before. 'I realised the absurdity of the obsession, and fought with it; yet for several days it held me in its grip, nor can I exaggerate how real and strong it seemed. Both the dead men had been friends of mine, one a very great friend [probably Will Scarlett]. Whether it is correct to claim this experience as psychologic, or psychic, I know not.'

Then, on the eleventh night, as the trio made a forced march to get through a pass in the rugged Taurus Mountains, there was an even stranger occurrence. The night was wild and mysterious as the trio, hungry and thirsty, tried to skirt local Turks around watch-fires. Sighting signal lamps flashing, they feared they had been detected.

'In the midst of the night, I felt—not suddenly nor surprisingly—that we were not three men struggling along in line, but four,' said Stoker. 'There was a fourth man, following at the end of our line, in the correct position for a fourth man to be. When we stopped for a few moment's rest he did not join us, but remained in the darkness, out of sight; yet as soon as we rose and resumed our march he dropped into his place forthwith. He never spoke, nor did he go ahead to lead us; his attitude seemed just that of the true and loyal friend who says: I cannot help, but when danger is at hand remember always that I am here, to stand by—or fall—with you.'

The trio made it through the pass and down to safer country before daylight. The fourth man had disappeared by the time they made camp and brewed hot cocoa. Amazingly, Stoker's two companions revealed that they too had seen a fourth man. 'We were agreed as to his general movements, the sense of friendliness and comfort he'd given us, and that the moment he vanished was when we felt we'd put the main danger behind us,' Stoker said in a 1930s radio broadcast. 'We also felt he'd brought us luck.'

It was an experience that stayed with Stoker for years. He later asked Sir Arthur Conan Doyle, author of the famous Sherlock Holmes detective mysteries and a convert to spiritualism, if he could explain it. Conan Doyle had heard of this phenomenon before. 'One of you was probably mediumistic without knowing it,' Sir Arthur told him.

Stoker wasn't satisfied with this explanation. Sir Arthur also told him that a sledge party of Sir Ernest Shackleton's 1916 Antarctic mission had told of a similar experience. Stoker eagerly read Shackleton's *South*, which tells how the sledge party was marooned on South Georgia. Shackleton set off with two others in a desperate attempt to find help. Stoker was fascinated by the following passage:

> I know that during that long and racking march over the unnamed mountains and glaciers of South Georgia it seemed to me that we were four, not three. I said nothing to my companions on the point, but afterwards Worsley said to me, 'Boss, I had a curious feeling on the march that there was another person with us'. Crean confessed to

> the same idea. One feels the 'dearth of human world, the roughness of human speech' in trying to describe things intangible, but a record of our journeys would be incomplete without a reference to a subject very near to our hearts.

To Stoker the similarities seemed extraordinary: a fourth man appearing to three who were hard pressed; none speaking about it until later; both incidents close together in time, with the Turkish episode in April 1916, the South Georgian a month later.

If the fourth man had brought them luck through that dangerous pass, it soon deserted them. Their progress was agonisingly slow. The three escapees were held up by bandits, threatened with death, robbed and released.

Stoker tells of one good day, when the trio sat on a mountainside and gazed at the blue Mediterranean Sea a few miles away—'a wondrous, soul-inspiring, body-inspiriting sight to three worn and weary sailors after a year of captivity ... for the sea was Home, was Freedom'. They could see fishing boats, and there was only one more mountain range to cross. Scrambling down a steep side of loose shale, however, all three suffered cuts and grazes.

Exhausted, they did not have the strength for the last range, so they decided to try to find a way around it. But through the next day and night they were still in the same valley. 'Our boots were in ribbons, food finished, strength ebbing fast,' Stoker said. 'Food must be obtained at whatever cost, or else we would only drop in our tracks and die.'

Years later, Stoker wrote in his scrapbook that it was Cochrane who cost the trio their freedom. Stoker said he wanted to increase their speed to reach the coast, but Cochrane disagreed. 'In the event, it was his complete physical exhaustion which stopped us covering the last few miles to the coast, and we were recaptured,' he wrote. Stoker never quite forgave Cochrane, although he acknowledged his influence in Stoker's later dramatic change in career.

Stumbling upon a goatherd's hut, the dishevelled trio told the herdsman they were German surveyors. But he would not sell them food. The trio fell on the herdsman's mercy, admitting that they were escaped British prisoners. They threatened that if he did not give them food they would die on his doorstep.

'Whereat food was produced,' said Stoker. 'A simple, kindly old man he seemed, for he bade us stop the night in one of his huts, while he killed and cut up a goat.'

The following day, supplied with bread, sour milk, meat and goatskin for new moccasins, the trio left. But the herdsman doublecrossed them. As the three lit a fire at a new camp to cook meat and make their new shoes, their camp site was surrounded by gendarmes. Turkish authorities paid bounties for escapees.

The three quietly surrendered. Stoker's arms were bound behind his back, while Cochrane and Price were handcuffed together by the wrists. They had been on the run for 18 days.

Under guard, the recaptured prisoners were taken to Constantinople, straight into Stoker's old prison, where they were put into solitary confinement. 'Not a nobleman now, but a dangerous man, and to be treated as such,' said Stoker.

Always an optimist, Stoker thought that at least in two ways he was better off than during his earlier solitary confinement. His cell opened onto a yard so that he had light and air. The prison wing, however, contained three other large rooms for about twenty prisoners, with whom Stoker had to jostle for a place 'in the loathsome common lavatory'. Secondly, he had more food than before. 'I was thankful for these mercies, yet depressed, as the effects of the physical strain and starvation took long to wear off.' The bugs were the same, however. Stoker found out they were fewer in daylight, so he took to pacing his room throughout the night.

The Constantinople prison commandant, Djevad Bey, against whom Stoker later laid charges, took to sending him newspapers containing news of British defeats. The Battle of Jutland (inconclusive, but reported locally as a great German victory), the fall of Kut-el-Mara with its surrender of an entire British army, and the death of Kitchener all added to Stoker's depression. 'One was able to read between the lines, but still the enemy's exultation was hard to bear.'

Stoker was unaware, however, that back in Ireland his father had been caught up in the Easter Rebellion of 1916. Crossing the line to treat the wounded, Dr Stoker's top hat was knocked off by a bullet, although he was uninjured.

Djevad Bey refused fresh clothing for Stoker, leaving him for three weeks in solitary confinement dressed in the rags in which he had struggled across 300 miles [480 kilometres]. Stoker's later formal charge against the commandant noted that he was given no towel or washing utensils for these three weeks, adding lice to the vermin already in his cell.

Stoker took to composing desperate verse again. In 'A Prison Prayer' he wrote of God's love and mercy coming like the dawn, concluding:

Standing by my window, gazing at the stars,
Winking now more faintly through the iron bars,
Somehow things seem better, sorrow's soothed away,
Dawn is surely coming, it will soon be—Day.

After three weeks solitary confinement, the escapees were moved into the same cell. Companionship, said Stoker, made prison life a little more bearable. Two months dragged by before a court martial, presided over by a Turkish general, slowly started to question them individually. Stoker at first found it somewhat comical, with repeated questions about parentage, and why they had escaped. The answer to the latter—that it was their duty, never seemed to satisfy the general. Repeatedly the court martial asked about outside help in the escape, not believing the men's assurances that there had been none. About the fifth sitting, Stoker was suddenly jolted by a new line of questioning.

'Do you know Mademoiselle Bertha?'

'I've never heard of the lady,' Stoker said truthfully.

'And yet,' the general said through an interpreter, 'two sentries have sworn before the court that they saw you pass a letter to Mademoiselle Bertha when they were escorting you in the bazaar at Afion Kara Hissar.'

Stoker repeated that he had not even then slightest idea who Mademoiselle Bertha was.

'Do you know the Greek stationmaster at Afion Kara Hissar?'

The penny dropped. 'So this was Mademoiselle Bertha . . . we knew of the existence of the Greek stationmaster, and, which had always been of *great* interest to us, we knew of his pretty daughter; for she, to the fluttering of our prisoners' hearts, used frequently to pass in sight of our exercise ground,' Stoker wrote. 'On one occasion I had met her, face to face, in the road when I was returning under escort from a visit to the commandant. I had raised my hat, which brought a rush of dimples to her cheeks, and as she passed I caught a glimpse of twinkling eyes, dark and beautiful. But neither note nor word—perhaps I should say spoken word—passed between us.'

The court martial questioning quickly implied a romantic liaison. 'There is no use your denying that you knew Mademoiselle Bertha,' the interpreter told Stoker. 'The court is fully aware that you ran away from camp many times by night to meet her on the hill behind the town. Now will you admit that she helped you to escape?'

Stoker realised he was on very dangerous ground. If he implicated Mademoiselle Bertha in any way both she and her family could be exposed to reprisals. He strongly denied any liaison, but questions about her dominated the court martial for several sittings. Stoker later learned that Mademoiselle Bertha and her father, as well as several other Christian residents of the town, had been imprisoned immediately after the trio's escape.

During the long days and nights in his cell, Stoker had plenty of time to fantasise about the beauties of Mademoiselle Bertha. Not surprisingly, he fell to verse.

Imagination now, sweet maid, endows thee
With virtue's every grace and beauty's charm
Perchance, perchance, sweet maid, did I but know thee
I could not then for ever more embalm
In memory's crypt a dream of gracious faery

Who, will she nill she, cast her faery shade,
At moment when all life was sad and dreary,
Across my path—then vanished to her glade.

Constantinople Prison, December 1916.

For six months, as the Battle of the Somme raged on the Western Front, the court martial dragged on. Finally, after the inquisitors had caught out Price and Stoker on a discrepancy in their evidence, they came up with a verdict. The discrepancy? Stoker had said the moon hadn't risen when they escaped, while Price said it was up.

As the three marched across the prison square to hear the verdict, Stoker was distinctly edgy. While he regarded the court martial proceedings as Gilbertian, would the punishment fit the crime? 'We were in Turkey,' Stoker thought, 'where amazing and very unpleasant things could happen.' Stoker and other POWs had already witnessed ill-treatment of Armenians.

The president and other members of the court martial were waiting for the prisoners when they arrived. Stoker and his two accomplices were stood to attention while the president, in solemn tones, read a long statement in Turkish. Stoker thought the interpreter was very nervous as he translated, first of all reciting the names and ranks of the prisoners, details of their 'fearful crimes', and then the sentence.

Stoker was sentenced to 25 days imprisonment, and his companions to 20 days each!

The court was in silence for a moment. Then the three prisoners burst out laughing. Stoker reported that even the president of the court martial managed a smile. Still laughing, Stoker turned to the interpreter.

'Will you please point out to the President that we have already been in prison six months!'

The president was aware of this. 'Then,' said Stoker, 'I take it we will be released at once?'

'Yes,' said the president.

Full of smiles, Stoker, Price and Cochrane saluted the court and marched back to their prison cells. 'And,' said Stoker, 'in prison we remained for another five months!'

They were exacting months. As Germany unleashed unrestricted submarine warfare, which in April 1917 led to America's entry into the war, the three prisoners held prolonged negotiations with Commandant Djevad Bey on their release. The sticking point was the commandant's demand they sign a parole not to escape again. Djevad Bey maintained that as the three had forfeited all rights as prisoners of war they should be treated as ordinary prisoners.

Stoker does not mention this in his memoirs, but other POWs, including Wheat reported the three held out against inducements that they could have their liberty (liberty, that is, to return to POW camp) if they gave their parole not to try to escape again. Finally, the three gave their word, and were released. Stoker said in his 1918 charge sheet against Djevad Bey that the commandant had also made certain promises. 'As these promises were not carried out the paroles were withdrawn some time later,' he noted.

Stoker and Cochrane clearly felt their paroles carried no validity. Both again tried to escape, Cochrane successfully. Price died in POW camp just before the end of the war, with Stoker nursing him during his final illness.

The three, however, would have been left in little doubt about how brutal civilian prison life could be if they had failed to reach some deal with Djevad Bey for their return back to POW camp. Their cell was immediately below a room where floggings took place. Each week the three would dread the evening when shrieks of pain could be heard overhead. 'I had never before heard full-grown men cry out in torture,' said Stoker. 'We covered our ears at the horror of it.'

Stoker also saw a man 'bastinadoed'. 'The memory of it will never leave me,' he said. The victim is partly raised off the ground, with his ankles secured to a pole. A cutting cane then lashes the bare soles of his feet. 'I believe the pain to be indescribable, and that few men retain consciousness for more than fifteen blows. The usual number inflicted in the prison seemed to be twenty-five or thirty. It is at least a week before the victim can walk again.'

Despite negotiations over a parole, Stoker planned an escape from the prison using the disguise of shaving off his bushy beard and moustache and trimming his long hair. But if he got away Price and Cochrane would be punished. He had to ask their permission. Price agreed, but Cochrane would not, claiming Stoker's planned disguise would be absurdly ineffective. They argued, but Stoker would not attempt escape without his permission. Stoker wrote later that Cochrane was a strange man who kept himself 'so tight inside that he could never relax'.

'For the subsequent year in prison in Constantinople he was not a cheerful cellmate,' Stoker wrote in 1959 after learning of Cochrane's death. 'Price and I were able to play cards, write silly doggerel and jabber nonsense, but he did not.'

One piece of happiness, however, came the prisoners' way. They petitioned Commandant Djevad Bey for permission to attend church on Christmas Day 1916. To their surprise, he agreed. The three groomed themselves for the occasion, and were escorted late in the morning across the bridge spanning the Golden Horn to Pera, and to the church of Reverend Dr Frew, whom Stoker remembered fondly from his earlier confinement in Constantinople.

The three prisoners arrived late, and Reverend Frew was already well into his sermon. He gave no sign of noticing their arrival. Stoker reported that Frew discreetly beckoned a small boy to his side, whispered something to him, and continued with his sermon. The boy disappeared, and Frew's sermon stretched out for quite a time. The congregation was fidgety and glancing at their watches as Frew discarded his written notes and simply chatted to his audience. Suddenly the boy reappeared, and Frew quickly wound up.

The three prisoners were forbidden to speak to anyone, but as they filed out the front door Frew was there. 'Smiling all over his Scotch face ... he held a large basket, which he thrust into my arms as I marched past,' said Stoker.

Back in their cell, the three enjoyed a Christmas repast of cake, crackers, biscuits, butter, cheese, chocolate and plum pudding. Stoker admired the clergyman's quick thinking. 'Frew, on spotting our arrival in church, had sent the boy to his house to collect supplies as quickly as possible, and had kept the sermon going until his return.'

13

'Look For a Man Carrying *The Times*'

'Straws in the wind'—Stoker's trademark expression for his breezy approach to life—blew again shortly after the three were finally released from prison in Constantinople in February 1917.

Yozgat, their new POW camp, was even deeper into Asia Minor than Afion Kara Hissar. But as prison camps go, it was at the better end of the range. Yozgat is situated at the head of a rocky valley in rugged mountainous country. It was the most isolated of all the camps, five days march from the nearest railway station, at Angora (now Ankara, the Turkish capital).

The prisoners were kept in detached houses in large grounds on the side of a hill, with picturesque views. While officers still had to scratch out a living, paying for their own food and upkeep, they were allowed pleasant diversions such as a rabbit 'hunt club', sports, and even their own theatre group. Turkish guards, however, took a dim view of a cricket ball sent by the American embassy. 'Bomba' was the word whispered as the ball was examined with great suspicion.

Shortly after arrival, Stoker was anxious to show Cochrane that his plan of shaving off his beard and long hair in order to disguise himself for an escape would work. He decided to play a trick on the entire camp. After breakfast one morning he left the camp, changed clothes, shaved his beard and hair, put on a pince-nez and presented himself to the camp as a newly-caught prisoner.

The senior officer of the prisoners, a colonel with whom Stoker had shared breakfast only a few hours before, greeted him very warmly. Had he had breakfast? the colonel asked. Stoker knew his disguise was working. The colonel took him to the exercise ground and began introducing him to the other prisoners. Stoker spun a yarn that he was a flying officer who had left London three weeks before and had been shot down over Constantinople ten days ago.

'It went splendidly,' Stoker said. 'There had been no fresh arrival in the camp for many months, and the prisoners crowded round me with eager questions to elicit my red-hot news. And red-hot it certainly was! Wondrous tales I told them of the progress of the war on all fronts, of the state of affairs in England, etc, etc, becoming more and more daring in my statements as each new story was swallowed ... The "have" was complete—far more so than I had dreamed might be possible. Not a soul recognised me.'

Stoker later rejected criticism that this was a cruel joke to play on POWs. 'In the ghastly monotony of a prisoner-of-war existence anything that breaks the monotony and gives one something to talk and laugh over is a heaven-sent blessing; and this provided the camp with a topic of amusement for days afterwards.'

He was soon caught out, of course. After a few hours some of the airmen among the prisoners started to ask him about the new aircraft in use, and the type he had been flying when shot down. Stoker knew the gig was up, and confessed all. 'There was a gasp, a silence ... I was a little nervous as to what was going to happen, as some men had made amazing fools of themselves—and then a big laugh burst over the whole camp ... For several days afterwards anyone looking at my shaven face invariably grinned heartily.'

Cochrane's reaction is not known.

Stoker later acknowledged that the dispute with Cochrane culminating in his prison prank blew the greatest 'straw' in his life, ultimately leading him to resign from the navy and take up a stage career. That straw quickly became apparent. The 'new' prisoner had told only one fellow POW, a major, of his little joke beforehand. The major was an amateur actor who had won permission from the camp commandant to stage theatricals. Some days after the joke the major approached Stoker with an offer to play the leading female role in an adaptation one of the prisoners had written of W. W. Jacob's popular play *The Monkey's Paw*.

'My dear chap,' replied Stoker, 'I've never acted in my life.'

'What about the newly caught flying officer?' the major asked. 'Wasn't that acting? Whilst watching you then I decided you would be absolutely capable of doing this part—it is a pathetic old lady, her son is killed . . .'

Stoker agreed, no doubt flattered that his practical joke had worked so well. In rehearsals for the show, Stoker made a wig from goats' hair, borrowed a padre's cassock for a dress, and applied liberal flour for face powder. His aim was to look like a white-haired old Irish woman mourning her lost son.

'The curtain rose and, before a packed "house", we sobbed and moaned our way through the little tragedy,' he said. 'In agonised tones I called on my dead son, my only che-ild, to come back to me. And, again to my amazement but the major's content, nobody laughed. In fact, the audience, though they voted the play as excellently done, requested that in future some lighter and less harrowing fare should be supplied.'

The next play was indeed a farce. Stoker played the lead of a surly, pious gentleman ridiculed in the play. It ended with Stoker climbing out a window in his colourful underpants. Stoker said the 'artistic taste of the prisoner public was hit to a nicety' by the sight of his 'wondrous-hued' backside trying to wriggle though a window.

Stoker spoke glowingly of the months at Yozgat after the long imprisonment in Constantinople. Literature, exercise and companionship filled his days. Stoker even joined the prison choir. But in the autumn of 1917 as the Allies and Germans slogged it out at the battle of Passchendaele, regarded as the last of the 'old-fashioned' set piece slaughters of the war, Stoker was transferred back to Afion Kara Hissar.

Conditions at Afion had improved since his 1916 escape. A theatre group had sprung up there, too, so Stoker could maintain his new interest. The Afion prisoners had even discovered an old American organ in the town's hardware store, which was promptly bought [on the time payment system] to add to musical and theatrical evenings.

In his book *Guests of the Unspeakable*, T. H. White, the Australian airman, said Stoker had somehow acquired a guitar, which he strummed to songs of his own composing. A Russian prisoner had taught Stoker how to play. Stoker later delighted in hearing one of his compositions played professionally in London.

'A cheerful and lovable Irishman and an optimist always, he early showed signs of that histrionic ability that caused him to forsake a brilliant career in the navy for the stage, when he wrote, sang and played for the "shows" that did so much to lighten interminable hours,' wrote White. Stoker's willingness to dress up as a woman, and his ability to be convincing as one, may have helped foster the tale that he had escaped in a dress.

* * *

Like Stoker's amazing adventures, the experiences of the *AE2* submariners as Turkish prisoners of war have almost been forgotten. The *AE2* crew, like their captain, was catapulted into a completely alien and unknown situation. Their lives were in constant danger, and they were mentally and physically shocked.

The Turkish attitude to the crew was complicated. Very few Turks had any knowledge of Australia, and they must have been extremely angered by the *AE2*'s exposure of their Gallipoli supply lines to submarine attack. Individual Turkish responses to the submariners tended to be good at first, but deteriorated later.

After the shock and alientation of their capture, the *AE2* crew began the slow process of acceptance and adaptation to their predicament. They were supported by being part of a strong-knit and flexible group, a simple fact, but one that would enable them to survive the next three and a half years in captivity.

According to Red Cross agreements, prisoners were supposed to be treated similarly to ordinary Turkish soldiers in terms of food and punishment. After their capture, however, the *AE2* men soon discovered a wide gap between theory and reality. The Turks allowed no independent inspections of POW camps.

Initially the submariners, a disciplined and fastidious group selected for their mental and physical abilities, were appalled by the filthy conditions at Afion Kara Hissar. Army corporal George Kerr, who was held in the Belemedik camp with many of the *AE2* crew, kept a secret Pitman's shorthand diary, later transcribed and published by his grandson as *Lost Anzacs: A Tale of Two Brothers*. In this, Kerr noted: 'Most of the crew of the *AE2* were initially intolerant of the harsh conditions, they seemed a cut above the rest, and as members of a "Royal" navy might have felt it beneath them to work building roads and supplementing labour shortages on farms.'

The process of adaptation was fast. Officers were separated from the men almost immediately, and spent almost all their time in Turkey apart from the ratings. Later the strange separation of Catholics and Protestants, and then more predictably petty officers from ratings would follow, but there were always enough men in each group to offer mutual support.

The Turks, applying to some degree the international rules for prisoners of war at that time, required all enlisted men, but not officers, to work, and paid them a small wage. This money was supplemented by various international payments that sometimes reached the men, and money cobbled together by Stoker and his officers. But the *AE2* crewmen were angered at the exorbitant prices they were often charged for necessities.

The first major camp experienced by *AE2*'s crew, Afion—the black opium castle—was not only the largest POW camp in Turkey, it was the clearing and distribution centre for all other Turkish camps. Before the war it had been a flourishing town controlled by wealthy Armenian families and a central market for both the opium and carpet trades. Afion's climate was extreme, with heavy snows in winter and searing heat in summer. In the spring and summer, poppy fields surrounded the town in a showy haze of purple and white.

The unsung hero for all the *AE2* prisoners (including the three officers) was Captain Francis Haworth Booth, the Australian navy's London representative. Haworth Booth discovered a conduit through a London City friend whose bank had a branch in Constantinople. Although its Turkish assets were frozen during the war, the bank could release funds locally. These lifesaving funds were paid via the Red Cross, and American and Dutch embassy sources to *AE2* coxswain Chief Petty Officer Harry Abbott, and then distributed to the officers and men.

Camp life at Afion developed its own social complexity. For entertainment, there was a library as well as the theatre group. One British officer, John Bott, noted that, despite the absence of women, the camp resembled a suburb in a Midlands city. Bott's description of camp life is entertaining: 'Innumerable cliques formed, from each of which gossip spread outward ... how X had received a pair of pyjamas from the Red Cross ... and supposedly sold them; how Y had climbed over the rooftops and met that Armenian girl with the big eyes ... how three men had experimented with opium smoking ... how Yeats Brown ... for weeks went about dressed as a girl.'

But no prisoner could really escape the psychological depression of confinement. An Australian Flying Corps officer, J. Halpin, described this syndrome: 'We lie around, solitary, silent, motionless, absorbed like dead men from whom has passed every urge to live, every voice of hope ... death is always with us as a constant menace; it is our whispered topic in the lengthened shades of evening, the drab and lonely solitude of night, the restless quiverings of early dawn.'

At the end of 1915 nearly all the *AE2* men, who had been working on roadmaking, were shipped out of Afion. Some went for a short stint at Çankiri, an agricultural prison near Ankara, but eventually most ended up at Belemedik, a forced labour camp in the remote Taurus Mountains of south-eastern Turkey. Crewman C. A. Bray claimed Belemedik meant 'nowhere', from *bele*, no, and *medik*, place. It seemed appropriate to him.

Belemedik was the main construction camp for the Berlin to Baghdad Railway Company, a German group building the crucial single gauge rail line to transport both Turkish military supplies and vital Middle Eastern oil. The main camp was set on the banks of a river, in a deep valley under towering mountains. The terrain was so inhospitable that the Turks had no need to put fences around the camp. It was a bad place for malaria: hot, humid and airless in warm weather, and always filled with mosquitos.

The aim of the construction work was to drive twelve tunnels through solid granite mountains. The work was extremely dangerous, and the men were required to work 12 hours a day, round the clock in shifts. Men who could not work or who became ill were simply unwanted, useless to the construction company, and at grave risk of their lives. Life suddenly became a matter of desperate survival, every man vulnerable. For Australian POWs, Belemedik was to have ghastly echoes in the Japanese slave labour camps of the Burma railway in World War II.

Some Belemedik prisoners died in badly supervised rock explosions. Conditions were dreadful, and the food poor. Many of the *AE2* men had valuable technical and engineering skills, and were allocated good jobs. Others tried to escape, despite overwhelming odds, which included a large bounty offered to Turks to turn them in. At the height of construction some 30 000 prisoners, including Greeks, Armenians and even Turks unfit for military service, were pressed into railway construction.

The worst scourge at Belemedik was disease. Although all the *AE2* men had been inoculated against typhoid, the overcrowded camp was riddled with malaria and meningitis, amongst other diseases. Four of the crew, three Englishmen and one Australian—Gilbert, Varcoe, Knaggs and Williams—died as prisoners. Nearly all the submariners left Turkey as little more than walking skeletons, and many suffered for the rest of their lives from malaria, internal problems, and the effects of injuries.

Corporal Kerr's diaries give some account of the most poignant and personal details of life in the camps. At Belemedik, as at Afion, the *AE2* men struggled to maintain morale by organising entertainments like concerts, and in the case of Kerr's mess, drinking parties, boxing and football matches. There were other preoccupations too, like personal relationships. Kerr writes frankly that Belemedik at the beginning of 1916 was rife with rumours and innuendo about sodomy, and that some (female) prostitutes enterprisingly turned up nearby.

By February 1916 the English prisoners at Belemedik had begun printing a camp newspaper called the *Belemedik Bugger*, a weekly that cost two piastres. Copies were made by hand. When Kerr tried to get the German bosses to produce it on their office copying machine all hell broke loose. The Germans and Turks showed no appreciation of the clever articles that were causing so much mirth amongst the prisoners. The paper was short-lived.

The final prison camp experienced by six of the *AE2* crew—Nichols, Churcher, Harding, Wilson, Wishart and Mitchell—was San Stefano. It is now called Yesilkoy. The prison camp, located near the current Ataturk International Airport south-west of Istanbul, had an airstrip nearby, used by Turkish and German airforce units. Some of the mostly Catholic Australian airmen sent there planned to escape by getting hold of these planes, but were unsuccessful. San Stefano, supervised by Germans and where the prisoners were used mostly as labourers or orderlies, was considered to be the least harsh prison camp in Turkey.

It is impossible to glamorise the Turkish prison experiences of the *AE2* crew. A bitter poem, written at Afion by an RAF flight lieutenant, Leonard Woolley, who had been shot down in Mesopotamia and force-marched to Turkey, summed up the feelings of many.

> Famished and spent across the waste, beastlike you drove us on,
> And clubbed to death the stragglers by the way.
> Our sick men in the lazar huts you left to die alone,
> And you robbed the very dying as they lay.
> Naked and starved we built you roads
> And tunnelled through your hills,
> And you flogged us when we fainted at our work.
> Fevered beneath the sun we toiled, wrecked by winter chills,
> Till death released us, kindlier than the Turk.
> And the tunnels we drove for you, the roads that we have made,
> Shall be highways for the armies of your foe.
> We shall mock you in our graves, that in what we did as slaves
> We helped, we too, to work your overthrow.

* * *

In spring 1918, as the war ground on seemingly endlessly, Stoker was moved from Afion back to Yozgat. Inevitably he was caught up in the question of escape again, agonising on whether to make a second bid for freedom.

The war appeared to be going badly. In November 1917 the Bolshevik revolution put Lenin into power. Lenin signed the Treaty of Brest Litovsk with Germany, ending the war on the Eastern Front. Germany quickly transferred troops to the fighting in France just as American troops were arriving in large numbers.

Seventy per cent of prisoners in Yozgat, Stoker said, thought they had no right to escape. Chances of success were seen as hopeless because it was so remote, and any attempt would bring punishment on fellow prisoners. Stoker's own failed attempt from Afion was cited as proof of the first point, and the punishment meted out to Kastamonu inmates after a successful escape by four British officers as proof of the second.

'My own personal view was that the feat showed such infinitesimal chances of success without outside assistance that it was no man's duty to try, and that the certainty of inflicting hardship on brother officers was a serious responsibility to undertake,' Stoker said.

There were cases where POWs were treated harshly just for thinking about escape. *AE2* crewman Wheat recounts the misfortune of Lieutenant Haggard of the *AE2* at Afion. Suspected of planning an escape, Haggard and two other officers were 'sentenced' to nine months close confinement. 'During this harsh treatment they were allowed one hour's exercise per 24 hours under guard,' said Wheat. Eventually news of the unjust punishment got out, and the Afion commandant was removed.

Thanks to his past experience, Stoker was besieged with requests to join new escape bids. He declined, calling many schemes absurd and doomed to failure without outside help. A plan by officers in one camp called for the POWs to seize the barracks and lay out sheets in squares as a landing signal for RAF rescue planes.

Cochrane, Stoker's accomplice in the failed 1916 bid, teamed up with two captains, Johnston and Yearsley, as part of a mass break-out from Yozgat on 7 August 1918. While at Afion, Cochrane had somehow managed to arrange a scheme for British rescue boats to rendezvous with escaping prisoners off the Turkish coast at the end of August 1918. Twenty-six officers escaped in separate parties. All were recaptured except for Cochrane's group.

The story of this group as told in Johnston and Yearsley's *Four-Fifty Miles to Freedom* is one of amazing endeavour. They were robbed by shepherds who seemingly befriended them, had a shoot out with ruffians and inevitably ran short of food in a 23-night march to the coast. There, they stole an old motor boat, ran up a sail and headed for Cyprus. After 190 kilometres at sea, and with Cyprus in sight, the engine failed. But they made it to shore, sending a message via villagers to British officials of their arrival.

Stoker at first thought their success had made him a false prophet, as he had claimed that nobody could escape without outside help. But reading *Four-Fifty Miles to Freedom* after the war Stoker was delighted to find the escapees believed that only divine intervention had brought them through. So, Stoker rationalised, God was the outside help for their successful escape!

God, however, was little help for the prisoners remaining in Yozgat. Restrictions were tightened, and for some time prisoners were denied letters.

When mail was again distributed, Stoker received a mysterious postcard. The writing on it was nonsensical to him. Suspecting a code, he soaked the card in water, splitting it open to find a secret message inside. Colonel Keeling, who had been part of the successful 1917 escape from Kastamonu, had worked out a plan of escape from Yozgat to the coast. Details of the plan, complete with maps, would follow in postcards to be sent to all officers whose surnames commenced with C or S.

Subsequent mail days, said Stoker, became a real excitement as, section by section, the map and plan came through. Keeling had arranged for food, arms and ammunition to be stored at a coastal hiding point. On given days in October and November a vessel would be ready to rescue escapees.

While the plan was obviously in deadly earnest, it has a comical slant to the modern eye. It detailed how an agent would be on an uninhabited island some 180 metres off the coast on certain dates. 'He will show recent copy of *Times*,' it declared. Just what one might expect to find on an uninhabited island off the Turkish coast in wartime—a person carrying a recent copy of *The Times* of London!

Despite these theatrics, Stoker welcomed the plan as the outside help he had been looking for. Two fellow officers, Hickman and Marsh, agreed to go with him. Given the farce of what happened it is not surprising the escape attempt was finally made on Friday 13 September 1918, two months before the Armistice.

Extra sentries were on duty after the earlier mass escape. Stoker and his colleagues made elaborate plans to sneak past them. They would break into a cellar underneath their house, and then out through a door that was locked only by a hook latch on the outside. A sentry patrolled some 9 metres from the door. The aspiring escapees drilled two holes through the door, and planned to spring the latch with a black thread passed through the holes. Fellow prisoners in the house would make various signals via laughter, song and thumping to indicate when the sentry's back was turned.

The three crept down to the cellar on the thirteenth. 'Behind us stretched a series of helpers forming a line of communication to each room of the house,' said Stoker. 'At every window was a look-out, whose duty was to report unexpected movements amongst the sentries.'

Stoker crept forward in the pitch black cellar, finding the two ends of the thread. Amidst laughter above to indicate 'go ahead' he began jerking the threads. The latch rose, and the laughter stopped, indicating the coast was clear. 'Ready,' Marsh whispered in his ear. Just as the three were about to bolt, a 'thump, thump, thump' could be heard from above. Stoker recounts the finale.

'What's wrong?' I whispered. But the words had barely left my mouth when I knew.

Footsteps could be heard approaching without on the path passing the cellar door. I stood stock still, hands upraised, each one still grasping an end of the thread holding up the latch lock. The footsteps made as if to pass; stopped a moment; and then came closer.

'There's a man at the door!' ... 'There's a man at the door! ... 'There's a man at the door!' ...

All along the line of communication I could hear the words being passed from mouth to mouth. In their nervousness our kind helpers were not guarding their whispered tones too carefully. I was aware there was a man at the door. I was painfully aware of it, for I could hear his laboured breathing; he seemed to be excited about something.

Stoker was later to learn that the guard's attention had been caught by the latch on the door bowing at him. In the excitement of the moment, Stoker's hands on the cotton threads were none too steady.

The guards, also hearing the 'whispered' warnings, burst into the darkened cellar with their bayonets ready. Stoker and his two accomplices scurried for the safety of the house upstairs.

* * *

The Great War was drawing to a close in Europe, but another tragedy remained for Stoker before freedom. A few weeks after the escape farce, influenza swept Yozgat, catching almost every prisoner. Stoker was laid low. Marsh, one of his recent escape bid colleagues, died. 'Poor Marsh—dying, it seemed before the sound of his eagerly whispered "Ready!" had left my ears.'

More were to follow. Price, who had accompanied Stoker on his 1916 escape, battled to tend other influenza victims despite being ill himself. Stoker got permission to transfer to his house to help Price as his condition gradually worsened.

'And there I watched him make his last courageous fight, gradually sink away and die … The cruelty of it—after three and a half years captivity—with the end, as we then knew, in sight. Price, great-hearted, generous, true and loyal friend, had crowned his life of service for others by making the supreme gift to his comrades.'

As the prisoners buried their dead, news of the Armistice of 11 November 1918 reached them. The Great War was over.

14

Monkey Tricks

The England Stoker knew before the war was almost another country when he returned just before Christmas 1918. The war had wrought vast changes. Stoker thought none was bigger than the change in English women. 'I shall never forget the impression it made on my mind when I first heard the then popular term of endearment between a maiden and her swain — "old bean",' he said.

This may have been Stoker's way of alluding to a personal crisis that he was either too embarrassed or too gallant to talk about. On return he discovered that his wife had had three children by other men in his five-year absence. If the three and a half years in prison camps had been traumatic, this was a real kick in the head.

Not much is known about Stoker's pre-war marriage to a woman called Olive. Whether or not it was a youthful indiscretion, Stoker later virtually wrote it out of his life. There is no mention of the marriage in his memoirs or personal notebooks. Stoker may have also tried to keep it quiet from the Admiralty. In May 1915, the Admiralty cabled his father in Dublin rather than his wife with the next-of-kin message about *AE2*'s disappearance. But Admiralty records reveal later letters from a somewhat distressed Olive seeking information about Stoker.

Did Stoker first hear the expression 'old bean' in his reunion with Olive when he discovered her wartime infidelity? It is not known. But he was clearly rocked by the news of the three children, two girls and a boy. A photograph taken just after the war shows a convalescing Stoker slumped in a hammock at his brother's home, a vacant expression on his face. His niece, Primrose, remembers him at the time as being disconsolate, and sleeping a lot. Unlike the pre-war Stoker, he did not want to play with his brother's children.

Stoker instituted an immediate divorce from Olive. 'When we got back from Turkey I had to divorce my first wife,' Stoker wrote to C. A. Bray, an *AE2* colleague, years later. 'The knowledge that I'd have to do that did not make the years of captivity any easier.'

But, being Stoker, over the years he kept in touch with the three children, particularly the two girls. 'He was very good to them,' said Primrose. 'They didn't look on him as their father, but he was the only father they ever knew.' Asked whether Olive had been forced into seeing other men for support, Primrose replied, 'No, she just liked men.'

Return to navy life was equally rough. 'The altered conditions of life, of love, of manners, of service, all seemed very unsettling,' Stoker wrote. Stoker's personal crisis compelled him to stay in Britain, and it was one of the reasons he gave Australian authorities for not wanting to remain in the Australian navy. He also felt that the years in captivity had cost him dearly, with many of his contemporaries promoted. 'He feels that unless some reward is given to him for his past services it is useless his leaving this country,' Australia's London naval representative cabled home.

The reward Stoker had in mind is unclear, although over the years many have suggested he should have received a Victoria Cross (VC) for the *AE2*'s pathbreaking attack on the Narrows. Stoker was awarded the Distinguished Service Order (DSO), although the submariner who preceded him and failed to breach the Narrows, Holbrook, and the two who immediately followed his lead, Boyle and Nasmith, were all awarded VCs. Whatever he may have felt privately, Stoker never complained about his DSO.

Interestingly, the citation for his DSO said it was in recognition of Stoker's 'gallantry in making the passage of the Dardanelles', not the *first* passage. The Australian Naval Board, however, gave Stoker due credit. It wrote to him in August 1919, expressing 'very high appreciation' of his performance 'in very exceptional danger'. It specifically cited Stoker achieving the honour for the service of 'an Australian submarine being the first to pass the Dardanelles Strait'.

The Australian navy's Vice-Admiral Creswell, who had originally opposed the acquisition of submarines, wanted Australia to offer Stoker more than just a letter. 'Although so late in the day ... in view of the frightful suffering endured by this Officer and the long continual infliction of cruel barbarities by the Turks, probably prompted by Germans, that the sympathy of this country and Government be accorded or marked in some special manner,' wrote Creswell in July 1919. Apart from scribbled notes on the Creswell recommendation that Stoker had already been awarded a DSO, and that a letter be sent to him, nothing further appears to have been done.

Stoker was given command of *K9*, one of the new K class submarines, the largest yet built. The Ks were a disaster. They were steam driven with a top surface speed in excess of 20 knots. The aim was to keep up with the fleet, but the K class was dangerously unmanageable, unstable, and leaked. After many casualties and disasters the K class was abandoned. 'I thought them bad submarines, slow to dive, clumsy to handle, and dangerous,' said Stoker.

One of the six J class subs which Britain gave to Australia after the war was adapted from the newer K class hulls. The Js also proved unreliable. Incidentally, Commander Boyle, VC, was appointed commander of the new Australian J class flotilla, with the intrepid Lieutenant D'Oyly-Hughes of *E11*, who staged the audacious railway attack from a submarine in the Marmara, volunteering as his first lieutenant.

Stoker's quick return to service in February 1919, a bare two months after returning from three and a half years in captivity, was a mistake. Things seemed to go well at first. His service records report that his superiors regarded him as 'zealous, loyal and reliable', showing considerable judgement, and popular with the men. He was strongly recommended for promotion, and in December 1919 was made a commander.

Although promoted, Stoker was fast falling out of love with active submarine command. 'My methods of dealing with my officers and men did not seem to work as well as in the old days,' he says. 'I somehow failed to understand them, and they failed to understand me. I had never before had to use punishment as a means of obtaining best work out of the men under my command. I had to use it now, and hated doing so.'

Perhaps Stoker's disenchantment was linked with *K9*'s accident under his command. The clumsy submarine collided with HMS *Terror*. A court of inquiry was mild on Stoker, but his commander-in-chief was not. 'I do not concur with the findings of the court,' said the commander-in-chief. 'The eddy referred to ... was probably a contributing cause to the accident but the margin of safety allowed by the commanding officer was too small. I therefore consider that Commander Stoker was to blame for not allowing more room for his turn.'

Against that sort of damning report, Stoker, by the beginning of 1920, applied to be transferred as second in command of a battleship or cruiser. Apart from three and a half years in captivity, he had been in submarines since 1906. 'I was tired of them,' he said. Stoker was relieved of *K9*'s command, but found he was 88th on the waiting list of officers for new ships. It looked like being about three or more months before a ship became available.

The prospect of months of idleness had little appeal after years as a prisoner of war, so Stoker 'roamed about London trying to fill in time in odd ways'. Stoker appears to have tried his hand at several new jobs, including work in an advertising agency.

Old naval friends wrote generous letters of recommendation for him, although one of these must have left Stoker spluttering. Admiral Mark Kerr, recording Stoker's excellent sports achievements and his ability to get on with both sexes, noted with English upper class condescension: 'In addition to this, he has the humdrum but valuable quality of zeal and hard work, and great dependability, which, as he has a lot of Irish blood in him, is almost unique.'

Straws in the wind were to blow again for Stoker, this time into an entirely new career. A chance meeting with the stage manager of the Ambassadors Theatre rekindled Stoker's POW interest in the theatre. He talked his way into sitting up the back of rehearsals, pretending to be an understudy for the H. M. Harwood play *The Grain of Mustard Seed*, a political satire.

Above: Prisoners of war at Afion Kara Hissar. In top row, fourth and fifth from left: Captain Stoker and Lieutenant Fitzgerald. Bottom row: Lieutenant Price, Lieutenant Cary, Lieutenant Haggard.
(STOKER COLLECTION)

Left: Belemedik prison camp in the remote Taurus Mountains.
(GEORGE KERR; BRAY COLLECTION)

Above: Local hill people, or 'Tartagees', at Belemedik prison camp.
(GEORGE KERR; BRAY COLLECTION)

Above: Belemedik was a place of extreme conditions—frozen in winter, scorching in summer. (GEORGE KERR; BRAY COLLECTION)

RIGHT: The sinking of *AE2*. Sketch by crew member A.N.C. Thomson. (MRS RUBY EDWARDS)

BELOW: Food—the prisoner's obsession. Sketch by CERA Reg Ballantyne. (VINE COLLECTION)

LEFT: Turkish leader Enver Pasha.
(BRAY COLLECTION)

BELOW: The grave of CPO Charles Varcoe, who died as a prisoner of war in Belemedik in 1916.
(AUSTRALIAN WAR MEMORIAL, P1645.003)

Right: Going home—the hospital ship *Kanowna* bringing POWs back from Turkey.

(*SYDNEY MAIL*, 9 APRIL 1919; SRL REF. BN 336, STATE REFERENCE LIBRARY, STATE LIBRARY OF NEW SOUTH WALES)

Below: Transferring POWs from Turkey to Allied ships.

(*SYDNEY MAIL*, 9 APRIL 1919; SRL REF. BN 336, STATE REFERENCE LIBRARY, STATE LIBRARY OF NEW SOUTH WALES)

ABOVE: The Melbourne society wedding in September 1923 of Lieutenant Geoffrey Haggard and Miss Marjory Syme (of *The Age* newspaper family).
(SMYTH-HAGGARD COLLECTION)

Above: Afion prisoners in their 'Turkish' suits, made in prison from cloth donated by Reverend Frew and the Red Cross. (STOKER COLLECTION)

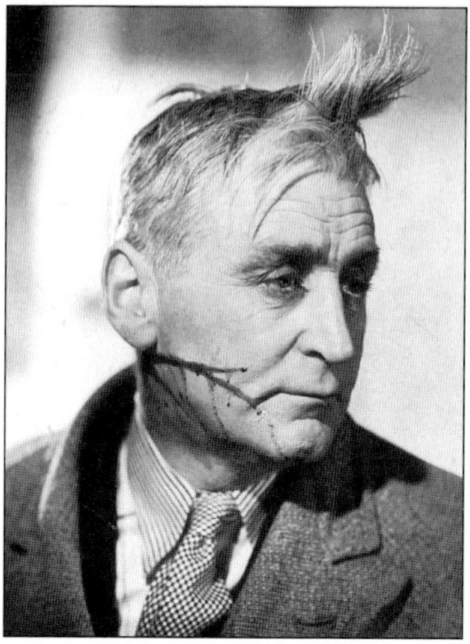

Above: Stoker as the villain in the 1936 film *Crackerjack*. (STOKER COLLECTION)

Above: Stoker as the easy-going husband in the 1921 play *A Social Conscience*. (STOKER COLLECTION)

Right: The wedding of Commander Stoker and actress Miss Dorothie (Peg) Pidcock on 22 April 1925. The marriage lasted over 40 years. (STOKER COLLECTION)

Harwood was to become a lifelong friend and tennis partner. Stoker often joked about Harwood's 'volatile and erratic serve'. One day at the Queen's Club he pulled Harwood into a partnership with the recently deposed King Manuel of Portugal to play a doubles match. Stoker forgot to properly introduce Harwood to the king, and then watched in horror as Harwood whacked a ball into the royal backside with a 'terrific crack'. Harwood said a casual sorry, and then proceeded to whack him again.

Sitting up the back of the Ambassadors Theatre, Stoker set about watching the actor-director, Norman McKinnel, go about his work. He wanted to compare his prisoner of war camp thespian experiences to the production of a real play. Stoker had seen McKinnel acting in the blood-freezing role of a cruel husband, and expected him to be a terror to the cast. Instead he found him the soul of gentleness.

One day, as Stoker was sitting in on rehearsals, one of the actors in a small part became unhappy, and quit. 'Here,' someone on stage yelled at Stoker in the stalls, 'just come up here and read this part, will you?' Stoker read it, apparently confidently and without stammering.

Rehearsals continued, and nobody arrived to take the part. 'And then, one day, the business manager sent for me and, to my amazement, produced a contract for my signature,' said Stoker. 'The situation appealed intensely to my sense of humour. I temporised with the business manager, and took the contract away with me to consider what I should do.'

Stoker was still on the active list of the Royal Navy, awaiting a new ship. *The King's Regulations and Admiralty Instructions*, the awe-inspiring book governing duties of naval officers ashore, offered no clue to Stoker's dilemma other than that he should behave in a manner befitting an 'Officer and a Gentleman'. Obviously the Lords of the Admiralty had never envisaged a situation in which an officer wanted to also act in a West End play.

Stoker quickly devised a handy subterfuge. 'What can prevent a man called, say, "Hew Gordon" [adapted from two of Stoker's actual names] acting at the Ambassadors, provided Commander Stoker presents himself to the authorities immediately when called for?' he asked. But to make sure there were no misunderstandings, Stoker took his plan to the Admiralty.

'Their Lordships' representatives whom I interviewed were distressed,' said Stoker. 'There was no precedent to be referred to in dealing with such a quaint proposition.' But the Admiralty eventually accepted the idea, saying it was refreshing to find an officer who would not keep bothering them to find him a ship. Feel free to do your 'monkey tricks' for a few months, they said. If anything cropped up they would give him plenty of warning.

A delighted Stoker immediately signed his contract as Hew Gordon, and the play opened to good reviews. For a few weeks Stoker found himself in receipt of two pay packets, one from the Admiralty to Commander Stoker, and the other from the Ambassadors to 'Hew Gordon'.

But a fortnight into this happy situation Stoker was walking through Piccadilly when a naval friend stopped him to offer his congratulations. Stoker at first thought he was referring to the new play, but then found to his horror that he meant the appointment as captain of the cruiser *Royal Arthur*, the depot ship for the Atlantic submarine flotilla.

'What about the eighty-seven other commanders before me on the list?' an exasperated Stoker cried to the Admiralty when he telephoned for confirmation of the news. 'Very sorry,' came the reply, 'you were the only suitable man on the list.'

This was a real dilemma—the sea or the stage? Personal reasons—the divorce from Olive—dictated remaining in England. As well, a special retirement scheme designed to clear the backlog of surplus officers after the war made retirement attractive. 'And lastly, it must be confessed that an Irishman's heart was drawn by the attraction of the huge gamble of the [stage].'

Stoker decided to take six months leave on half-pay to consider his future, remaining in the play.

Three months later he knocked on director Norman McKinnel's door during an interval to ask his frank opinion of whether Stoker could ever make a living out of the stage. 'Make a living out of the stage?' McKinnel repeated the question as he sucked on his pipe. Stoker was glad he had carefully phrased his question.

'There are two things necessary for that,' advised McKinnel. 'Firstly, you must be able to act; secondly, you must obtain engagements. As to your acting, I can only say you have shaken my old views. I always said that it took about fifteen years to make anything approaching an actor, but you have apparently stepped right into it. I have nothing against you on that score.' Stoker lapped up the flattery as McKinnel continued.

'How are you going to obtain fairly regular work? I don't quite see that. If you were a young and beautiful man you might obtain engagements because you were a young and beautiful man—but, you know, Stoker, you're not.' Stoker burst into laughter.

McKinnel's summary was that, given luck and hard work, Stoker had as reasonable a chance as anyone else. This was mildly discouraging: McKinnel was really saying he had little chance of eking out more than a living—and even for that luck and hard work would be required.

Stoker thought about it for another month or so, and then, in October 1920, he asked the Admiralty to put him on the retired list. 'As much to my own surprise as anyone's, I had given up the Sea for the Stage.' Six months before the change he'd had no thought at all about becoming an actor. Yet, as he acknowledged some years later, 'the straws had been guiding me towards the stage for years past'.

The wrench from life at sea was hard. For Stoker, the sea was both a mistress and a mother. 'Few of those who go down to her withstand for long the claim she makes on their hearts,' he wrote. 'I doubt if human wives and sweethearts ever realise the strength of the rival they have to fight in winning and keeping a sailor lover. For the sea, though a woman, is straight and true; she does not lie or cheat; she has beauty and grandeur in all her myriad; she appeals always to the best, never to the worst, of the men who meet her; she helps a man to be a man, and never tries to undermine his strength or play upon his weaknesses ... A dangerous rival, Miladies.'

Stoker, however, had taken a calculated gamble. At that time, 1920, future prospects in the navy did not seem encouraging. He certainly called this right. The Royal Navy was downsizing after the war. 'Another war within my lifetime was definitely inconceivable,' said Stoker. This, he called wrong. Years later, Stoker's family would tease him that had he stayed in the navy he might have risen to admiral or higher, like some of his Dardanelles submarine colleagues.

15

The Place All the Straws Led To

On leaving the navy Stoker ditched 'Hew Gordon' as his acting name. In his second play, *A Social Conscience*, one H. G. Stoker was listed playing the easygoing husband. Opening at the Royalty Theatre in 1921, this was also a Harwood script.

'H. G. Stoker is exactly right as the stupid husband—an excellent piece of casting and acting,' said a press reviewer of Stoker's performance, complete with plus-fours attire. In a following Brendan Fleming play *The Eleventh Commandment*, listed as a comedy-tragedy, a reviewer said Stoker was an 'ever most cheerful actor'.

Stoker quickly carved out a niche with character roles. His forte was playing the part of a professional, whether an officer, doctor or even Watson to Sherlock Holmes. A Sherlock Holmes play at the Princes Theatre required both Holmes and the good Dr Watson to use a periscope to spy on villains. Producer Eille Norwood took Stoker aside: 'I'd better tell you about periscopes, and how one uses them.' Stoker merely sighed.

In *The Eleventh Commandment* Stoker found himself playing alongside a beautiful young actress, Dorothie Pidcock, the daughter of a clergyman whom reviewers said 'arrived' in the play. Later they also played together in *Spring Cleaning* at St Martin's Theatre. They married in 1925 in a ceremony at the Savoy Chapel. Stoker, always with an eye to ceremony, married 'Peg' (Dorothie's middle name was Margaret) in full naval uniform. The couple stayed together until Stoker's death in 1966. There were no children.

One press commentator at the wedding of the two West End actors wrote: 'Those who know what Commander Stoker did [in the war], think a VC should have been a just reward.' Another noted that he had commanded a 'British submarine'.

In the mid 1920s Stoker's career blossomed in both literary and theatrical directions. In March 1925 his *Straws in the Wind*, a highly readable account of his early naval life, the *AE2*'s brief but dramatic journey up the Narrows, imprisonment and life immediately after the war, was published to widespread acclaim. The *Daily Mail* described it as a 'breathless story'. The more sedate *Daily Telegraph* called it a 'delightful volume', noting that Stoker possessed not only the cheery optimism of the Irish but had the ability of being able to put it in writing.

Favourable reviews rolled in from Cairo to Auckland as the book went into several editions. The *Melbourne Herald* said, 'There is an unfailing appeal to Australians in the story of their own submarine, the *AE2*, which after achieving the passage of the Dardanelles, was sunk by the Turks and its crew captured.' In Ireland, Stoker was hailed as 'our countryman', and *Straws in the Wind* as 'a spirited and engrossing book'.

Very few of the British reviews referred to *AE2* as an Australian submarine. Somehow the impression was given that the submarine was British. There were doubts even in Australia that compatriots had been aboard *AE2*. In 1928, the Australian War Memorial, then located in Melbourne, wrote to the Naval Accounts Branch to seek details to disprove 'a statement made to us that there were no Australians in the *AE1* and [AE]2'.

Visiting New York in 1922, in the cast of John Galsworthy's drama *Loyalties*, Stoker was hailed in the local press as the man who 'drove the first Allied submarine under the minefields of the Dardanelles into the Sea of Marmara'. The American newspaper interviewer reported Stoker calling him 'dear'. Stoker was appalled. 'Beware of American reporters,' he noted in his scrapbook. 'This is the first time I have ever been accused of calling a newspaperman "dear".'

The American press seized on Stoker's war record. One paper interviewed him in his hotel room as Stoker was 'poring over maps', following the war news as Ataturk fought to expel the Greek army from

Constantinople, occupied in the postwar division of Turkey. His strategic view of Gallipoli, according to the reporter, was that the Germans had made the Turks hold back, requiring the Allies to keep forces in the Dardanelles and away from the Western Front.

Loyalties was a huge success in New York, with the Irish-born Stoker reviewed as the 'typical Englishman'. Stoker and the cast were at first puzzled by the shrieks of laughter at the opening scene when Stoker, partially disrobed, calls to his wife, Adela.

'It turned out to be a joke to them seeing a man taking off his dinner jacket to show a pair of braces (which they never wear) and coming out with English sounding words,' said Stoker.

Back in London in 1928 Stoker launched into his most famous stage role, as the colonel in H. C. Sherriff's *Journey's End*, the sensationally successful play of life in a frontline trench in March 1918. A young Laurence Olivier played the captain. Stoker described Olivier as a 'lad of 21, with very little stage experience'.

Journey's End, with its cut-away trench facing the audience, was a psychological thriller about a varied group of men facing battle and perhaps death. Sherriff had shopped his play around West End theatres, but all had refused it. The play had no female role, then considered essential for box-office success. An American stage entrepreneur, Maurice Brown, whom Stoker described as an arty type, heard about the play, bought the rights and staged it. The play, said Stoker, became a financial goldmine. Sherriff is said to have made the fabulous sum of £150 000, as well as landing a Hollywood contract at £5000 a year to write film scripts.

Every reviewer heaped praise on Stoker. 'His is a piece of acting which, small in itself, may well serve as a standard by which to judge the rest,' said one. 'H. G. Stoker as the deep-feeling, unemotional colonel, achieved portraits of an actuality almost uncanny,' said *The Times*, rather ungrammatically.

The fame of the play spread to Australia, where the *Sydney Pictorial* under the headline 'Ex-Naval Man's Triumph', said: 'A feature of the remarkable wordplay was the appearance in the part of the colonel of

Commander Stoker, who commanded an Australian submarine in the Dardanelles.'

One night all of Britain's Victoria Cross winners attended, causing such commotion that the play was late starting and did not finish until about midnight. The press put this down to the historic nature of the event. But Stoker had the inside story. 'The problem with this "historic" occasion was that the VCs had all dined with HRH Prince of Wales on the night before, and were apparently still all tiddley,' he said. 'They made so much noise all through the play that any decent performance was impossible.'

The *Daily Telegraph*'s review of the night lamented that there was not a VC on the other side of the curtain. 'Indeed, if it had not been for a piece of cruel misadventure there would have been one in the person of H. G. Stoker who played the small part of the colonel so perfectly,' said the *Telegraph*. Putting Stoker in the Royal Navy, the newspaper claimed that in 1915 it had been well known there was a Victoria Cross waiting to reward the first man who took a submarine through the Turkish minefields in the Dardanelles Strait. But after several unsuccessful attempts, the Admiralty had decided not to risk any more lives in such a forlorn hope. Stoker gained a reluctant consent and succeeded, only to spend three and a half years in a Turkish prison. 'His claims to be given a VC were somehow forgotten—though both the next two officers who followed where he had shown the way got their VCs,' said the *Telegraph*. 'The DSO which came his way much later must have been a poor consolation for the loss of the highest military honour, so worthily earned.'

The fame from *Journey's End* stuck with Stoker throughout his career. Stoker remembered the time as particularly happy. 'We were all tremendously friendly in the company—possibly because it contained no female disturbing influence,' he wrote sardonically.

By the late 1920s Stoker had become a regular fixture around West End plays. The *Sketch*'s 'Literary Lounger' columnist devoted an entire page to his burgeoning career. 'The playgoing public is becoming accustomed to the intermittent appearances of a smallish man, very neatly dressed, who has a perpetual elevation of the eyebrows, an unaffected drawl, a tone of gentle reasoning, and a smile that only comes off when some situation in the play renders assumed gravity absolutely necessary,' said Literary Lounger. This, said the *Sketch*, was the West End's latest *raisonneur*, the perpetual character-actor who could lounge in and out of scenes with a cigarette muttering lines such as 'Dash it all' and 'I say, old girl'. The *Sketch* said every cast was delighted to have Stoker in the company, not only because he was London's 'most cheerful actor', or because he was the very man for the part, but also because it was so romantic to have a leading personality from the Dardanelles invasion 'sitting condescendingly on the ends of chesterfields, and raising his eyebrows to an enviable height, and trickling cold water mingled with the warm milk of human kindness down the impetuous backs of the loveliest leading ladies of the moment'.

Small wonder that the Literary Lounger review made it into Stoker's scrapbooks. His reputation as the consummate player of the professional character stuck with Stoker. In early 2000, Sir John Mills recalled that Stoker was a wonderful actor. 'If you wanted a captain in a play or something like that, get H. G,' said Mills. 'He was the best ... very good indeed.'

Stoker may have been a late starter, but he was undoubtedly a gifted actor. McKinnel's advice—to work hard and trust to luck—held true for him. The parts rolled in. Stoker was clearly a precursor of the more famous David Niven.

Not content with merely being an actor, Stoker in 1932 teamed up with another former submariner, J. L. Hunt, to write *Below The Surface*, a play about pressures for promotion amongst rival submariners. A feature of the play was the submarine stage set, complete with periscope, dials and equipment from a bridge.

Below the Surface was initially performed by the Repertory Players, a Sunday night acting group. Mainstream theatres rejected the play, claiming the submarine setting and the play's action and dialogue made it too technical for an ordinary audience to understand.

An incident at one Repertory Players performance showed Stoker's gift of seizing the moment, as he had in the Dardanelles. With some West End promoters in the audience, Stoker came out after the final curtain and told the audience the sad tale of the rejection of *Below the Surface* by the big theatres. 'Of course,' said Stoker with a smile, 'this is not an ordinary audience, but will you please tell me whether, in your opinion, this play would be perfectly and easily understood by an ordinary audience?' The theatre thundered a 'yes'. One of the West End managers present got the message, and *Below the Surface* was immediately signed up for a run.

The play opened at the Prince of Wales Theatre in February 1932, with Stoker playing the part of Captain Radpole, commander of the submarine flotilla. The program featured a cover photograph of the *AE2*. Indeed, there was at least one fascinating analogy with *AE2*. In the play Stoker posed the question of how far a submarine captain was justified in taking extreme risks with his boat.

Reviewers were generally enthusiastic: 'Painfully realistic ... the real stuff ... fascinating stage spectacle ... you fairly hold your breath with excitement.'

The mock submarine set was a winner with audiences, the diving needle convincing them that the submarine was actually submerged. 'I had guessed this would be so from remembering how visitors to a real submarine had eyes for the diving gauge only, and the movement of its needle,' said Stoker. At one performance the stage submarine, complete with gauges and needles, crashed to the floor. A group of navy men in the audience roundly applauded.

Below the Surface ran for three months, first at the Prince of Wales and then at the Apollo. Despite the generally good reviews, the play did not draw good audiences. Stoker said the loss of the submarine *M2* with all hands the week before the play opened was the deterrent. It was too late to postpone the production, and although the first night's takings were donated to the fund for the families of the lost submariners, the play was effectively doomed.

In the 1930s, Stoker turned his hand to new forms of media, as well as the business of the theatre. In 1932 he made his first BBC radio broadcast, *Hazard*, recounting how *AE2* breached the Narrows. Another favourite was *The Fourth Man*, the story of how he and his two fellow escapees from a Turkish prisoner of war camp in 1916 felt the mysterious presence of a fourth man, just as Shackleton had in the Antarctic at about the same time. Stoker was developing the knack of plucking episodes out of his adventurous life and turning them into short dramatic stories.

Stoker's first cinema appearance was in *Channel Crossing* in 1933. *Brown on Resolution* followed in 1935, based on C. S. Forester's adventure yarn about a wounded British sailor delaying the German battleship *Zeithen* in the Galapagos Islands until the Royal Navy arrives to sink it. Stoker played the captain of an outgunned British ship sunk by the *Zeithen* on the way to the islands. The scene showing him on the bridge crying 'Abandon ship' must have been poignant for Stoker, given his real life experience. A young John Mills played the British sailor who delays the *Zeithen* by rifle fire as it tries to make repairs to damage sustained in its battle with Stoker's ship.

Later retitled *Forever England*, the film still appears on daytime television in Australia. In all, Stoker played in eight films, including *Crackerjack* in 1938, *Brighton Rock* in 1947 and *Call of the Blood* in 1948.

The late 1930s was probably Stoker's golden era. His milieu was the Chelsea-Knightsbridge set of well-to-do tennis and golf amateurs, as well as the Garrick Club, the home of the theatre and literary set. Apart from acting in stage and film parts he had become the business manager for the Repertory Players, whose popular Sunday shows discovered actors like Robert Morley. In 1938 he also took on the job of managing the Apollo Theatre. It was Stoker's fourth profession—sailor, actor, author, theatre manager. One critic said he 'must be one of the busiest people in the theatre today'.

At the Apollo, Stoker staged *Black Swans* by Geoffrey Kerr. The show opened to encouraging reviews ('devastatingly funny') but failed to attract big audiences. Stoker wanted to move it to the Shaftesbury Theatre, but the show became the first West End production caught in a tickets war between rival theatre owners. Stoker lamented that a 'managerial battle made it impossible to comply [with the move] without antagonising the chief theatre proprietors'.

Just before the outbreak of World War II, Stoker was acting in *The Flashing Stream* at the Apollo, a play about tensions between naval officers on an island, while managing the theatre as well. In his spare time, he was directing (his fifth profession) A. A. Milne's *Gentleman Unknown*. The words 'H. G. Stoker Presents . . .' began to appear on theatre programs. His *Only Yesterday*, a play about a father who lost his son in World War I, played right up until the outbreak of war. Stoker directed, as well as playing the role of the father. 'It should have played to Hitler in Berlin,' said Stoker as the war loomed.

The pace was obviously cutting into his two other great loves, golf and tennis. Stoker apologised for a loss at Wimbledon due to a heavy morning rehearsal and a heavier matinee show. Stoker was deadly serious about tennis, organising the naval tennis group and playing at Wimbledon several times, winning the doubles one year against a Spanish pair.

Peg gave up the theatre in 1931. Stoker was very disappointed: 'Pity, she was a very good actress,' he said. Stoker's second marriage, however, proved a great success. Niece Primrose remembers them as a very happy couple, always off to parties and hosting dinners amongst the theatre set. Stoker also kept up with old navy and POW mates, often sailing with his 'reprisalist' companion, Fitzgerald.

Stoker's civilian world was swept away in a few hours in September 1939 when he was recalled to active service. 'It was good to be in the thick of things, rather than looking on,' said the 54-year-old Stoker.

His first assignment was as Chief of Staff to Admiral King, staff officer in Belfast. Stoker quickly fell back into the familiar naval routines despite a 19-year absence. Under his command was Tommy Wishart, a Belfastman and old *AE2* crewman. The two compared notes about their Australian odyssey in 1914. 'It was no pleasure jaunt, I can assure you,' recalled Stoker, 'but we were banking on what might be more or less a holiday stay in Australia.'

Stoker, however, soon found himself disapproving of Admiral King's 'habits and actions', and applied for a transfer. The navy 'rewarded' him with command of HMS *Minos*, the naval base at Lowestoft in East Anglia for minesweepers and gunboat operations against the Germans in the North Sea. Lowestoft is Britain's closest point to Germany and was a likely site of invasion.

Like all senior officials, Stoker received a sobering note from Winston Churchill: 'On what may be the eve of an attempted invasion or battle for our national land, the prime minister desires to impress upon all persons holding responsible positions in the government, in the fighting services, or in the civil departments, their duty to maintain a spirit of alertness and confident energy.'

There was no problem staying alert at Lowestoft. The Germans sent in snap air raids almost daily. One day in September 1941 the dockyard was bombed and wrecked only twenty minutes after the workers had left. All civilians were evacuated from the area. Undaunted, Peg came to live with Stoker. She was the only woman in town.

Stoker was shocked by Lowestoft's lack of defences. 'When I arrived to take over command there was virtually nothing with which we could hope to even hamper the enemy if he did come,' he said. 'The general told me of his shortage of men, ammunition and equipment, and my ships—mostly converted trawlers—had antiquated guns.'

Stoker set about a building program for minesweepers. By August 1942, he was exhausted after two years in an exacting command with regular air raids, and the Admiralty decided to give him an easier job. He was put on the lecture circuit to brief people around the country on what the navy was doing.

While Stoker found public relations work distasteful, it enabled him to visit many ships at sea as well as prepare radio broadcasts on his travels around the fleet. 'Here are a few yarns about my travels—greatly shortened for security reasons,' one broadcast began.

In April 1944 Stoker's association with big amphibious invasions turned full circle when he was appointed to the staff of the navy command for the Allied expeditionary force for the invasion of Europe, known by the mouthful ANCXF. Stoker, then 59, typically dubbed himself the navy 'old fool' in the party.

One of his tasks was to prepare a war diary for future historians. His notes of 15 May 1944 put Stoker at one of the most momentous meetings of the war—the final conference of all military chiefs to approve Neptune, the code name for the navy's task of landing the huge Allied army for Overlord, the invasion of Europe. All the great names of the European war were present—Eisenhower, Montgomery and Churchill. King George VI also attended.

Despite the seriousness of the occasion, and fears that bad weather might delay the invasion (it finally took place on 6 June), Stoker managed to find a light-hearted side to events. Churchill was in full rhetorical flight, exuding confidence in the impending invasion. Churchill, of course, had always lamented the 'ifs' of Gallipoli, including what might have happened if the military had shown more speed in some of its attacks. Perhaps this was in his mind when he urged the D-day army commanders to 'press on' when they got to France.

'For example,' Stoker records him as saying, 'don't bother about reports and records, let 'em slip, let 'em wait—press on—don't give the enemy a second to catch his breath.' For Stoker this was vastly amusing, as one of his other duties was to send morning reports to Churchill's office on how many troops, vehicles and stores had been put ashore each day. 'If the Old Man didn't have that signal each morning with his breakfast one of his minions was on the phone forthwith.'

On 5 June Stoker had the job of guarding the door to the final meeting to decide the go-ahead for invasion the following day, and passing messages in and out. In the back of his mind were two midget submarines, positioned off the coast of France to set flashing lights to guide the Allied invasion force. The submarines had already been told of delays due to bad weather, and Stoker felt keenly for their crews.

After D-day the naval role wound down. Stoker returned to his job of visiting the fleet to brief crew and officers on upcoming operations against the Japanese in the Pacific. He had not lost his theatrical touch. One of his broadcasts about this time likened the operations of an aircraft carrier to a ballet performance, referring to the landing deck crew in their coloured caps and with arms extended to guide returning aircraft. One of Stoker's comments, however, almost landed him in hot water. Visiting Portsmouth he told officers that the Japanese were virtually beaten, with most of their ships sunk. It was a security breach, and could have damaged the final war effort against Japan. The local commander signalled the Admiralty for disciplinary action, but as Stoker said, 'their Lordships took no action, and within weeks the Japanese gave in'.

Returning to civilian life, Stoker quickly became absorbed in new stage roles in the plays *Green Room Rags* and *Dog's Delight*. But the real life drama of war had jaded Stoker's taste for the theatre. 'Play acting didn't seem so interesting after the war, nor, I'm afraid, did theatre folk seem quite so attractive.' As well, chances for new theatre management opportunities had dimmed; costs were up, profits slimmer and wartime had pretty much reduced the West End to one monopoly operator.

Wartime stories were very popular, however, and Stoker collaborated with K. B. Woollard on the submarine escape drama *Morning Departure*, which opened at the Adelphi Theatre. It later became a film starring John Mills, and was serialised in the *Daily Mail*. Although Stoker was co-author of the original play he disagreed with Woollard on some of the content and refused to put his name to it. He sold his half share to Woollard before it became a hit. 'I suppose it was a pity I didn't leave my name on it,' he later lamented.

Television, however, opened new horizons, and Stoker, in the late 1940s, launched himself into TV dramas. In 1949, he collaborated with Gilbert Hackforth-Jones on the hit television drama *Deep Waters*, a psychological thriller about a submarine commander who has to order his flotilla into oblivion. Stoker felt this a much superior story to *Morning Departure*. 'In fact, the latter would never have been produced if I'd had this story to work on first,' he said. 'Hackforth-Jones supplied the story, and I wrote the play. He was supposed to collaborate on the dramatisation, but didn't.' One reviewer called it 'first class television'.

Although the theatre and TV work continued through the early 1950s, Stoker took up other, more leisurely pursuits. In 1951, aged 66, he played his last serious golf tournament, finding croquet 'more attractive to my ageing limbs'. While one critic of that era described croquet as an 'impossibly difficult exercise played to incomprehensible rules by venomous old people with a tendency to swear', Stoker was fascinated by it.

The type who never does anything in a half-hearted fashion, Stoker went on to become one of the leading croquet players in the British Isles. He won the Irish championship in 1962, aged 77. 'Champion of Ireland at 77 . . . grand,' he said. 'To be champion of my native country at anything, even tiddlywinks, would have thrilled me.' Although still active in tennis, Stoker wrote to friends that at his age croquet was 'the finest game of all for keeping the doctor at bay'.

The 1950s were crammed with croquet, holidays and parties at country houses with the theatre set for Stoker and Peg. Stoker effectively retired, and, although Anglo-Irish, his great fondness for the royal family began to bring out more of the 'Anglo' in him. In 1948 he and Peg were guests of King George VI at Windsor Great Park. Stoker described it as 'one of the most pleasant days I ever spent in my life', attending a service in the royal chapel and then playing cricket with the king.

Stoker was in at bat when the king was bowling. 'Sir, please remember that I was a shipmate with your grandfather,' he said, raising a laugh all round. Stoker revelled in such brushes with royalty, mixing easily in the king's circle.

As Stoker was chatting with J. E. Brown, editor of the *Sketch*, the king joined them to congratulate Brown on the popular Snodgrass wartime cartoon strip, featuring a pretty young woman in the navy. A particular cartoon praised by the king had the short-skirted female naval recruit up a ladder pinning flags on a wall map of fleet movements, with an admiral under the ladder looking up. To one side, a senior naval officer says to another: 'Either the admiral wants the fleet further south or we'd better put Snodgrass in bell bottoms.' Stoker said the *Sketch* editor didn't know how to respond to the king's compliment. 'Yes,' continued the king, 'I keep it in the downstairs lavatory.'

Stoker organised royal telegrams for the regular dinners of surviving graduates of the old training ship *Britannia*. These were worrying nights for Peg, anxious that Stoker not drink too much. She got a real fright after one reunion, keeping an eye out for Stoker as his taxi pulled up outside their home. Stoker had dropped his spectacle case, emerging from the taxi on all fours as he searched the floor.

In 1954, aged 69, Stoker was reflecting on his 'all-rounder life'. He was struck by Duff Cooper's remark that as a young man he had had the 'stupid idea that hard work at a given task was degrading'. Stoker felt he had the same 'stupid idea' that a good all-rounder was the ideal to be aimed at. But that precluded reaching the absolute top of any profession. 'There's certainly lots of fun in the all-rounder life, but no big bags of nuts—or nuggets.'

Stoker consoled himself on the lack of 'bags of nuts' in the theatre by playing the stockmarket. According to his niece Primrose, he was quite successful. Money, however, was not a big issue for him, as it was for others. Once he partnered Somerset Maugham at bridge in a game at the Garrick Club. 'Luckily we won,' said Stoker. 'He didn't like losing, although he was incredibly rich.'

HMS *Thorough* made headlines in 1957 when it became the first submarine to circumnavigate the globe. Stoker recalled *AE2*'s epic journey 42 years before when it almost achieved the feat. 'Most of our journey was in war conditions and without a quarter of their modern amenities,' he said.

Although Stoker spent most of his last 40 years in the world of the theatre, submarines were still a major tug on his heart. Visiting the chapel at Portsmouth dedicated to lost submariners—Britain lost 54 subs in World War I—Stoker said it was not all sadness. 'How could it be?' he asked. 'There is glory. Death can come in many less noble ways than these men found, facing dangers uncountable ... And there may be worse places to lie for the long sleep, with comrades about you, and the ship you loved forming a steel tomb maybe hundreds of fathoms deep. Comrades ... comradeship ... it plays such an immense part in the life of a submarine ... As you stand in the Shrine of Remembrance it is easy to believe that such comradeship far outlives death.'

True to his lifelong belief in straws in the wind, the last page of Stoker's personal diaries, apparently written the year before he died, contains a list of the things that provided him with the 'big thrill'.

These, said Stoker, were the 'odd and various things' that 'one can laugh—laugh a lot at'.

His nine-point list, in somewhat shaky handwriting, reads:

- To 'walk with kings'—and princes and princesses.
- In 1900, the practical birth of submarines, the thought of commanding one seemed thrilling.
- To win cups in lawn tennis and golf and croquet. To make centuries in cricket. To see packed stands at big rugby matches.
- To write a book and receive laudatory reviews in London, provincial and Dominion papers.
- To act in West End stage with stars of the day, in successful plays, and on television and radio, and in films, and in New York and Canada.
- To be given a role in history books.
- To hear a song one had composed sung by the leading baritone of the day—loudly applauded.
- To be a prisoner of war of the Turks, and to escape, and to be recaptured.
- To stand on the stage at a successful first night and receive cheers and applause of the audience as the author.

* * *

Dacre Stoker died in February 1966 in London. He certainly deserved cheers and applause, and more than for writing plays.

16

'North! North!'

On 2 July 1998 Selçuk Kolay reached out and touched the starboard side exhaust pipe of the *AE2*. He was 72 metres down on the floor of the Sea of Marmara, and the first person to see or touch *AE2* in 83 years.

Kolay relished the historical moment. He rubbed his diving gloves against the rusty hull, planning to keep them as a souvenir. Back on board his research ship, the *Soros*, he rushed to the bridge to telephone colleagues in Australia about his find. Returning to the deck he found that one of the crewmen had just washed his gloves. They looked rusty, the crewman said.

Kolay's find capped a three-year search that at times became more like a detective story. Frustrated with confusing historical data that turned up no sunken submarine, Kolay interviewed local fishermen and even Stoker's one remaining relative — his niece Primrose — to gain clues. But it was only a conversation with his own father that put the final piece of the jigsaw into place: many maps were based on a mistake in transcription from the old Arabic to the modern Latin alphabet.

Kolay then was the director of the gem-like Rahmi M. Koç Museum in Istanbul, where maritime and industrial artefacts, and items from contemporary life and Turkish history are lovingly restored and exhibited with flair. In his spare time, he is an avid naval buff and scuba diver.

In the Turkish navy as a young man for his compulsory military service, Kolay researched submarine warfare, where he learnt about the *AE2*. After graduating as an industrial engineer, he assisted the German author, Bernd Langensiepen, in researching his books *The Ottoman Torpedo Boats* and *The Ottoman Steam Navy*.

In the 1990s Kolay—combining his passions—refined his underwater skills in searches for lost craft, using side-scan sonars, proton magnetometers (which measure metal density) and global satellite positioning systems. In 1993 he identified the remains in the Black Sea of the German World War I submarine *UB 46*. Later the same year he found the sunken Turkish cruiser *Midilli*. This was the former German ship *Breslau*, which the British navy chased into Constantinople, setting the scene for the eventual Dardanelles operation. Kolay also found the remains of the Turkish submarine *Atilay* from World War I.

In December 1994, at a reception for the opening of his Istanbul museum, Kolay fell to chatting with the Australian ambassador to Turkey, David Evans. It was the spark that led to the hunt for *AE2*; all earlier attempts to find the submarine had failed.

Kolay talked with his boss, the wealthy industrialist Rahmi Koç, about taking up the challenge to find the wreck. For Kolay, *AE2*'s feat in breaching the heavily mined and protected Dardanelles Strait was 'one of the most daring and successful submarine exploits of its time'. Koç agreed.

When Kolay over the next few months sat down to study the Turkish, Australian, British and German archives he got quite a shock. These not only gave various locations for the sinking of *AE2*, they were wildly different. The Turkish and German locations were about 18.5 kilometres apart. Stoker's position, according to British and Australian records, put the *AE2*'s sinking 6.4 kilometres north of Karaburun Point, just before the Sea of Mamara leads into the top of the Dardanelles Strait. This was 12.8 kilometres east of the Turkish position. German records even showed one position of the sunken submarine as right on top of a small island!

Using all possible positions, Kolay worked out a search area across 35 square kilometres, a very large area to scan. The Turkish navy had looked in this area before, but found nothing. Maybe *AE2* was covered by the thick soft mud on this part of the floor of the Marmara. The side-scan sonar and proton magnetometer on board *Soros* would detect *AE2* even if it was totally buried in mud.

Using a global satellite positioning system, Kolay started the long grind of scanning the search area one quadrant at a time. It was frustrating work. Bad weather and rough seas caused delays, while new sonar gear imported from the US at first did not work. By June 1995 he had eliminated about 80 per cent of the area, enabling him to concentrate more on the Stoker position of 7.4 kilometres north of Karaburun Point.

But by the end of August he had had no luck. A sunken coaster turned up not far from Stoker's position, but no submarine. Kolay took to spending evenings with local fishermen trying to find locations where their nets had snagged, but drew a blank. Friends advised him to spend more time on the Turkish position since Stoker had been in enemy waters desperately trying to escape a torpedo attack. Surely the Turkish navy's position would be more reliable.

Kolay disagreed. Stoker had sailed his submarine around the world twice and guided it through the Dardanelles without touching a single mine. 'This man will know by the inch where he sank,' Kolay told himself.

Confident that Stoker would somehow lead him to the lost *AE2*, Kolay began researching the captain's life. In London, a friend working on a BBC documentary of *AE2* had found Stoker's last relative in Britain, his niece Primrose, then 85.

Primrose Stoker had adored her uncle, and was close to him in his later years in London. She responded enthusiastically to questions about his life, producing photos from her collection. Kolay's search impressed Primrose. She suddenly produced Stoker's old leather bag full of manuscripts and suggested Kolay examine them. They included Stoker's personal diary, letters he had received while a prisoner of war and maps showing planned escape routes.

Kolay pressed her for more. 'Can you remember him telling you anything about the *AE2* after he came back from imprisonment?' he asked.

'As a war hero he never talked about this incident, he was too secretive,' Primrose said. 'But as a little girl, I can recall Captain Stoker would sometimes shout "North! North!" in his sleep.' The nightmares were a vivid recollection for Primrose. As a child she had been frightened by them.

Over the next 48 hours Kolay studied the material with almost no sleep. While many were documents Kolay already had copies of, he was able to see Stoker's handwritten changes on the originals. He was struck by a discrepancy in the depth of the sinking position. Stoker said his boat sank in about 55 fathoms [100 metres] 6.4 kilometres north of Karaburun Point. But at that point the depth of the water is more like 70 metres.

Back in Istanbul, Kolay decided to extend his search north. Maybe Stoker had deliberately misled people about the sinking location, and that might explain his cries of 'North! North!'. After all, in 1915 *AE2* was state-of-the-art submarine technology. Stoker would not have wanted his boat recovered by the enemy. The British had gone to great lengths to destroy *E14* when it ran aground in the Dardanelles Strait only a few weeks before Stoker's voyage.

Scanning north, Kolay hit a wreck that looked on the sonar remarkably like a submarine. It even had similar shape and dimensions to the *AE2*. Diving on the wreck, he found it densely covered by old fishing nets. It still looked like a submarine. Kolay called in an Australian diving team, but on closer inspection the wreck turned out to be an old steamer.

Kolay was in the third year of his search, and feeling mightily frustrated. He was convinced that Stoker, although wrong about the depth, was right about the position 6.4 kilometres north of Karaburun. Even a sketch made by *AE2* signalman John Thomson while in prison showed the sinking location somewhere north of Karaburun Point. But there was no *AE2* to be found there. Kolay decided to scan the area again. 'I knew this was the hardest case I ever had,' he said.

In fact, all the charts gave positions north-west by north of Karaburun. Ali Riza, captain of the *Sultanhisar* torpedo boat whose gunfire damaged *AE2* before Stoker decided to scuttle, also gave this as an approximate area. *Zuhaf* and *Aydin Reis*, the two other Ottomon torpedo boats that arrived on the scene had also taken bearings, but Kolay could not find these in archives.

'It was funny, but every passing month I was becoming more determined than desperate,' said Kolay. On Marmara Island, a local fisherman told Kolay that his friend had experienced snagging problems in the area north of Karaburun a fortnight before. It was dark, and without electronic navigation they were not certain of the exact location. But they had the feeling it was slightly north-west of Karaburun.

On a fine day in May 1998 Kolay dropped a marker buoy exactly 6.4 kilometres north of Karaburun, telling the *Soros*'s captain to stop the engines. He wanted time to work out a new search pattern. Kolay worked on his charts for a while before noticing that the *Soros* had drifted a couple of hundred metres to the west.

'There was no wind, no waves—it was just like the day of *AE2*'s sinking,' said Kolay. This was probably due to a weak natural current towards the Dardanelles. 'Suddenly I remembered the Turkish position approximately 12.8 kilometres west of that of Stoker, which I had classified as wrong and had not considered as a possible sinking site!'

Kolay at once ordered the *Soros* to go to Aksaz, a village about 11 kilometres west of Karaburun. He had visited the village three years earlier to ask if the fishermen knew of an obstruction north-east of Karaburun. This time he was asking about obstructions to the north-west. Two brothers immediately told him of an obstruction where they had snared their nets, but could not remember the exact location.

With this information, Kolay knew he had to scan further to the west than he had scanned before. The latitude of the Turkish position seemed right, but the longitude was surely too far west. Why was that? Kolay wondered.

The position was taken from a book published by the Turkish General Staff in 1936, twenty-one years after *AE2* was sunk in 1915. But no source was shown. Kolay was certain it had been taken from Ottoman naval archives and transcribed from Arabic script into Latin script after 1928, when Turkey switched alphabets in the modernising reforms of Kemal Ataturk.

The Turkish longitude, given as 27° 10' seemed to Kolay to be too far west by at least 8 to 11 kilometres. If it had been given as 15, 16 or even 17 instead of 10' he would have considered it a possible sinking site. Had a mistake been made in transcription?

As older Turks can read Arabic script, Kolay called on his father and asked him to write down the Arabic figures for 10 and 15. 'When I saw the figures he had written, I knew that a mistake was made during transcription,' said Kolay. 'Figures 10 and 15 are almost identical, so the east longitude should read 15' instead of 10! Now I had a new area of approximately 4 square miles to search.'

On 11 June 1998, Kolay had been scanning in the new area all day. Just after 5pm, as he was thinking of packing up for the day, a slim profile started showing up on the screen. A few seconds later the magnetometer went mad. 'I knew I had found the *AE2*,' he said.

Magnetometer readings revealed the wreck was approximately 540 tonnes. Side-scan sonar showed the shape of a submarine of 50–55 metres lying at a depth of 72 metres, 6.4 kilometres north-west of Karaburun. Kolay checked his old plottings. They revealed that three and a half years before he had been within 300 metres of the wreck, scanning in the other direction.

'Everything now became obvious,' said Kolay. 'When the *AE2* was hit and damaged by shellfire from the Turkish torpedo boat, Captain Stoker decided to scuttle it and not to let it fall into enemy hands. He steadied his boat on the surface, gave the signal to *Sultanhisar* that he was ready to surrender and gathered his crew on the deck. Then he probably took his bearings to know his exact position before opening the valves.

'At that time he was north-east by north of Karaburun as marked on the charts. It took some time before the last of Captain Stoker and his crew swam across to the torpedo boat, and the slowly sinking submarine disappeared from the surface. During this time both the sub and the torpedo boat drifted westward, just as our research ship did 83 years later—and the two torpedo boats closing in just after the sinking took the actual bearing of the sinking point.'

AE2 had drifted west in the current from the time of scuttling to sinking to the bottom. The Dardanelles outflow, the very thing that had bedevilled Stoker and other submariners in 1915, had foxed searchers over the years relying on official maps.

* * *

AE2 may have been found, but it is still reluctant to reveal its secrets. Two attempts to dive on *AE2* failed. It was not until 2 July 1998 that Kolay was able to secure a line to the wreck and take a cameraman down with him to see *AE2* for the first time. The two toured the aft deck and conning tower. 'The submarine was in excellent condition,' said Kolay. 'It was like stepping back in time. The morning of 30 April 1915 was frozen here.'

AE2 must have floated down without turning. The submarine is lying almost bolt upright with mud up around the natural waterline. The stern is high off the mud floor, with the two blades of the portside propeller and even larger portions of one blade of the starboard propeller protruding above the mud. Kolay found a few irregularly shaped holes that could be the shell damage from the *Sultanhisar*. Parts of the hull are covered in old fishing nets, while heavy encrustration has set in.

Kolay found one surprise. The main hatch is still slightly ajar, just as Stoker left it when he was the last man to climb out 83 years previously. The only inhabitant inside the hatch these days is a 2 metre conger eel.

An Australian diving team arrived in October 1998 led by Dr Mark Spencer, a Sydney dentist who had taken up the fate of *AE2* as a hobby. He launched Project *AE2* to drum up government and commercial sponsorship to help identify the wreck, prepare an archaeological report for the Australian government, and build a wreck site condition model. Accompanied by Tim Smith, maritime archaeologist with the NSW Heritage Office, the team quickly confirmed Kolay's finding of the *AE2*. John Thomson, grandson of *AE2* signalman Albert Thomson, was in the Australian diving party, giving a personal connection to the original crew.

* * *

Why has *AE2* been virtually forgotten? Professor Robert O'Neill, the military historian and academic, says the 'Anzac public relations' has largely obliterated the role of the British and French at Gallipoli. It has also obliterated the navy and *AE2*.

The Australian navy has only itself to blame. *AE2*'s exploits suffered from excessive naval secrecy and failure to appreciate the magnitude of the little submarine's achievement. By the time the navy was releasing details of the *AE2*'s loss the news was understandably swamped by reports of the Gallipoli landings.

For some years the Australian navy seemed unsure that *AE2* could lay claim to being the first submarine to make the hazardous Dardanelles passage underwater, much less in wartime conditions. In 1919 the navy noted on a London report that it 'appears to definitely establish that *AE2* was first submarine to achieve the passage of the Dardanelles successfully'. Yet this had been known to the Royal Navy since receipt of the *AE2*'s crucial message on the night of 25 April 1914.

It may be that Stoker and the *AE2* suffered from war weariness. The Marmara submariners who received VCs all returned quickly to tell their tale. The story of *AE2*'s daring passage was locked up with its crew for three and a half years. By the time they straggled home in 1919 the Dardanelles campaign was the epitome of failure. The world by then was not looking for war heroes; it just wanted to get on with postwar life. Returned British submariners like Nasmith might have been lionised as the 'Scourge of the Marmara', but those who failed to return until years later had stories few wanted to hear.

For many—particularly in Britain—*AE2* was regarded as a British submarine anyway. This may be understandable, but the lapse in Australia beggars belief. Despite the notoriety of Stoker's book *Straws in the Wind* in 1925, the fledgling Australian War Memorial a few years later was asking the Australian navy to confirm that there were Australians aboard the submarine.

Could it be that *AE2*'s role in the embarrassing near-withdrawal after the first day's fighting condemned it to slip through the net of the Anzac legend? The message from Anzac Cove to Hamilton on the night of

25 April—if evacuation is planned, do it now—is not something that is highlighted in most Gallipoli accounts. Most historians agree that the evacuation message was alarmist and unnecessary, and that Hamilton's famous 'dig, dig, dig' response had little effect on the determination of the troops to fight on.

Whatever the reason, *AE2* has been 'lost' for 85 years. Thanks to Selçuk Kolay—awarded an Order of Australia for his efforts—the little submarine has been located. It is quite well preserved in the Marmara mud, although obviously it will deteriorate if not raised and perserved properly.

AE2's achievements cannot be measured in terms of Turkish vessels sunk. In fact, Stoker sank only one; possibly a second. Stoker's achievement, as noted by Rear Admiral C.V. Usborne in 1932, was that he led the way into the Marmara. '[He] started the paralysis which soon swept over Turkish sea communications, and his exploits must rank high in the annals of naval achievement,' said Usborne.

Turn the issue around. What would have been the Turkish position if *AE2* had not pioneered what became a major Allied submarine campaign on its Gallipoli supply lines? There is no doubt the Turkish defences would have been better equipped and reinforced. The Allied invasion faced a tough—and widely underestimated—opponent at Gallipoli. That opposition would have been ever tougher without *AE2*'s breakthrough.

Is there one final straw in the wind for Stoker's submarine? Kolay's location of the wreck has sparked a debate between Turkey and Australia on whether *AE2* should be raised and displayed, and if so, where. Ideas abound, from leaving it as a 'living museum' on the floor of the Marmara, to displaying it in Istanbul, perhaps in association with the Australian War Memorial. It could become a magnet for the many thousands of Australians who flock to Turkey each year to visit the Gallipoli landing site; a symbol of the permanent co-operation between former enemies.

That, of course, was not Stoker's aim as he headed towards the Golden Horn with his one remaining torpedo on the day he met *Sultanhisar*. But Stoker's devilish sense of humour would be tickled if *AE2*'s final resting place were to be Istanbul's Golden Horn.

Whatever befalls the *AE2* next—whether she is raised and placed on display or left as a living museum beneath the sea, whether she belongs to Turkey or to Australia or to both—Australians can be proud that so many straws in the wind blew *AE2*'s extraordinary captain and brave crew to Gallipoli.

17

Stoker's Men

After sailing around the world, breaching the Narrows of the Dardanelles and then spending three and a half years in Turkish POW camps, the crew of the *AE2* epitomised the comradeship that marks submariners.

Stoker, who went out of his way to praise his crew in the *AE2*'s hazardous voyage up the Narrows, summed up this feeling: 'Men living together in closely confined quarters, sharing in absolute equality the hazards of every danger, each one holding the lives of all in their hands ... comradeship comes firmly and with depth of meaning to such men.'

The stories of Stoker's men are a crucial part of the history of one of Australia's greatest naval feats.

Cary, John Pitt MID; Lieutenant/Commander; RN/RAN

Lieutenant John (Jack) Cary was third officer of the *AE2*. Unlike other members of the submarine crew he was not a specialist submariner, but a naval hydrographer, map-maker and draughtsman. He was assigned to *AE2* from the Admiralty because of the lack of accurate charts and maps of the Dardanelles region, a factor which was impeding the Allied cause in general, and naval strategy in particular.

Cary was born in Donegal, Ireland, the son of an Anglo-Irish family originally from Devonshire. His father Arthur sent him and his brother Joyce (later to become the famous novelist) to an English boarding school, Hurstleigh Preparatory School in Kent. On arrival at the school, the brothers had strong Irish accents which at first made them figures of fun. They soon adjusted however, and Jack went on to win prizes, although Joyce didn't. At age 14, Jack was interviewed at the Admiralty and accepted for officer training at Britannia Royal Naval College, Dartmouth, fulfilling his boyhood ambition.

Joyce, a slight and physically weak boy, was unable to get in to the navy. As he wrote: 'It was my brother who became the sailor . . . his first appearance . . . in blue and gold, made him my hero.' Surprisingly, perhaps, they always remained friends. Joyce Cary later wrote to his wife about Jack: 'He's shy, you know, and has no great fun of conversation, but [is] a dear boy, unselfish and affectionate . . . I never knew him to make an enemy in his life.' By 17, midshipman Jack Cary was serving aboard the *Albemarle*. Then followed tours of duty aboard the *London*, *Venus*, *Agamemnon* and the *Endeavour*, when he was promoted to sub-lieutenant. He served on the *Thunder*, *Daisy* and the surveying ship *Fanborne* until 1913 when he became a lieutenant, a skilled hydrographer.

He was lent to the RAN in 1913, but did not sail on the *AE2* for her voyage to Australia. He was assigned instead to the *Berrima*, the submarine escort ship. Cary joined *AE2* as third officer only in January 1915.

At Afion Kara Hissar prison camp, Cary was interned with a group including his fellow officers Stoker and Haggard. He was able to cope with the years of deprivation both physically and mentally, and produced some sketches and paintings. His laconic personality was shown in a letter to Miss Chomley of the Red Cross in 1918:

Dear Miss Chomley, I have just received your letter of May 28th. I regret to state that I was not wounded. In my prolonged visit to this country I have put my knee out once, I don't know the medical term, but it's my left knee and something to do with a semi-lunar cartilege. I am also at this moment recovering from a serious attack of the Spanish Grip, and in consequence am slightly deaf: this I think will yield to treatment. If you can get me exchanged, please do, but it is no good my being medically examined as they only laugh at me. Home sickness and incipient lunacy are really my main illnesses.

Cary was known in the camp for his dry wit. He found a tortoise which he made his pet, and began to race it against all challengers for appropriate odds. Apparently his tortoise proved spectacularly unsuccessful as a speedster, because a letter to his half-sister Shiela reported that he had eventually roasted and eaten the poor animal. The meat, he wrote, 'was quite acceptable, rather tasteless but quite tender'.

After his release from Afion Kara Hissar and return to London, he was fit enough to re-enlist in the RN and returned that same year to the Australia Station on the *Merlin*, a survey vessel. He then spent several years charting the Torres Strait region in particular. His brother Joyce wrote with some pride that Jack had discovered a small island there that he named Cary Island. But later he informed Joyce 'with mock dismay, that it had been renamed Kareng Si Ajar ... he was slightly peeved considering he had buckled the rudder of a motor boat on it, and so thought it most unfair'.

Jack returned to England in 1922, served in the Shetland Islands, then in West Africa. Promoted to commander in 1924 he served in Scotland before accepting a posting to the Admiralty's hydrographic department. In 1935 he retired to live with his father and Shiela at their home in Somerset. He never married.

Cary came out of retirement to serve again in WWII from 1939 to 1945. He died in 1953 of a heart attack while on the golf course.

Haggard, Geoffrey Arthur Gordon DSC; Lieutenant/Commander; RN/RAN

Geoffrey Haggard was born in London on 4 May 1888, the elder son of Major Edward Arthur Haggard and his wife Emily (née Calvert). He was the nephew and godson of novelist Sir Rider Haggard.

Although he suffered from asthma as a child, Haggard was accepted into the Royal Naval Training College, Osborne House at the age of 13 and graduated as an officer trainee four years later. His first naval postings included HMS *Britannia* (1903), *Isis*, *Implacable* (1905), *Swiftsure*, *Excellent* (1908), *Foam* and *Mercury*, before he transferred in 1910 to submarines in search of more adventure, first on *B2*, then *B11* in 1911, and then *AE2* in 1915.

To Haggard, the surrender of the *AE2* was a moment of great personal anguish. He clearly disagreed with his captain's decision, and was heard to argue that they should all fight on to their deaths in true adventure-novel style. But Stoker knew that there was no real choice: the warship with its then state-of-the-art technology could not be allowed to fall into enemy hands. Besides this, the sub had nothing left to fight with.

In the prison camp, Haggard joined Stoker and fellow officers in working hard to keep up morale. They formed an amateur theatrical group, for which Haggard wrote, and acted in, productions. For the most part, Haggard coped well with prison life, but all the men were ultimately at the mercy of whichever Turkish commandant was in charge. At the end of 1916 the Afion prison commandant was Bimbashi Musloum Bey, who targeted Haggard and made his life miserable. Asserting that Haggard seemed likely to try to escape, the commandant had him arrested without questioning, gave him a mock trial then locked him up in a small dark building which was strictly guarded and cut off from all communication. News of the behaviour of this individual was finally leaked to the Turkish authorities and he was removed from his post. Haggard's daughter Jenny Smyth says that during this terrible period of solitary confinement her father feared for his sanity: 'all he had to read was a tin that had contained plum jam. He forced himself to read its label over and over again to keep his mind alive.'

Worse still for Haggard was that he was considered to be English and so missed out on the Red Cross parcels and money that came via the RAN representative in London. He was also overlooked by the British. This bureaucratic bungling seriously affected Haggard who had become weak and run-down following a bout of malaria. He was also devastated by the news that his only and younger brother Major (Rider) Lancelot Haggard had been killed in action at Passchendaele in France.

On 24 April 1919 Haggard was awarded a DSC in recognition of his gallantry on *AE2* during the passage of the Dardanelles. After the war, he was keen to remain in RN submarines but after examination by the Admiralty, it was decided that 'his long stay in Turkey as a prisoner of war has reduced his powers of concentration, although [he is] temperate, keen and zealous'. Haggard was accepted for service but not in submarines. Disappointed, he retired at his own request on 27 November 1920, when he was offered the post of aide-de-camp to the Earl of Stradbroke, who was governor of Victoria. Haggard accepted the post and returned to Australia.

In September 1923 he married Marjory Syme, daughter of David Syme, a Victorian newspaper baron. He was 35 years old, she just 20. He then began another career, this time as a gentleman farmer and grazier at Pendleside, the Syme family property at Woori Yallock in the Yarra Valley, about 40 miles from Melbourne. He became a successful country squire, running a prime sheep, cattle and horse stud there for many years.

By 1938 his previously good health had begun to fail, and he was hospitalised briefly, attributing this bout of illness to his time as a prisoner of war. By 1939 he was pleading with the RAN to take him back on active service, but was not successful. Undaunted, he then applied to the RN and was eventually accepted. His letter of acceptance arrived on 10 October, stating ominously that he would be posted to the British Naval Base at Singapore. Daughter Jenny Smyth recounts: 'That evening he was walking back home along the railway track after celebrating his call-up. As a train approached, the heel of his boot caught in the track. The train just missed him, but a rock thrown up by the wheel of the engine hit him in the temple and he was killed instantly.' Haggard left a very young grieving widow and a family of three small children.

Herbert, Douglass Phillips; Engineer Lieutenant/Principal Naval Engineer; RAN

Born in Sydney on 11 November 1888, Douglass Herbert was an academically gifted student who graduated with a double honours degree from Sydney University in engineering and science in 1908. He joined the RAN in 1912.

Herbert left Australia to oversee the construction and commissioning of both *AE1* and *AE2*. Although not aboard the submarines, he and Lieutenant Paterson always accompanied either of the depot escorts or bases and he was, according to his son Jock, 'in all the major steps' and therefore an integral part of the *AE2* story. His task was to organise and plan for the whole squadron as well as individual submarines, design new equipment, and propose future improvements.

Herbert was at Kokopo (Rabaul) in New Guinea when the *AE1* was lost, and also in the Dardanelles, although not on board the *AE2* when she was last in action. He proceeded through the Dardanelles with the Allied fleet in 1919, conveying intelligence officers from Constantinople to Sebastopol in the Crimea. During and post-WWI, he continued service in the RAN all over the world, including New Zealand, the Falkland Islands, Jamaica and the UK. By 1919 he had been promoted to engineer lieutenant commander. He returned to Sydney with his Scottish wife Jean and their boys Colin and Jock in 1924, and saw service in Japan and Hong Kong before returning to Geelong and then Garden Island, Sydney.

By the late 1930s Herbert was naval engineer officer at the High Commission in London, and rejoined the navy when war broke out, seeing active service at Naval Headquarters in Darwin in 1939 and 1940. He was transferred in 1941 as principal naval engineer in Adelaide, overseeing wartime shipbuilding.

He retired in 1953 and moved to Melbourne. He died on 22 October 1964 after a long and distinguished career.

Paterson, Halliday Gunning; Engineer Lieutenant; RN

Halliday Paterson was born in Rio de Janeiro, Brazil. He joined the RAN from the RN as an engineer officer in 1913, serving at the London Depot from 7 May 1913 to 27 February 1914, then aboard the *Sydney* and *Penguin* submarines from 25 May 1914 to 31 December 1916. After 1916 he continued service with the RAN at *Penguin*, *Egmont*, *Psyche* and *Cerberus*. He was promoted to lieutenant commander in June 1916, and resigned on 27 July the same year.

Stoker thought highly of Paterson's engineering capabilities and wrote a detailed technical report on the *AE2*'s problems to the navy on 24 November 1914, clearly stating that he wanted Paterson to be involved with the submarines: 'I would further submit that Eng Lieut Paterson should be appointed to oversee the building of the next submarines, and that he should be sent at an early date in their construction. This officer is now conversant with the necessities of the boats peculiar to the station, and I am of the opinion, which was shared by the late Lt Commr Besant, that it was largely owing to the work of this officer in attending personally to every detail in the construction of *AE1* and *AE2* that their steaming performances were due.'

Paterson's last known address was San Francisco in 1920.

Abbott, Harry DSM; Chief Petty Officer; RN/RAN 8268

Harry Abbott, coxswain of the *AE2*, was also one of the oldest crew members. He was born on 18 April 1876 in Devon, England.

Abbott joined the RN at the age of 18 in 1894 and rapidly rose in rank to the position of chief petty officer by 1913, when he was officially loaned by the RN to the RAN to serve aboard its newly built and commissioned submarine, the *AE2*.

Taken prisoner of war, he was first interned at Afion Kara Hissar. At Belemedik, Abbott became the paymaster for all the *AE2* crew, as well as their guardian. The money was delivered to the men only through the ingenuity of the RAN representative in London at that time, Captain Francis Haworth Booth. Haworth Booth wrote:

> *I ... discovered that there was a Firm in the City who had a Branch in Constantinople, Messrs G. P. & J. Baker Ltd, and that this Firm has some special influence with the USA Embassy in that Town – also that they had some 'Dead Money' which they could not use in Turkey, or get out of the country, and that they were glad to effect remittances to prisoners, as long as the funds at their disposal permitted ... I then decided on [payment] of 5 pounds each for the 29 crew of the AE2 captured on 30th April last, and 5 pounds each for the two RAN members of spare crew of AE2 captured with HM submarine E7. This was in addition to 30/- per month for each. I am now informed that the American Ambassador in Constantinople was requested to make payment to Harry Abbott as indicated above on 9th November.*

Abbott also tried to shield his men. In his shorthand diaries, Corporal George Kerr records on 9 July 1916 that two Australian submariners, Thomson and Gywnne, had 'set out [escaped] nearly a month ago, and had been gone a fortnight before the man in charge reported them missing. The Turks knew nothing for a long time, despite the fact that the men were counted every night. Two men from the night shift used to come off work and take their place for the counting. A few days after Abbott reported their escape we received news that they had been taken near Adana ...' The cover-up was a dangerous gamble by Abbott, and showed real courage.

Abbott returned to England on 10 December 1918 via Alexandria in Egypt, and re-enlisted in the RAN. The navy approved passage for both his wife and son by April 1919, and the family later settled in Neutral Bay, Sydney. Abbott continued his career as chief petty officer on *Platypus*, *Cerberus* and *Penguin* until 1923.

Bell, Stephen Thomas MID; Chief Engineroom Artificer 2nd Class; RN/RAN 8272

Stephen Bell, born on 16 February 1880 in Bermondsey, London, was one of a select group of experienced RN men lent to the newly established RAN in 1913. Bell's diary, now in the RAN Submarine Museum at Gosport, Hampshire in the UK, gives a unique insight into the last moments of the AE2:

> *The Captain told someone to get ready with something white. A. B. Cheater, the officer's servant, was the man who opened the conning tower. Two gunboats were still firing at us. The torpedo boat was much nearer and stopped firing then hoisted a signal to the others and launched a boat, taking off all they could [three non-swimmers] ... When they were all gone we went on deck, stopped the blow and opened the vent. There being then the three officers and two CERAs, and the Captain said, 'Come on then, it is no use stopping here'. I then dived and when in the water I looked around but the boat had gone.*

As a prisoner of war Bell suffered badly from recurrent but unknown health problems, and on 24 June 1916 Corporal Kerr described his involvement in a serious accident: 'Steve Bell has run into an engine coming from Belemedik. The motor was badly smashed and he sustained several injuries to the hands, body and head.' A further entry in Kerr's diary noted: 'Steve's injuries did not turn out to be so bad after all. He had the skin knocked off his scalp, his thumb crushed, and several bruises on the right side ... After three days in hospital he is now convalescing with the CPOs.'

Bell survived both injuries and prison, although he contracted malaria which plagued his health for the rest of his life. He returned home to London via Malta at the end of 1918, where he re-enlisted in the RN. Bell must have been a good engineer, because the navy sent him back to sea several times in spite of increasingly poor health.

Bell was mentioned in despatches on 17 October 1919 'for valuable services in the prosecution of the war whilst serving on HM Australian submarine, *AE2*'.

Bray, Cecil Arthur; Able Seaman/Chief Petty Officer; RAN 7296

Cecil Arthur Bray was born at Bourke NSW, on 3 April 1890. Abandoned by his parents and raised as a foundling, he grew up in government welfare homes and foster families.

His fortunes began to change when as a teenager he was fostered by a wealthy Coogee chemist, a Mr Alexander. At age 18, Bray joined the new navy. He was chosen for submarine service and joined the commissioning crew of the *AE2* in 1913, after training in Portsmouth.

Bray developed an affinity with his captain, Dacre Stoker, and the two stayed in touch throughout their lives. A hard-working and trustworthy prisoner, Bray was bizarrely given a reference by the German Construction Company at the end of his time in Turkey. During his incarceration, he kept an illustrated diary. In it he noted that in the name Belemedik, 'Bele' stood for 'No' and 'Medik' for 'Place'. He thought the name appropriate for the desolate prison high in the bleak Taurus Mountains. His work was hard and tedious, and like nearly all the prisoners he contracted malaria which remained with him throughout his life.

Prison life revolved around obsessions with food which was always in short supply. Bray befriended the local hill people and was able to obtain extra cheese and yoghurt to supplement his diet. Impressing his German supervisors with his work ethic, Bray was put in charge of some of the camp's electrical systems, which included setting up a cinema. He ended up with a team of Turkish workmen under him who had to address him as 'Bray Effendi', a title of respect. Bray's prisoner of war experience demonstrated resilience under extreme conditions.

Bray returned to Australia in 1919 and had no hesitation in re-enlisting in the navy. He stayed with submarines, and went again to England in 1925 for specialist training as a crew member of the then new generation of RAN submarines, *Oxley* and *Otway*. He came back to Australia as torpedo coxswain on *Oxley* in 1928, staying with her until compulsory retirement at the age of 40. In 1930 he joined the Naval

Dockyard Police. Always patriotic, at the outbreak of WWII he re-enlisted as a naval regulating officer, serving at the Brisbane Naval Department until 1945.

On 22 March 1965 Bray received a letter from a very elderly Stoker:

My Dear Bray,

Your letter arrived yesterday and caused me the very greatest pleasure. It is good to know the world has gone well for you, and I am quite sure you have well deserved it. The years have treated me kindly too and I'm in almost indecent good health considering my 80th birthday was last month. I've always been keen on games, won a lot of cups at golf and tennis between wars, and was lucky to discover croquet at the age of 65 – and that's the finest game of all for keeping the doctor at bay. Four years ago I was thrilled (and lucky) to win the Championship of Ireland – to be Champion of my natural country at anything, even tiddlywinks, would have thrilled me!

Of course the sad part of living so long is watching old friends die off. Nichols very kindly wrote me two very long letters last year telling me what he could about all our grand chaps of AE2 – including you of course. The sad list of deaths, too. Wheat and his wife had called on me some years ago, so I was particularly sorry to hear that he had slipped cable. Nichols seems understandably proud of the grand progress Australia is making, and I was proud of the successes most of our chaps seem to have made of their lives after leaving the navy.

After we got back from Turkey I had to divorce my first wife – the knowledge that I'd have to do that did not make the years of captivity any easier. But in 1925 I married again and we happily celebrate our 40th year next month. Then I'd a lucky career on the stage until called back for service in 1939. I'd several interesting appointments (serving as a Captain), got to sea many times, was on Commander-In-Chief's staff for the Normandy invasion, and afterwards was sent by the Admiralty to lecture to every ship and establishment in the Home and Mediterranean fleets, explaining to them about development and progress of the fighting against Japan. So I got about a bit! After the war I only did a little acting on TV and film, but wrote three plays, two about submarines which were produced on stage, TV and film, then I found I'd made sufficient to retire permanently and take up croquet!

But naval contact is not quite broken, so until last year I was President of Navy Lawn Tennis Association, and have regularly attended the annual dinner of the S/M Old Comrades Association, the only officer who has done so since its inception. They always make me say a few words, then the reigning Flag Officer S/M comes up each year to take the dinner, and tells us what is going on.

When he told us the Polaris S/Ms are going to be 7000 tons it reminded me of how incredibly big we thought the E boats were at 700 tons. Admirals Nasmith and Boyle are still alive, but I somehow feel they haven't had quite as much fun as I have through the years. I have been visited several times by a man writing yet another book on the Dardanelles submarines. And have just been invited by the 29th Division to attend their 50th (to be their last) anniversary dinner of their captivity.

The receipt of our signal that we were through just stopped the Anzacs being withdrawn that night. What a tragedy that campaign failed. It would have altered all history. No Russian revolution and possibly no communism.

And now I'm off to the garage to take density of my battery on charge! Hoping this may just catch you to wish you Good Luck on April 3rd [Bray's 75th birthday].

Very Sincerely,

H. G. Stoker

Bray was one of Australia's longest-serving submariners. Because of this long service and accumulated knowledge, the elderly Bray, like Stoker in Britain, was often sought out by writers and researchers wanting details of naval history, language and procedures. He became the unofficial expert for the ABC, and took part in a radio play.

Broomhead, Harry Burton DSM; Chief Engineroom Artificer 1st Class; RN/RAN 8278

Yorkshireman Harry Broomhead was born on 25 May 1876. He was one of the skilled RN group lent to the RAN for the new *AE2* submarine.

A handsome man, he had a quiet, conscientious temperament. He suffered greatly as a prisoner of war, and in 1918 his distraught mother wrote to the Central Prisoners of War Committee, begging for their assistance. She had received a letter from Broomhead telling her that he was 'practically starving' and weighed only 4 stones, 11½ pounds.

Broomhead did survive, although it must have been a close call in his weakened skeletal condition. He was reunited with his wife in Southsea, where he slowly recuperated, only to later discover that his RN seniority had been compromised by his years as a prisoner of war and there was a question mark over his medical fitness. He decided to return to Australia, as did many of his fellow *AE2* crew members, although he remained with the RN. On loan, he re-enlisted in the RAN where he rose in rank to commissioned engineer officer by 1924.

Although he officially retired from the RN in August 1924, Broomhead went on to be re-appointed temporarily from that same date, followed by a series of 'temporary' appointments in the same way until he finally transferred to the retired list on 25 May 1936. He died in 1946.

Brown, Herbert Alexander (Bert) DSM; Stoker Petty Officer; RN/RAN 8096

Bert Brown was the quintessential tough sailor. One of the older crew members, he was born on 19 August 1882 at Higham, Kent. He entered the RN as a boy before rising to the rank of stoker petty officer. He was amongst those lent in 1913 to the RAN to man their newly commissioned submarine, *AE2*.

A hard and seasoned submariner, Brown was a trusted worker. He wrote in his diary that the *AE2* was 'his pride and joy'. This loyalty was rewarded in 1919 when he received the DSM 'for distinguished services in HM submarine *AE2*'.

As a prisoner of war Brown's technical skills were quickly detected by his captors. Initially assigned to roadmaking tasks, he was reassigned to the repair and maintenance of machines, at first near Çankiri on a large tract of agricultural land near Ankara, which was being planted with grain crops by the Turkish Red Crescent Society. Here he discovered, oddly enough, that some of the machinery had been made in Australia.

From this rural camp Brown was next sent to Belemedik, where his term of imprisonment became much more difficult. His diary records the severe living conditions, poor food and lack of adequate clothing, all of which left many men susceptible to ill health. In August 1916, Brown wrote: 'The illness about now is terrible, there have been sometimes as many as 5 or 6 Russians dying in one day . . . over the last 6 months over 800 deaths'. He also claimed that prisoners working in the tunnels which were being blasted through the mountains 'often lost their sight, while others had their brains affected'.

Brown survived the epidemic of 1916 that claimed many of his colleagues, partly due to the arrival of parcels from the Red Cross, subsidised by the Australian government and delivered with the help of both the American and Netherlands embassies in Constantinople. As Brown became resigned to life at Belemedik, he wrote of a 'strange pride in seeing the [railway] line completed, the first train going through between Stamboul and Aleppo'.

In July 1918 he wrote to the Red Cross asking to be sent 'a small consignment of garden seed, anything that is eatable . . . we may be able . . . to grow a little vegetables if you will label them all, what they are and time for planting'. He received these, and later sent Miss Chomley a photograph of his garden.

In 1918 Brown was released, arriving in London via Alexandria at the end of December. He re-enlisted in the RAN and relocated to Australia with his three children. A widower, he remarried after completing his tour of duty in 1923. He and his wife Maude became farmers on an orange orchard near Gosford, NSW.

Cheater, William Thomas; Able Seaman–Petty Officer; RN/RAN 7999

Tommy Cheater was one of the most colourful members of the crew of the *AE2*. Born on 20 March 1883 at Ringwood, Hampshire, he was the middle child of a large family.

He joined the RN as a cabin boy in 1898, at the age of 15. He transferred to the submarine service in 1904, and served on Holland A class and B class submarines. He recalled that in the earliest Holland class subs, a little cage of white mice would always be taken aboard to detect the presence of poisonous fumes.

In 1913 Cheater heard that the new Australian submarines were seeking experienced crew and would be paying extra rates. Along with thousands of other hopeful sailors he applied, and was accepted after a rigorous selection process. By April 1913 he had signed up for five years' service with the RAN where he was assigned as batman to Captain Stoker and the officers. According to his daughter Gladys, Cheater enjoyed working for Captain Stoker and 'thought the world of him'.

In the Afion prison camp, Cheater's duties as batman included going to the local markets to buy food and clothing for the officers. As months passed in captivity, the Afion officers staged plays and concerts for which Cheater bought all the materials for props, sets and costumes, including women's clothing and veils. Apparently, Stoker and his fellow officers at that time were already planning to escape dressed as women. Gladys Hall remembers her father telling her that he was sent specifically to buy long Arab-style women's garments.

After three officers, Captain Stoker, Lt Price and Captain Cochrane (both from the *E7*) escaped, Cheater was singled out and held partly responsible by the Turkish warders. The Turks had traced the escape disguises back to his market excursions. He was beaten badly and thrown into solitary confinement. He later told his family that he was lucky to have survived this, the worst time of his life.

Stoker was recaptured and transferred to officers' camp at Yozgat. Strangely, Thomas Cheater was allowed to accompany him as his orderly. In a twist of their roles, Stoker visited the recuperating Cheater in England after the war, taking his family food parcels from Ireland.

Cheater re-enrolled in the RAN for a further five years' service in 1919, and he and his family moved to Australia with assistance from the government and set up home in Mascot, Sydney. Cheater rose in rank to petty officer at the end of his tour of duty in 1924. He re-enlisted in 1939 and served during WWII as a probationary constable in the Naval Dockyard Police. He kept in touch with Captain Stoker.

As Cheater grew older he suffered recurrent nightmares about his past experiences. Researcher Bill Sellars tells a story about how, in extreme old age, Cheater became obsessed by the fear of drowning. When he took his bath, the story goes, he would tie a piece of string between the tap and his big toe so that if he fell asleep it would jerk him awake.

In fact, Cheater remained hale and hearty well into his eighth decade. Each year on Anzac Day he would join his old friends at the RSL club for 'a drink or two or three', and he participated in every Anzac Day parade as a genuine Gallipoli hero for as long as he could. When he could no longer physically walk in the parade, he was driven by taxi. He passed away in August 1972, aged 89.

Churcher, Lionel Stanley; Able Seaman; RN/RAN 7970

Lionel Churcher was a cook on the *AE2*. A Cockney, born in Bermondsey on 11 March 1883, he joined the RN as a boy and served aboard a number of ships before being selected for submarine service.

By all accounts, Churcher was a fiery and temperamental POW. He clashed particularly with Australian corporal George Kerr, the Belemedik camp caterer who kept a detailed shorthand diary of events. The two adversaries were also drinking buddies and their imbibing sessions often led to fights. Churcher also liked to complain, loudly and often: his litany of irritations included 'inadequate bedding', 'being ignored' and 'lack of assistance' in his job as cook. Kerr wrote in February 1916 that 'another binge drinking session ended in yet another brawl, where Churcher was knocked over'. By March this behaviour had been noticed by the warders and the camp authorities. On 11 March, Churcher's birthday, he celebrated by really hitting the bottle. Kerr wrote in his diary: 'When he was led away to prison Churcher cried out, "This is a bastard, isn't it, on a man's bloody birthday!"'

Shortly after this incident Churcher was among a party of Belemedik prisoners sent back to Afion Kara Hissar. From there he was sent with his *AE2* crewmates Nichols, Wishart, Wilson and Harding to San Stefano prison near Constantinople. All these men had been in trouble at Belemedik but, ironically, they ended up in one of the best POW camps in Turkey. It appears they were selected because they were at risk of becoming habitual targets for the Turkish authorities, not for religious or other reasons as was previously thought.

In 1919 Churcher returned home to London. He must have been still reasonably fit and healthy at that time because he immediately re-enlisted for service in the RN for another tour of duty as an able seaman.

Cullen, James; Stoker; RAN 2826

Born on 24 May 1894 at Lang Lang, Victoria, Jim Cullen was the great yarn-spinner and larrikin of the *AE2*, both attributes which he displayed frequently during his three and a half years in captivity in Turkey.

One of seven children in a large Catholic family he grew up on a farm outside Perth, WA. All four boys in the family served in WWI. Cullen was selected as crew to join the new *AE2* submarine, going aboard in Sydney as a 19-year-old stoker.

As a POW, Cullen was sent to Belemedik as one of a Catholic group. This peculiar separation was the result of intensive lobbying of Enver Pasha and the Turkish government by the Catholic Apostolic Representative in Constantinople, Monsignor Dolci, to try to secure more favourable treatment for his flock, which also included a large number of French submariners.

It's thought that Cullen spoke German, which would have been a great advantage in the camp. AIF Corporal George Kerr's shorthand diaries record many personal details of life in the prison camps. In December 1915 Kerr wrote that Jim had an 'amazing ability as a yarn-spinner ... most of Cullen's stories were an hour's vigil ... One tale concerned a goat which followed the sailors into a hotel, demanded beer, and when it did not receive it, signalled its despair by butting whoever was shouting. But the best [story] of all was a cockatoo which had for its vocabulary two very objectionable words. One day the bird got covered with coal tar, and one of the men received orders to have the bird cleaned before devotions the next morning. He cleaned it, but dipped it in caustic soda, which took all the feathers off the poor thing. At devotions next morning, there was the bird sitting on the floor by our mess table without a feather on, except two on the head, and uttering very bad words, which, in the circumstances, we found appropriate.'

Cullen and Kerr soon became regular, boisterous and indulgent drinking partners. This led to boxing matches and fights which caused gradual mental and physical deterioration. From this low point onwards, Cullen left Kerr's group in that mess and was next recorded as working in the hospital at Belemedik under the protection of an outstanding POW doctor, Captain Clifford of the Indian Army. Cullen contracted malaria during an epidemic which swept the camp at this time.

He was next assigned to a group working along the railway line at Kelebek, which included the *AE2*'s John Wheat and a Private Samson of the AIF. The three began to hatch an escape plan after secretly building a boat; they hoped to reach the coast some 35 miles away. It took the trio three months, working secretly at night, to construct the boat from stolen materials, all of which had to be carefully hidden away every day. They did escape on the night of 29 April 1918 and almost made it to the coast, but were at the last minute foiled, both by incredibly heavy rain and by Cullen falling ill with an attack of malaria. They were forced to return to camp, where Cullen was able to hide his absence as he worked separately from the others at the hospital. Both Wheat and Samson, however, were punished.

Cullen was released from the camp at the end of 1918, still far from well. He arrived safely back in England but was hospitalised for many months. He never returned to his family home but re-enlisted in the RAN for a further five years' service in 1919. He left Australia to live and work in New Zealand some time during the 1930s. He was killed in an earthquake in New Zealand in 1945, aged 61.

Falconer, William Wolseley; Telegrapher; RAN 1936

If one man could claim to have influenced the course of history with a single deed, it would be *AE2*'s telegrapher William Falconer. Falconer was born on 14 October 1892 at Richmond, Victoria. He enlisted in the RAN at age 18 for a tour of seven years' service.

It was Falconer's Marconi wireless message on the night of the Anzac offensive that figured in the midnight meeting aboard the flagship on whether the Anzacs should be withdrawn.

Stoker wrote: 'At nightfall we again commenced to establish wireless communication with the fleet, but with no more success than before. Every possible test and overhaul of our instruments was carried out, but to no avail.' But the message had got through.

Falconer's role was never acknowledged as the feat it actually was, but it was known about. Captain Francis Haworth Booth, the RAN representative in London, wrote to Naval Command in Melbourne on 17 December 1917: 'John Kerin and W.W. Falconer were both nominated for awards, the [Admiralty] Naval Board rejected this because the Admiralty had not proposed to take similar action for their personnel.'

As a prisoner of war in Turkey, Falconer was interned first at Afion Kara Hissar, then Belemedik. His technical expertise made him a valuable asset to the German engineers contracted to build the railway through the Taurus Mountains. Falconer survived these bitter years, and after his release returned to London by the end of 1918. He arrived back in Australia in April 1919 and was demobilised at his own request in September 1919.

Fawns, Peter; Engine Room Artificer Class I; RN/RAN 8285

Peter Fawns, born on 3 August 1874 in Dundee, Scotland, was one of hundreds of applicants who, attracted by the promise of travel and adventure, applied to join the new Australian submarine service.

An artificer, Fawns was eminently qualified and very experienced. His work on *AE2* was that known in submarine parlance as 'outside wrecker', responsible for all engineering systems outside the engine room. Lt Commander Barrie Downer notes: 'It is probable that Peter Fawns would have been manning the driving and control panel of *AE2* during its unsuccessful attempts to regain trim and control during the attacks by the *Sultanhisar*.'

Fawns was interned first at Afion Kara Hissar, then sent on to Çankiri by October 1915 to work on agricultural machinery for the large scale wheat and grain crops being sown in the area. His wife Jeannie was told that the prisoners there at that time were unable to receive any parcels from home, and his only source of income was a monthly sum of three pounds from the Australian Naval Board, distributed through the American Ambassador in Constantinople. After Çankiri, Fawns was sent to Belemedik, where his expertise as an engineer artificer was a valuable commodity to the German construction company. It's likely he would have received some payment for his work. By February 1916 his wife was advised that he was being 'looked after' by the British Emergency Navy League, and in March she heard he had been moved to another camp at Pozanti, also in the Taurus Mountains. In January 1917 he was again back near Ankara, possibly seconded to servicing agricultural machinery.

Peter Fawns arrived in London from Turkey on Christmas Eve 1918, after a tortuous journey via Salonika. After recuperating, he was demobilised on 27 March 1919 at the age of 45 and worked thereafter as a coppersmith. He is thought to have died in 1949 at the age of 75.

Gilbert, Stephen John; Petty Officer; RN/RAN 8053

Stephen Gilbert's story is one of the horror of war. He died as a prisoner of war at Belemedik in 1916.

Born at Broadwater, Sussex on 13 May 1878, Gilbert entered the RN at the age of 17 in 1895. He began training as both a gunnery and torpedo operator, becoming a leading torpedoman by 1903, and by 1910 had become a submariner expert in the electrical circuitry systems of torpedoes.

After being selected for service on the new E class submarines, Gilbert transferred to the RAN on 15 April 1913 for a five-year period, and travelled to Australia, German New Guinea and the Pacific with *AE2*.

Gilbert kept a diary of his years on the *AE2*, which detailed his service in the Pacific, including the horror he and his crewmates felt after the sudden and inexplicable loss of their sister ship the *AE1* and all hands: 'This came as a great shock to us as the only two boats in Australia, and leaving England together. After the loss *AE2* did not go out on patrol duty, but stood by each day [in case needed] before the order came for us to proceed back to Sydney.' Gilbert's theory about the *AE1* was that it had accidentally surfaced under the accompanying ship.

After the sinking of *AE2*, Gilbert began life as a prisoner of war. His diary records harsh conditions, agonising hunger, incessant vermin and hard, enforced work. The camps, he wrote, were 'not fit to put pigs in'. After working with road-building gangs of Russian, French and English prisoners, he was sent with some of his *AE2* crewmates to Çankiri, travelling by train, cattle truck and foot, the latter a shockingly cold forced march over four days on bread and water. The men arrived in 'very weakened and poor condition'.

From Çankiri, he was taken to Belemedik and forced to work for German contractors on the construction of the railway and its 12 tunnels. Conditions were extreme: cold and windswept with heavy snow in winter, and blistering heat in summer. The crowded camp was swept by a three-month period of illness and disease including malaria, typhoid fever and possibly cholera.

Gilbert's wife Beatrice wrote in desperation to the navy in January 1916 to say that she had heard nothing from her husband since August: 'Could not something be done ... it is a great worry ...' Some corrupt camp warders were confiscating mail and parcels which made life even more intolerable.

Worse was to come. By August 1916, the camp had become a cesspool of disease. Hundreds of prisoners died, including Stephen Gilbert. Corporal George Kerr recorded in his shorthand diary: 'Gilbert of the *AE2* died this morning. It is thought to be typhoid. He had been in hospital for a fortnight.' Gilbert was buried in the Christian Cemetery, Belemedik until 1922, when his remains were moved by the Imperial War Graves Commission to Baghdad North Gate Cemetery. Gilbert's diary was brought back to his widow in Australia by his returning shipmates.

Gwynne, Ernest Alfred; Able Seaman/Petty Officer; RAN 7475

Victorian-born Ernest Gwynne joined the Royal Australian Navy on 1 January 1913 for a period of five years as an able seaman. He was selected for training as crew for Australia's new *AE2*. Returning with the submarine to action in the Dardanelles, he was unexpectedly listed for service as 'spare crew' for another Allied submarine, the British *E7*, under the command of Lieutenant Commander Archibald Cochrane.

The *E7* followed close behind the epic voyage of *AE2*, and Gwynne soon found himself in the thick of battle. *E7* was a later and improved vessel with upgraded weapons, especially guns and torpedoes. It entered the Sea of Marmara and bombarded trains, a railway viaduct, the Constantinople naval arsenal and an ammunitions store—action which created havoc among the Turks—before it was caught in nets across the Narrows. *E7*'s crew was taken prisoner and Gwynne was reunited with his *AE2* mates.

Gwynne clearly identified himself as belonging to the *AE2*, and remained with those submariners as a prisoner of war for three and a half years. He moved with them from his first camp at Afion Kara Hissar to Belemedik, and it was from Belemedik that he made an escape attempt with his friend, *AE2* signalman A.N.C. 'Bunts' Thomson in June 1916.

Sent to a railway punishment camp at Adapazari near Pozanti, Gwynne wrote in December 1917 to thank the Red Cross for getting two parcels and money to him, but adding that nothing had been received from his mother in Melbourne for two and a half years. He was desperately in need of both clothing and boots. In a second Red Cross letter on 22 September 1918 he reported that he was surviving his extremely dangerous circumstances and was fit and well.

Back home in February 1919, Gwynne promptly re-enlisted in the RAN. Promoted to leading seaman by 1921, he served another tour of duty during which he was promoted to petty officer. His record of service was one of longest and most consistent of all the *AE2* men. He was discharged at his own request in 1937, but recommenced duty with the navy's shore-based auxiliary services during WWII. He died on 18 November 1951, aged 60.

Harding, Horace James; Stoker; RAN 7216

Horace Harding could be termed the wild child of the *AE2* crew. One of the tallest crew members at almost six feet, he also had by far the most tattoos. Harding's service record shows that his career was volatile – good conduct badges were granted, deprived, restored, deferred and granted again, and there was a good deal of 'time forfeited'. He was chosen for service on the *AE2* in 1913 after signing on for a tour in the fledgling RAN in 1912, aged 22.

Life in the prison camp did not dampen Harding's exuberant behaviour. In a mess with a group of crewmates who also liked to party and enjoy themselves, he soon got into scrapes. Camp caterer Corporal George Kerr recorded Harding's drinking antics with great glee. On 24 February 1916, he wrote: 'Harding grabbed me then a fight ensued . . . a general brawl took place . . . Afterwards those still standing looked around to see who needed help . . . Harding was not in the room and [Cullen] scoured around and finding no trace of him looked behind the building, and found him asleep on the ground. He was brought back inside.'

A few days later, Kerr and Harding met in a violent boxing match, during which Kerr apparently defeated his opponent. There was yet another brawl, this time involving *AE2* men from another of the Protestant frames. Harding came to the attention of the Turkish warders, was punished then removed from Belemedik and sent back to Afion Kara Hissar. This probably saved his life, even though at the time it was thought to be further punishment.

Harding was transferred from Afion Kara Hissar in 1917 to San Stefano. After release, he reached London early in 1919 via Malta. He re-enlisted in the RAN for a further tour, and was officially granted passage for his wife Blanche to join him in Australia, where they lived at Surrey Hills in Melbourne. Serving at *Cerberus*, and on the *Melbourne* and *Sydney*, the tough and resilient Harding's naval career continued until 1926.

Holderness, Charles; Leading Seaman; RN/RAN 8270

A senior *AE2* rating, Charles Holderness was born on 22 July 1878 in Kent. He was one of the experienced submariners lent by the RN to the RAN in 1913.

At Belemedik POW camp, conditions were difficult for Holderness, then 37 years old. Although it cannot be verified, he appears to be the Charlie referred to in mid 1916 in George Kerr's secret diary: 'Charlie has had several stints in the hospital with very high fever'—probably a virulent form of malaria that swept the camp at that time.

Holderness just survived the traumatic prison experience and recurrent bouts of serious illness. On release, he made his way home via Alexandria in Egypt, where he was reunited with his wife Daisy in time for Christmas 1918. His Naval Service Record reveals that he was one of the few returning POWs from Turkey to be granted a full pension when he was finally demobilised in March 1919, at the age of 41.

Jenkins, William Brown; Stoker; RAN 2080

William Jenkins emigrated to Australia from England, where he was born in Hull on 26 August 1912. After selection and training as a submariner in the new Australian navy, he joined the *AE2's* commissioning crew at Portsmouth, where he also must have married for he later applied to the RAN for an assisted passage to Australia for his wife, Kate Elizabeth.

A prisoner of war in both Afion Kara Hissar and Belemedik, Jenkins spent three years working as a labourer on the infamous Berlin to Baghdad railway's horror stretch through the Taurus Mountains. George Kerr's diary records that Jenkins was one of a small coterie of 'good time boys' at Belemedik who spent their leisure time drinking and card-playing. At one stage Kerr recorded a fairly hefty debt (50 Turkish pounds) that Jenkins owed him, perhaps for alcohol and cigarettes, but it could also have been a gambling debt.

Jenkins was repatriated to London via Alexandria in Egypt by December 1918. He served again briefly at the London Depot, and on the *Dolphin* and *Bonaventure*, before returning home to Australia aboard *HMAS Platypus* on 2 May 1919. His tour of duty ended on 20 October 1919. He did not re-enlist in the RAN, and was last heard of in Malvern East, Victoria.

Kerin, John; Leading Stoker; RAN 7391

John Kerin was an Australian country boy, born the second son in a farmer's family of five at Currawarna near Wagga Wagga NSW, on 5 November 1885. Tall and rangy at six foot one, and strongly built, he towered above his fellow *AE2* crew members and was promptly nicknamed 'Tiny'. At 27, Kerin was chosen for submarine service in the RAN, enlisting in December 1912 for a tour of five years. He underwent six months' specialist training in Portsmouth, during which period he also gained qualifications as a diver.

Kerin was the gentle giant of Belemedik camp, and also a peacemaker who looked out for his submariner mates. George Kerr recorded Kerin's intervention in a fight between the *AE2*'s young Bill (Michael) Williams and Ben Talbot: 'Tiny interfered and then Williams wanted to have a go at him, and told him that even if he were as big as a tree he would [still] fight him . . . It was funny to see Tiny standing there waiting . . . with [Williams] afraid to do more than to tell him he didn't care.' But pressure of camp imprisonment did get to John Kerin on one occasion at least, as shown by an entry in Kerr's diary in March 1916: 'Another drunk—Tiny Kerin this time. This is his first offence . . .'

After release, Kerin arrived back in London in December 1918, via Alexandria. He was very ill with influenza and was hospitalised for a month. He returned to Australia as soon as he had recovered, and left the navy at his own request when the term of his period expired on 30 June 1919. In later life Kerin worked as a boilermaker for an engineering company. He died in May 1947, aged 62, and is buried in Rookwood Cemetery, Sydney.

Kinder, Henry James Elly MID; Stoker Petty Officer; RAN 7244

Harry Kinder was born on 17 January 1891 at Kogarah, Sydney, the third in a family of four children. Kinder joined up at the age of 17, and was selected for submarine service four years later, having 'put up his age'.

His diary records some of the colour of the submarine training of the Australians in Portsmouth, England:

> *Candidates had to be physically pretty good, and detailed family health histories were extracted from everyone. A six-month trial period was then required before anyone was considered capable of taking a place on a submarine. The slightest mistake on the part of one crew member could mean the loss of many lives and the boat.*
>
> *Submariners were issued with unusual clothing because of the extreme cold. There were extra thick woollen underclothes, and thick stockings which came up to the thigh and which had very big feet, so they could be doubled back to keep the feet warm. This outfit was finished by a pair of*

leather seaboots a couple of sizes too big, which gave you the chance to kick them off if you should fall overboard.

I was pleased at having volunteered because of the extra allowances as danger money, or blood money as it is commonly called. Accidents were frequent, as [the submarines] were practically still in the experimental stage, and could not be relied upon. One was nearly as much in danger in peacetime as in wartime. The Australians had their share of narrow escapes while still under training.

Kinder enjoyed the kudos of being accepted as a submariner. An artistic man, he used the long hours during the journey to Australia to complete the most amazing pieces of exquisitely worked fine embroidery, including table-cloths. His family still treasure them.

Kinder was never able to speak or write about his terrible experiences as a POW, and his diary stops abruptly after he wrote of the *AE2*'s passage through the Narrows of the Dardanelles in April 1915: 'In terror I counted 18 sets of scraping, menacing mine cables as I crouched in the darkness of the submarine . . .'

He never lacked courage, however. As the sub was sinking he actually returned to the vessel to retrieve important ship's papers for Captain Stoker, and for this was mentioned in despatches on 11 January 1919.

Kinder was severely beaten in the prison camp, and suffered kidney damage as well as contracting malaria. He was very lucky to survive his Turkish experience, and was so ill on release that he was the only *AE2* submariner sent directly back to Australia. Still suffering from his experiences, he left the RAN voluntarily at the end of his service period in July 1919. Although he never spoke of his years as a prisoner of war, he marched every year on Anzac Day, often accompanied by his little fox terrier.

Kinder settled with his wife and family in the Dorrigo and then Casino areas of NSW, where he was first a farmer and later a telegraph linesman. In old age he became increasingly eccentric and went off to live in a tent by himself at a beach near Evans Head, where he entertained the locals by producing large beach sand drawings and sculptures. He died on 25 April 1964—Anzac Day.

Knaggs, Albert Edward; Able Seaman; RN/RAN 7893

A war casualty, Albert Knaggs left an important diary of events up until his death in October 1916. He filled a very small notebook with almost microscopic writing; its value lies in being a contemporary eyewitness record whereas most of the other diaries of *AE2* men were written years after the war.

Knaggs was born in Bristol, England, on 12 August 1881. At the time he was selected for submarine service in 1912, on loan from the RN to the RAN, he was already an experienced able seaman who had seen service on at least a dozen RN ships.

Taken prisoner from the sinking *AE2* on 30 April 1915, Knaggs' diary entries show the treatment meted out to the ordinary enlisted men, Protestant and English. Of all the classifications, this grouping was treated the most harshly. In the almost 18 months of captivity before his death, Knaggs was shunted from camp to camp and, from his own account, always seemed to be allocated the heaviest and most difficult tasks.

Jailed first in Constantinople, the submariners found themselves, as Knaggs described: 'Nearly eaten alive with bugs and lice before supplied with soldier suits, overcoats, slippers and red fezzes, marched through the streets of Constantinople to a prison and given food not fit for pigs ... heads shaved like criminals.' When the men arrived at the camp in Afion Kara Hissar, their problems continued: 'Impossible to sleep at night with the cold and wind ... packed 32 in a room which would accommodate 16 healthily.'

Knaggs was put to work roadmaking and breaking stones. Without proper clothing or protective footwear, conditions were tough. The men were on near-starvation rations and became progressively weakened. In July Knaggs was given a second, similar assignment. He wrote: 'All English left to work in the country, marching all day, before sleeping in the cold outdoors at night. Then began more roadwork, from sunrise to sunset, on bread and water.' On 14 July he wrote, ominously: 'We refused to work.'

This was a dangerous tactic to adopt in the prison camps. Knaggs and his group were sent back to Afion Kara Hissar, but then re-assigned to another group of English prisoners who were being shipped by rail to Angora. From there they were marched 80 miles to an old army training barracks in Çankiri, again a cold draughty place full of lice and vermin. All the men arrived there in a weak and exhausted state.

Later Knaggs was shipped back from Çankiri with a group of men who were ill or injured. Some were carried the 80 miles back to Angora by wagon, but others were made to 'march through snow so heavy you would sink to your boot-tops'. From there they were put on a heavily overloaded train which headed for Konya, and then continued in the direction of Pozanti in the Taurus Mountains. Knaggs wrote optimistically from there in February: 'Here we are allowed plenty of liberty, no sentries allowed to interfere with us as long as things run smoothly. The work consists of drilling and blasting tunnels, navvying etc . . . The name of this place being Belemedik.'

Shortly after this entry, Knaggs was transferred to labouring work at the sawmills, a less demanding job. He began to report continually on the disease sweeping through the camp, now seriously overcrowded with thousands of prisoners living in sub-standard conditions. Malaria and typhoid fever were rampant, especially in the Russian and French quarters.

At the end of March 1916, he was placed at the First Tunnel camp, working as a cook for German carpenters, and from there was sent at the end of May to Kula Maghera, a Second Tunnel camp along the railway line. It is not known why he was moved around so frequently, more so than any other *AE2* prisoner of war. His diary entries end abruptly on 18 July 1916.

Knaggs' poor health may have been one reason for his difficulties as a POW. He had contracted malaria, probably in the first wave of the illness that swept Belemedik in early spring, and although he had been inoculated against typhoid fever at Afion Kara Hissar, he died in the makeshift camp hospital at Belemedik on 22 October 1916. He was buried at Belemedik in the Christian Armenian Cemetery. The Imperial War Graves Commission later relocated his grave to their official Baghdad North Gate Cemetery.

McGregor, John Thomas; Leading Seaman; RN/RAN 7532

John McGregor was born on 25 May 1879 in Southampton, one of a large family of six boys. He enlisted in the RN on 10 September 1896, aged 18, for a 12-year period. His RN career included service on a dozen ships and by 1909 he was recommended for service with the Royal Fleet Reserve. He had special qualifications as a gunnery and torpedo expert when he began service as a submariner in 1909. In 1913 he was one of the group loaned by the RN to the RAN as founding crew members of the new *AE2* submarine.

McGregor travelled to Australia with *AE2* and saw action off German New Guinea and in the Pacific. He returned to the Dardanelles with *AE2*, but according to his granddaughter Joan Colmer, contracted an odd skin complaint which caused all his hair to fall out. He spent some months in hospital and was precluded on medical grounds from joining *AE2* on her final voyage. Like all spare crew, however, he was seconded by the RN and consequently found himself part of the actual Gallipoli landings. He found the experience 'utterly horrific'.

He served again in the RAN after the Dardanelles, at the London Depot, *Sydney*, *Cerberus* and *Penguin*. At his own request, he was demobilised on 18 September 1919. He returned to Australia with his wife and family soon afterwards, and settled at Concord, Sydney.

Mitchell, Reuben Joseph Edwin, DSM; Able Seaman; RAN 7476

Reuben Mitchell was one of the most courageous submariners of WWI. Born in Ballarat, Victoria, on 28 July 1894, he was selected for submarine service on the *AE2* in 1912. He served aboard *AE2* for her voyages to and from Australia, including action off German New Guinea and in the Pacific. At the time of the Dardanelles campaign he had been temporarily transferred to the submarine repair ship, *Penguin*.

After the capture of *AE2* and his former crewmates, Mitchell served aboard the *E14*, which subsequently followed *AE2*, entered the Sea of Marmara and sank many ships. In 1918, *E14* was sent to attack the German ship, *Goeben*. *E14* was hit by enemy fire and sank with the loss of 22 men, including the captain and two officers. Mitchell was one of only nine survivors. A fellow crew member recorded his heroism:

> *Reuben Mitchell acted most gallantly. He was on the conning tower with the three officers, passing orders below to the helmsman. All the officers were swept off the bridge by shell fire and he was left alone. Although the enemy had the exact range and he was clearly visible he stuck to his post, and took charge of the doomed boat until she sank. When in the water, he then rescued the wireless operator who was unconscious from head wounds. There was no senior officer [left] to recommend him for his outstanding gallantry, and his only reward was the self-evident fact that he had done his duty.*

Taken prisoner by the Turks, Mitchell survived harsh treatment and recovered from his wounds. While imprisoned in solitary confinement at Samatyra, the battered submariner one day heard a familiar tune being whistled—'Waltzing Matilda'—followed by a broad Australian accent. Calling out, he discovered it was the RAAF's Captain Thomas H. Piper. This small incident proved such a psychological boost to Mitchell that he never forgot it. Years later back in Australia he contacted Piper in Tasmania and asked him to be best man at his wedding. While still in Turkey in 1918, Mitchell also met up with his two closest friends and *AE2* crewmates Alex Nichols and John Wheat, before all three were finally released.

Mitchell reached London where he recuperated, and received a DSM on 12 December 1919. He returned home to Ballarat, where he and his wife Hazel raised three children. In the 1930s the family settled in Port Kembla NSW, where Mitchell renewed his friendship with John Wheat. He re-enlisted in the navy's RAFR from June 1935 until June 1940, serving at both *Cerberus* and *Penguin*. He died on 16 August 1954, aged 60.

Nash, George Henry; Leading Seaman; RN/RAN 8056

A senior rating, George Nash was one of the experienced RN submariners loaned to the RAN in 1913 as crew for the *AE2*. Born on 31 March 1882 at Bristol, Somerset, of Scottish lineage, Nash joined the RAN for a tour of five years.

He was interned at Belemedik with fellow *AE2* submariners including Petty Officer C. A. Bray, whose diaries record that he and Nash were both studying maths in order to gain further expertise as electrical engineers. Their textbooks were supplied by the Red Cross, the British Prisoners Education Society, a charity attached to the Victoria and Albert Museum in London.

Nash survived the arduous camp conditions including epidemics of malaria and other virulent diseases. He returned to London at the end of 1918 and served out his full tour of duty at the RAN's London Depot. He was demobilised at his own request on 25 March 1919. He was awarded the RN medal, the 1914–15 Star, which remained unclaimed.

Nichols, Alexander Charles; Able Seaman/Petty Officer; RAN 7298

The only Queenslander in the *AE2* crew, Alexander Nichols joined the RAN in 1912 at the age of 19, for a tour of service of seven years. He was a good-looking young man with brown hair and eyes and a fair complexion.

Nichols was one of a trio of Australian ratings (with John Wheat and C. A. Bray) who wrote detailed diaries of their individual experiences, both on the submarine and later in various prison camps.

By May 1916, both Wheat and Nichols were working on the line at Haçikiri, about 12 miles from Belemedik. Conditions were appalling and the men began plans to escape. For months they pumped local peasants for information about their location, and began hoarding what food and utensils they could conceal. They made their escape attempt on 12 August

1916. It proved disastrous. The terrain was precipitous, impassable. It offered no shelter, water or food, and they quickly became hopelessly lost. They made it to within sight of the coast, but by that time were almost starving. After a week they were forced to return to Pozanti, where they were arrested and marched back to Belemedik. They were thrown into prison and fed only bread and water for a week. Nichols suffered a severe attack of malaria and collapsed. His poor health prevented him from working, and he was also now a security risk. At the end of 1916 he was sent back to Afion Kara Hissar with a group of fellow prisoners who were unable or unwilling to work, or who had proved troublesome.

After recovering his health at Afion, Nichols was again singled out for transfer. It was a move that probably saved his life. Together with fellow *AE2* submariners Churcher, Wishart, Wilson and Harding, he volunteered to go to the San Stefano prison camp near Constantinople. Nichols wrote in his diary: 'I was suffering from dysentery and fever, but determined to get away . . . I managed to secure a large opium pill which I managed to swallow a few minutes previous to the doctor's inspection, and so managed to get away . . .'

Arriving 'by cattle truck' at Haida Pasha, the men were marched through Constantinople to San Stefano, a distance of 16 miles, which took them 8 hours. San Stefano had previously been a Catholic convent and three priests remained there. One became a friend; Nichols called him Father Brickdust because of his ruddy face and red hair. The *AE2* men were grateful for his support, and attended his mass. Father Brickdust became a vital conduit to the Dutch Embassy, and through it to the Red Cross, facilitating delivery of parcels, food and money to the prisoners.

At San Stefano the prisoners worked for Germans, loading and unloading goods, or as ship's fitters, carpenters or orderlies. It was possibly the best-run prisoner of war camp in Turkey, but again this depended on the whim of the German commandant. One man, Count von Bennermann, wrote Nichols, 'was also very good, until his brother was killed . . . then he turned on us . . . He used to call us *Schweinhunder* and other choice names . . . and put us in prison for 14 days on the slightest pretext'.

By mid October 1918, Nichols noticed a definite change in attitude on the part of the Turkish civilians towards their prisoners, and a growing disdain among them for the Germans. In November, Nichols was released and began a homeward journey, first to Malta, then to Taranto, Italy, overland to Paris, then to London. There he spent several months recuperating before returning home to Queensland.

Nichols left the navy in 1920 but, according to his daughter Mrs Ena Henderson, 'he lived and died Navy'. He rejoined in 1939 as a petty officer with the RAFR, and spent the war years around the Pacific Islands and New Guinea de-activating enemy mines, and was in Darwin during the Japanese raids. Nichols completed this second period of active service on 21 August 1945. He kept in touch with Captain Stoker, and organised reunions of his naval colleagues. He was one of the longest-surviving *AE2* men, despite almost having died as a POW in Turkey. He died in 1971 at Woody Point, Queensland, aged 78.

Suckling, Charles George; Stoker; RAN 2148

One of two West Australians in the *AE2* crew, Charles Suckling was born in Perth on 8 June 1893. He joined the fledgling RAN at the age of 19 on 3 September 1912 for a five-year period of service.

Suckling kept a colourful record of his experiences, including his years as a POW in Turkey. In his diary he particularly paid tribute to Captain Stoker, of whom he wrote: 'Lt Commander Stoker was a man absolutely loved by his crew, and there was not one of us who was not willing to go anywhere he cared to take us . . .' Stoker spoke to all the crew before they left for the Dardanelles and 'told them each he was at liberty to leave the boat. Not one man asked to be relieved . . . All hands in the *AE2* knew that the chances were in favour of tomorrow bringing our death, so most of us had letters to write.'

Taken as a POW from the sinking sub, Suckling recalled:

> *Then began a life for us which was nothing but a sorry existence, and I don't think if we had known what was ahead . . . that one of us would have left the boat. And when we were released from Turkey three and a half*

years later, leaving four of our number behind, we were nothing more than living skeletons . . . The building we were in was built of wood and was absolutely alive with lice and as we had no way of washing our clothes or even our bodies, we were soon as much alive as the buildings. To break the monotony someone suggested that we start a competition to see who could catch the most lice off their own clothes and body, each man being allowed to strip twice a day. The record catch was 250 in a day ...

The first few months in captivity were the worst. 'How we survived without going mad I don't know.' An assignment to work at breaking stones for roadworks came almost as a relief although the work was heavy, and there were guards 'armed with sticks about three foot long and about two inches thick which they made full use of. I remember one day when the guards were more vicious than usual some wag started singing "Rule Britannia, Britons never shall be slaves ..." I am sure no-one would of recognised us as British sailors or soldiers'.

Within three months, Suckling and some of his group were sent by cattle truck train to Angora, then marched about 80 miles to Çankiri, a terrible trek that took them four days. At Çankiri, it began to snow heavily. The men were given quilts, but what they desperately needed was warm underwear. Always enterprising, Suckling noted in his diary: 'We were given quilts to keep us warm at night, and were not long in finding out that they were filled with raw wool. A few weeks later all the wool had been taken out and spun and knitted into warm underclothes.' Within a few months the men were moved by another march back to Angora, from where they were put on trains for shipment to Belemedik.

Suckling was lucky to get a job looking after an air compressor and switchboard, but later went to work on a drilling machine which was harder work and dangerous. It was common to drill into an unexploded charge and a few men were blown to pieces or crushed by falling rock. It was at this stage that Suckling apparently suffered permanent damage to his eyes, which would later result in total blindness.

Some of the men tried to escape, 'but none succeeded. Two seamen of *AE2* did actually reach the coast where they remained for about 10 days, but had to give themselves up for want of food. Myself and two others made an attempt from our camp and were away for four days, but could not get clear of the mountains, and our food running short we had to return, which we did without the Turks missing us.'

It was the enemy within the huge camp that was more lethal. Endemic malaria and other diseases swept over the men. Suckling wrote: 'Men began to die like flies, four of *AE2*'s crew were among the victims. After three months of malaria there was about 100 of those remaining who were too weak to work, myself among them, so we were put on the train back to Afion Kara Hissar.'

After he had regained his health, Suckling volunteered as an engineer to work on a farm with threshing machines. From there he was sent to a larger farm to service tractors, harvesters and ploughs. Always inventive, Suckling and his *AE2* mates became extremely cunning about getting more food. During the winter everything was covered with snow and work in the fields ceased. Suckling reported: 'as we could not get through to the villages we had to live on the Turkish food and anything extra we could steal ... One night we actually stole a bullock, killed it and salted the meat down, and buried the hide and bones before morning. The Turks thought wolves must have got it as there were quite a lot of wolves about.'

The men were eventually sent back to Afion Kara Hissar amid rumours that the war might soon finish. This was the case and Suckling was released. He took a train to Smyrna (Izmir) and was shipped onwards to Alexandria, then Port Said. He notes: 'The *AE2* men were told that we were to be sent to England to be decorated, but when we actually arrived a few weeks before Christmas 1918, the only ones to receive decorations were the three officers.'

Suckling arrived home in Fremantle, Western Australia on 19 February 1919. He and his wife Margaret opened a butchery and delicatessen shop in Fremantle, but his eyesight began to fail completely and in later years he was forced to live in a special home for the blind. He was granted a full disability pension, the navy and the government officially attributing his total blindness to beatings about the head he received as a POW in Turkey. Although disabled, Charles Suckling was the last of the *AE2* crew to die, in 1983, aged 92.

Talbot, Benjamin; Able Seaman/Chief Petty Officer; RN/RAN 8221

Ben Talbot was an experienced RN sailor when he was loaned to the RAN in 1913 for service on the new *AE2* submarine. He was born in Middlesex, England, on 31 May 1883. Talbot was slight in build but physically very fit—attributes which contributed towards his selection for service as a submariner.

In prison camp, Talbot was one of those Catholic POWs oddly singled out for favourable treatment. However, they remained normal prisoners of war, despite such privileges. Their enemy, as Greg Kerr wrote in his book, *Lost Anzacs*, 'lay within themselves, fuelled by boredom and frustration'. Kerr's grandfather, Corporal George Kerr kept a clear record of this insidious enemy, as both he and the mess turned to heavy drinking and drunken brawls:

> *On Christmas Day [1916] the boys had been drinking, and Talbot borrowed a suit of clothes from one of the Russians and with the help of a pair of glasses and a hat he aped the part of a dude very well. He had with him a young Russian dressed up as a woman and he looked the part as far as facial appearance went ...*

By 28 December Talbot was participating in a boxing match with the same Russian, much to Kerr's amusement. Talbot was a very good boxer and was able to defend himself. He also taught boxing to others in the camp. He survived the horrors of the prison camp, and even escaped punishment for his at times rowdy and belligerent behaviour.

He was released and returned safely to London and his wife Cecelia and three children by January 1919. He then re-enlisted in the RAN and, with government assistance, brought his family to Australia where they settled in Geelong, Victoria. Talbot continued his naval career after the war, rising in rank from able seaman to leading seaman, and finally became a chief petty officer in April 1928. He died on 7 August 1952, aged 69.

Thomson, Albert Norman Charles; Leading Signalman; RN/RAN 8271

Known as 'Bunts' (from naval slang for 'Bunting-Tosser') Albert Thomson was born on 24 May 1888 at Albury NSW. Sadly his mother did not survive the birth of her son, and Thomson returned with his father to Scotland in the mid 1890s. In 1905 he left his job as a painter's assistant to join the RN as a boy 2nd Class, for 12 years' service. He trained and qualified as a signalman on the *Victory*, and served on a number of RN ships, rising to leading signalman.

In 1913, possibly because of his Australian roots, he volunteered for service with the new RAN submarine *AE2*, and was selected as one of the original crew, officially lent by the RN to the RAN from December 1913 for a period of three years.

Thomson was one of two *AE2* men who recorded the historic moment of the sinking of the submarine in a series of graphic sketches which he drew later in the prison camps, first at Afion Kara Hissar then at Belemedik. At Belemedik Thomson gained a reputation for stepping into fist fights to help *AE2* comrades, and by April 1917 had been transferred to a remote railway camp, possibly as punishment for fighting. Conditions there were appalling and Thomson and Michael (Bill) Williams, also of *AE2*, tried to escape. In his diary, George Kerr related: 'They spent all one Sunday night roaming the mountains until Bill Williams lost heart, to use Bunts' words, and said it would be advisable to return . . . Bunts was cut up over Williams' lack of courage, and says he tried to keep his heart up but all to no purpose.'

By 9 July, however, Thomson and another submariner Gwynne had made another escape attempt. Kerr wrote:

> *They set out nearly a month ago, and had been gone a fortnight before the man in charge reported them missing. The Turks knew nothing for a long time [because] two men from the night shift [would] take their place for . . . counting . . . We [then] received news that they had been taken near Adana after having been seen wandering about for 3 or 4 days begging*

bread and water. Everyone believes them to be caught but they have not passed this way yet.

After Adana, Thomson was returned to Belemedik and there were no further escape attempts recorded. He was finally released and returned to London on Christmas Eve 1918. Despite being very thin, his physical constitution must have been strong for he re-enlisted on 25 March 1919 in the RAN for a further period of three years, during which he served on *Platypus* and *Cerberus*. His wife and family joined him in Australia aboard the *Zealandia* in 1920, and they set up home in Victoria.

After surviving against such terrible odds, Thomson died tragically young on 29 May 1922, when the bus he was driving overturned going around a corner.

In an interesting third-generation link, one of Thomson's grandsons, John Thomson, has been actively involved in the project to raise the *AE2* submarine from the floor of the Sea of Marmara.

Varcoe, Charles; Chief Stoker; RN/RAN 8275

Charlie Varcoe was a senior and crucial member of the *AE2* crew. Sadly, he did not survive the war.

Born at St Stephens, Cornwall, on 4 August 1879, Varcoe was one of the experienced submariners lent to the RAN by the RN in 1913 to man the new *AE2*. At that time, aged 32, he was already a chief stoker. As such, he was looked up to by the younger members of the crew, and he was often called upon to act as both mediator and father figure.

In Belemedik prison camp, Varcoe mixed with his fellow CPOs and ratings alike, often joining the group of young tearaways at the Catholic mess run by Corporal George Kerr. In the summer of 1916 a serious outbreak of disease swept through the overcrowded camp, which had been pushed beyond its limits of sanitation and hygiene by huge numbers of forced labour prisoners, mainly from the Russian front. Charlie Varcoe contracted what was thought to be a virulent form of meningitis.

George Kerr wrote in his diary on 18 September 1916:

Charlie Varcoe, who had been ailing for some time, went to the hospital yesterday, and on his way there fell down unconscious. He was picked up by one of our lads, and admitted to hospital. In the afternoon the doctor sent down a message to the effect that Charlie would die in an hour. He had not then regained consciousness. In the morning we were told that he had died at 7 o'clock that morning [of meningitis]. He was buried the same afternoon, Macklin reading the service ...

Although first buried in the Belemedik Armenian Christian Cemetery in 1916, Varcoe was later reinterred by the Imperial War Graves Committee in the official Baghdad North Gate Cemetery, where there is a plaque erected in his memory.

Vaughan, Charles MID; Chief Petty Officer; RN/RAN 8259

Charlie Vaughan was the senior ranked crew member of the *AE2*. At 40 years, he was also one of the oldest, a top RN submariner who was personally selected by Captain Martin Nasmith for loan to the RAN in 1913 to man their new E class submersible. Vaughan signed on with the RAN on 4 December 1913 for a period of five years.

After the initial shock of capture and internment after the sinking of the *AE2* in the Sea of Marmara, during which he displayed great courage and discipline, Vaughan adapted to the grim struggle for survival in POW camps, first at Afion Kara Hissar then at Belemedik. He was one of the petty officers who continued to keep a weather eye out for his young ratings during these difficult years, and like Charlie Varcoe mixed with them socially in order to do so.

Vaughan was lucky to have the physical and mental strength to last the distance until the end of 1918, when he was released from the camp and began the long voyage home. He arrived safely in London via Alexandria on 18 December 1918. On 22 April 1919, a month after he was demobilised, Vaughan was eventually awarded a mentioned in despatches, 'For miscellaneous services in HM Australian submarine *AE2*'.

Walker, Thomas Henry; Stoker; RN/RAN 8289

Born at Radford, Nottingham, on 10 April 1885, Thomas Walker served on HM ships from 2 January 1908, aboard the *Dolphin*, *Bonaventure* and *Maidstone*. One of those selected by Captain Nasmith for loan to the RAN, Walker's nickname aboard the *AE2* was 'Hookey', derived from the stoker insignia on his uniform, or perhaps also from his penchant for a scrap.

Taken prisoner with his crewmates after the sinking of the *AE2*, Walker spent a miserable three and a half years in prison camps at Afion Kara Hissar and Belemedik, where his technical skills made him valuable. With the help of his mates, and parcels from the Red Cross, Walker managed to survive the disease, discomfort and near starvation of the camps. He socialised with the notorious mess of Catholic *AE2* men nearby, and was mentioned by diarist, George Kerr on 18 February 1916:

> *At present Jim [Cullen] and Hookey Walker are adrift [AWOL]—have been absent from yesterday, when they set out to buy a padlock and some alcohol, with their hearts a good deal more interested in the latter, I think. They did not come home last night . . .*
>
> *[Later] Jim and Hookey Walker turned up last night, being only a day and a half adrift. They were a good time away, which may point to the amount of liquor they had drunk during the two days. I told them it was rather lowdown to come home after two days absence and tell us what liquor they had consumed. I had rather they spoke of what they had brought home. After a while [Jim] began telling me of the information he and Hookey had gathered during their trip, and telling me that he was thinking out a plan of escape.*

But guards prevented the escape and Walker, perhaps a victim of one of the many camp diseases, made no further attempts. He survived his experiences, however, and reached home in London, via Smyrna and Beirut, on 18 December 1918. He rejoined the RAN on 22 February 1919 and served at the London Depot on *Platypus*, but was finally invalided out and demobilised on 25 August 1919.

Wheat, John Harrison; Able Seaman; RAN 7861

John Wheat was one of the most complex and interesting of the *AE2* ratings. He tried twice to escape from POW camp, later writing in minute detail of his experiences.

Born on 3 August 1893 in Sale, Victoria, Wheat grew up on a smallholding in Gippsland, where he and his brothers cleared virgin bush to establish a dairy herd. He joined the RAN soon after his eighteenth birthday in 1911, and on 22 February 1913 volunteered for seven years' service as a submariner on the navy's new *AE2*. His diary records his emotion at losing *AE2*: 'She had been my home for nearly eighteen months, and I missed her . . . '

Wheat's first escape attempt was made in mid August 1916, with *AE2*'s Alex Nichols. Assigned to a tunnel camp at Haçikiri, 12 miles from Belemedik, they carefully investigated the terrain and found that they were about 45 miles from the coast—but would have to cross wild mountains to reach it. They set off with pilfered food and high hopes, but found the ravines, cliffs and gullies impenetrable. There was no water, food or shelter, and they were attacked by wild dogs. They finally reached the sea near Mersina (Içel) and made a raft, only to find it could not take their weight. 'It was a huge disappointment,' wrote Wheat. They were able to buy some food from locals, but then their luck ran out. Nichols was badly stung by a scorpion, and could hardly walk as they made their way to Tarsus. Both men were weak and hungry so decided to head back to the Baghdad rail line, where they met a party of English prisoners who gave them food. They were arrested by a sentry and paraded before a camp commandant 'who flew into such a temper he could hardly speak' at their audacity. Wheat and Nichols had been away for 19 days.

Both were severely punished. Tied up and locked in vermin-infested dark holes for many days, they were then marched back to Belemedik and imprisoned again. Nichols suffered a severe attack of malaria, and collapsed while being questioned. Then, bizarrely, both were released after promising not to escape again.

Wheat was sent back to Afion Kara Hissar which was suffering under the command of a particularly brutal Turkish commandant. Wheat wrote of him: 'He would send for the youngest prisoners to have secret and private interviews . . . conduct and morality so bestial and unnatural that . . . a revolt throughout the camp seemed imminent.' The commandant was eventually found out and removed.

Wheat was again sent back to the Taurus Mountains, this time to Bör, near Niğde on the northern side of the mountains, where he spent some time recovering from bouts of malaria. The climate was very hot, and the food so bad that Wheat wrote 'we wouldn't give [it] to dogs in Australia'. After transfer to a railway repair workshop, he began to plan another escape, fearing that he would not survive these conditions.

With *AE2*'s Jim Cullen and a soldier, Private Samson, Wheat began to collect items to build a collapsible boat. The project took the men seven months, working on it in secret at night.

Throughout the night of 29 April 1918, they carried the boat in pieces across rough country, then slept all the next day. The following night there was a thunderstorm, and the heavy rain continued all through the next day. They had reached flat ground but the continuous rain had turned the fields they were crossing into muddy bogs, and their food was saturated.

Cullen had an attack of malaria that night, and they were forced to leave the boat in the middle of a wheat field and return to their camp near Kelebek. Cullen had been working for the Indian Army doctor, Captain Clifford, who had been able to conceal his absence. But Wheat and Samson were not so lucky. Both were thrown into the 'Black Hole of Gelebek'—an infamous filthy dungeon crawling with lice and fleas. Captain Clifford finally rescued them, but both were so unfit that they were sent back to Afion Kara Hissar in May 1918.

Wheat was selected for exchange of 1000 men for enemy prisoners in October 1918, and made his way to Smyrna (Izmir) where he wrote that he was 'overjoyed to see the Australian hospital ship, *Kanowna*'. It took him to Alexandria then to London, before returning with its load of prisoners of war to Australia.

Wheat recovered quickly, and served again in the RAN until the end of February 1920, when he left Australia for Singapore to work for the British India Navigation Company where he rose to the rank of officer. In 1923 he married Matron Marie Hunstone, a nurse who had worked in Mesopotamia during the war and had received several awards for valour.

John and Marie Wheat returned to Australia after some years, and lived in a number of NSW coastal towns. They visited England in 1950, and met up with Captain Stoker. John Wheat died in the 1950s, when Marie moved back to Derbyshire to live with her family.

Williams, Michael Wright; Stoker; RAN 2305

Michael Williams (Bill to his submariner crewmates) was born at Dunkeld near Hamilton, Victoria, on 1 September 1894, one of a large Catholic family of nine children. The patriotic Williams family contributed four sons to WWI. All died on active service: Private John Williams at Lone Pine, Gallipoli; Stoker Michael in obscure circumstances as a POW in Turkey; Private Thomas in action in France, 1917; and Private Frank in action in France, 1918.

Bill Williams joined the RAN on 7 October 1912 at the age of 18, signing up for seven years. Captured after the *AE2* sinking on 30 April 1915, he was sent first to Afion Kara Hissar. Later he was separated from the majority of the crew because of his Catholic religion and sent to the 1st Division camp at Belemedik.

Corporal George Kerr complained of Williams in his diary: '[Bill] is an out and out loafer'. He also took umbrage at Bill's mates: '[They] took to reclining in carefree attitude on the ground or on their barrows quite regardless of the fact that they could be seen from the windows of Mr Imhoff [a German supervisor].' Williams' attitude was, 'the bastards made us work, but we'll take care they don't get too much out of us'.

Williams began to drink heavily after hearing of his brother's death, which led him into fist fights. His mates from *AE2*—Ben Talbot, Jim Cullen and Charlie Varcoe—tried to pacify him during these binges but were not successful. Williams finally lost his privileged position in the mess and was sent to a punishment labour camp near Pozanti (probably Bahçeli). From here, in March 1916, he and *AE2*'s signalman Bunts Thomson tried to escape. The attempt was unsuccessful and they were forced to return, with Thomson complaining of Williams' 'lack of courage'.

These accounts denote a young man showing signs of severe depression. In May 1916 Williams was involved in a serious accident at the tunnel camp. Kerr reported: 'A rock slide had smashed into the men's sleeping quarters. Len New [an Australian soldier] was killed and Williams [in the bunk below New] was seriously injured.' While he was still suffering from these injuries, Williams was further reprimanded for 'refusing to work' and shunted to another punishment camp, possibly Bahçe. This was known to be a camp of ill-repute and Williams may have become a target for ill-treatment by warders there, known for their callousness towards ailing prisoners. More importantly perhaps, it meant Williams had been moved beyond the protection of his mates.

His last days are a mystery. He may simply have succumbed to injuries, illness or disease in his last months, or he may have been killed. Allegedly he died of either dysentery or malaria on 29 September 1916, at only 21 years of age. Strangely his body could not be found; apparently he was buried in an unknown grave. *AE2* crewmate John Wheat wrote in his diary that it was common knowledge the Turks 'were doing away with' the sickest prisoners. Another fellow prisoner, CPO Sims, later told the navy that he 'had no knowledge of [Williams'] death'. Even the German commandant at Belemedik was unable to get further information. When Petty Officer Bray of *AE2* made enquiries he was told only that Williams was dead. There were no remains and no grave that could be traced.

The Imperial War Graves Commission later erected an engraved memorial to Stoker Michael Williams at the official North Gate Cemetery in Baghdad. Due to naval bureaucratic bungling, Williams' impoverished mother was denied any entitlements and pay owed to her son until more than three years later. In desperation she appealed to her local Member of Parliament, Bill Slater, and to the then prime minister,

Billy Hughes. Her letter of 1 September 1919 to Billy Hughes is reproduced below.

Mr Hughes Prime Minister

Sir, I want to put my case before you. I have lost my four sons at the front. Pte John, killed in Action at Lone Pine, 1915. Pte Frank, killed in action at Somme, 1916. Stoker Michael, late of AE2 submarine, died prisoner of war at Pozanti, 1916, and Pte Thomas, died of wounds received in France.

Sir, it's Stoker Michael I want to put to you about. I got paid up to June 1916, the Turks never reported his death. I can't get his pay from June as I have cards he wrote me in September 1916.

I received his cards regular until the 10th of September was the date he wrote the last one to me. I have one son married left, and I have four girls, the eldest as turned 15 years down to 7 years.

I want to write to you about the boys at the front. Mr W. Slater MLA has been very kind indeed to us. My husband receives an invalid pension and also 10s of pension for our son Stoker Michael he received Mr Slater got for him. At first it was refused to me and Mr Slater took it up and got for him. I bought into a home on my son's deferred pay, I owe one hundred pounds.

We left Dunkeld as I could not live in the bush under the terrible loss of my dear boys and we were twenty miles from the doctor and my husband wants medical attention also one of my little girls is not strong.

Sir, I think you will find my case a hard one, as brothers and nephews all done their duty.

Sir, I just heard my son who died a prisoner of war met with foul play, they blame the warders in the hospital and my son was burried as a Turk, which is hard on free Britishers.

I will close hoping you will look into my case. I remain Dear Sir Yours Truly,

Mrs M. Williams.

Mrs Williams did eventually receive some assistance (a 2/6 a week pension) following Bill Slater's representation, but her nephew, Frank Kranz of Geelong, cannot recall the family ever receiving a reply from Prime Minister Billy Hughes.

Wilson, Archibald McCullough; Leading Stoker/Petty Officer; RAN 7501

Archibald McCullough Wilson was born at Oamaru, New Zealand on 1 March 1888, into a family of Scottish Presbyterian ancestry. He moved to Australia as a young man, and joined the RAN in 1913 for a period of five years' service.

Known to his crewmates as 'Tug', Wilson was small but pugnacious. In the Dardanelles he was designated spare crew and re-assigned to the RN's *E7*. He was aboard this submarine as it followed the *AE2* through the Narrows under Captain Archibald Cochrane. A later and much better equipped sub than *AE2*, the *E7* sank several ships and shelled railway lines and a munitions factory, spreading terror among the Turks before being caught in Turkish nets and sunk. Wilson's daughter, Mrs Rose Walpole, wrote to historian Bill Sellars in 1987 that when the sub was sunk, 'my father told the Captain that he couldn't swim, and the Captain told him that now was a b—— good time to learn'.

Wilson linked up with his *AE2* crewmates as a prisoner of war at Afion Kara Hissar, where he found a relatively secure job working as a cook for a mess of air force officers. A strong and assertive character, he clashed at least twice with Turkish guards at Belemedik and was beaten badly. His daughter Rose recalled that 'he had a badly broken nose caused by a blow from a gun butt, inflicted by one of the guards'.

Following these incidents, Wilson was transferred back to Afion Kara Hissar, and later to San Stefano with fellow *AE2* men Nichols, Wishart, Churcher and Harding. Surprisingly San Stefano turned out to be, according to Alex Nichols, 'on the whole about the best prison camp in Turkey'.

Wilson and his mates were housed in what had once been a convent, from which, Nichols wrote, 'the nuns had fled in terror since the war, and the only occupants when we arrived were three priests of the Franciscan order'. Although not all Catholics, the men were befriended by the priests, who used their influence to enable them to receive aid parcels via the Dutch Embassy and the Red Cross.

On his release from San Stefano in November 1918, Wilson began a long voyage home, first on the *Adamant*, then the *Hird*, followed by a small boat which took him to Malta, and from there to Italy and overland to London. On arrival in London, Wilson's mate Nichols observed, 'Many of the men shed tears the Turks could not wring from them'.

Wilson re-enlisted in the RAN after the war on 1 January 1919 for a further five-year period, and advanced in rank to stoker petty officer. He set up home in Geelong, Victoria with his wife and seven children. In July 1924 he was approved to be discharged 'invalided'. During the Great Depression, Wilson fell on hard times, and although he was a 'jack of all trades' he enlisted the aid of both Commanders Stoker and Haggard to get assistance for himself and his family from the Repatriation Department. Both gave him strong references, and Haggard offered to personally represent him before a Commission hearing. Wilson died of a heart attack on 16 June 1953, aged 65.

Wishart, Thomas; Stoker; RN/RAN 8277

Tommy Wishart was born on 29 October 1882 at Partick, on the River Clyde near Glasgow in Scotland. His father worked as a boilermaker in the famous shipyards nearby so it was hardly surprising when young Tommy joined the RN in January 1903, aged 20. He actually gave his age as only 18, because as he was only five feet two and a half inches tall, he wished to give the impression that he still had time to grow. But Wishart was physically very strong, and a good worker. By 1906 he was a stoker, class I.

He transferred to submarines, where his size was an asset. He served first in A class submarines, and in 1913 volunteered to join the RAN and new *AE2* sub on loan from the RN for a period of three years.

As a prisoner of war, Wishart was taken first to Afion Kara Hissar, where he found work as an orderly for air force officers. At the end of 1915, he was transferred with most of the *AE2* crew to the 1st Division camp at Belemedik, where he was injured by a falling log. The accident placed Wishart at great risk as the Turks were notorious for their callous treatment of any prisoner who could not work. According to Corporal George Kerr's diary, on at least two occasions the fiery Wishart became incensed with his Turkish guards and punched them. On the second occasion he knocked the guard down. He was punished severely, beaten and placed in vermin-infested solitary confinement on starvation rations.

Following the second incident, and too weak to work, Wishart was shipped with a large number of other prisoners back to Afion Kara Hissar. With him were at least four of his *AE2* shipmates who had suffered similar difficulties: Nichols, Wilson, Churcher and Harding. It was a move that almost certainly saved Wishart's life, for from Afion Kara Hissar he was selected for transfer to the more humane San Stefano camp.

Wishart returned to London by the end of 1918, travelling via Alexandria in Egypt, and rejoined his wife Annie in Belfast. He returned to the RN in 1921, serving at sea again until 1926, and working in merchant ships until 1935. He then obtained a post with the Belfast Corporation dealing with local shipping, and stayed there until the outbreak of WWII, during which he served at HMS *Caroline* in Belfast. In October 1939 Wishart met his respected *AE2* Captain Stoker once again. Stoker was serving as chief of staff to Admiral King, the Fleet Flag Officer in Belfast. The two old submariners worked together again for the first time since the Dardanelles.

Wishart's son, Harry Wishart, recalls his father as a small strong stubborn man with a strong work ethic. He was a committed Christian, but also a severe disciplinarian with his five children. Tommy Wishart died in Belfast on 20 February 1952, aged 69.

Additional AE2 crew list

The following British and Australian submariners served as crew on the *AE2* in 1913 and 1914, but were not aboard during its last journey into the Dardanelles.

The first group of sailors all died when *AE2*'s sister ship *AE1* was lost with all hands off Rabaul in New Guinea, 1914:

Bray, John James (Jack), Stoker Class I, Melbourne, Victoria.

Dennis, Frederick George, Able Seaman, born Devon, UK, living in Melbourne, Victoria.

Jarman, Jack, Able Seaman, Dookie, Victoria.

Guy, William Elliot, Southsea, UK.

The second group comprises original crew members of the *AE2* in Portsmouth, February 1914:

Broughton, George William, Stoker, born Skerbeck, Lincolnshire, UK.

Hitchcock, William James, Petty Officer, born Flushing, Cornwall, UK.

Hopkins, A. H. Sub-Lieutenant, RN (trip to Australia only).

Hughes, George, Stoker Class I, born Belfast, Northern Ireland.

Johnson, Thomas, Stoker, born Newcastle-on-Tyne, UK.

McCready, George, Petty Officer, born Belfast, Northern Ireland.

Norris, Stanley Jefferies Vickers, Able Seaman, Devonport, Tasmania.

Peddie, Thomas Henry, Leading Stoker, North Carlton, Victoria.

Robinson, James Harold, Leading Stoker, Perth, Western Australia.

Smith, Albert Edward, Chief Stoker, Devonport, UK.

Todd, Joseph, Leading Stoker, Liverpool, UK.

Stiling, Herbert, Petty Officer, born Brent Knoll, Somerset, living in Gordon, New South Wales.

Notes on sources

One of the difficulties faced in tracing Stoker's crew members was the almost complete lack of secondary sources. The only information available was in Naval Service Records, which include a brief physical description (to enable bodies to be identified in case of death) and two group photographs of the crew, which were found to be inaccurately captioned.

Returning to grass-roots direct methodology, the descendants of the crew were tracked down mainly through requests placed in mass-circulation newspapers and magazines in Australia, New Zealand and the UK, as well as phone books, electoral rolls, post offices, returned servicemen's associations and other institutions. The response was rewarding. It has resulted in these men being identified for the first time and, more importantly, their personal stories recorded.

Doctor Michael White of the University of Queensland, Lieutenant Commander Greg Swindon and Commander Tony Vine were immensely generous and gave us access to their own research collections on the *AE2* and her crew. The diaries of Corporal George Kerr proved a surprisingly rich new source of anecdotes about the submariners as prisoners of war, and his grandson Greg Kerr was particularly helpful with other documentary and photographic evidence. Bill Sellars in Istanbul provided vital and accurate information about the Turkish prisoner of war camps. Other major sources were the RAN's Submarine Historical Collection (curator Peter Smith) and the RN's Submarine Museum in Gosport, UK (curator Margaret Bidmead).

As well as those sources listed in the full bibliography, credit is given to the following people who gave generously of both their time and family archival material:

Ashby, Mrs M., Avalon NSW.

Baker, Alec H., Dee Why NSW (Tel W. W. Falconer).

Bray Family, especially Mrs Gwen Simpson, Kiah NSW (PO C. A. Bray).

Cary Family, Professor Tristram Cary, SA; Anthony Cary, Brussels, Belgium; John Cary, Teddington, UK; Joanna Cary, Henley, UK; Colonel R. R. McNish, Warminster, UK (Lt John Pitt Cary).

Cheater Family, for research, information and photographs; Gladys Hill, Cherrybrook NSW (daughter); Norma Lynch, Castle Hill NSW; Brian Hazlewood, Yagoona NSW; Sandra Meurer, Kellyville NSW (AB Thomas Cheater).

Clarke, Joy, Dunkeld VIC, and the *Hamilton Spectator* newspaper (LSto Michael Williams).

Colmer, Joan, Manly NSW (LS John McGregor).

Cullen Family; Lillian Cullen, Busselton WA; Margret Teale, Busselton WA; J. W. Byrne, Riverton WA (Sto Jim Cullen).

Edwards, Barrie, Clarence Town NSW; Mrs Ruby Edwards, East Maitland NSW (L/Sig A. N. C. Thomson).

Gibson, Maisie L., Geelong VIC (ERA1 James Gibson).

Gow, Janet, genealogist, Auckland, New Zealand (Sto Jim Cullen).

Gregson, Patricia, Collie WA (AB Charles Suckling).

Haggard Family, Commodore Dacre and Mrs Jenny Smyth (née Haggard), Toorak VIC; Reverend Richard Haggard, London, UK (Lt Geoffrey Haggard).

Henderson, Ena, Woody Point QLD (AB Alex Nichols).

Herbert, Jock, Upper Ferntree Gully VIC (Lt Eng Douglass Herbert).

Hunstone, Michael, Tideswell, Derbyshire, UK (AB John Wheat).

Kinder Family; Ross Kinder, Nundah QLD; Ray Kinder, Casino NSW; Chris Jones, Newcastle NSW; Zoie Knuckey, Adelaide SA (PO Harry Kinder).

Kranz, Frank, East Geelong VIC (LSto Michael Williams).

Lightfoot, Christopher, Metropolitan Museum, New York, USA (Prisoner of War Camps).

McKenzie, Malcolm, East Gosford NSW (PO Herbert Brown).

Marshall, June P. (AB Reuben Mitchell).

Meyers, John, Gympie QLD (CERA1 Harry Broomhead).

Moore, Bernadette, Bellevue Heights SA (LSto John Kerin).

Naval Service Records, Queanbeyan Office, Department of Defence, Canberra ACT, with thanks to Veronica Bagshaw in particular.

Stoker Family, Patrick Stoker, Canada; Miss Primrose Stoker, London, UK; D. C. Stoker, Colorado, USA (Lt Cdr Dacre Stoker).

Thompson, J. A. (Jim), Coolamon, and the Coolamon RSL, NSW (LSto John Kerin).

Tubbs, Stephen Gilbert, Inverell NSW (PO S. J. Gilbert).

Wilson Family, Sandy Clifton, Corio VIC; Heather McKay, Elsternwick VIC; Rose Walpole and Bob Appleton, Geelong VIC (LSto, Archibald (Tug) Wilson).

Wishart, Harry, Bradford-on-Avon, Wiltshire, UK (Sto Thomas Wishart).

Bibliography

Adam-Smith, Patsy, *The ANZACS*, Thomas Nelson, Melbourne, 1978.

——*Prisoners of War*, Penguin, Melbourne, 1992.

Andrews, E. M., *The Anzac Illusion: Anglo-Australian relations during WWI*, Cambridge University Press, Melbourne, 1993.

Australian Broadcasting Commission, *Gallipoli: The Fatal Shore*, ABC documentary film, Sydney, 1992.

'Australian Soldiers and Sailors Freed From the Turks', *Sydney Mail*, 9 April 1919, p. 10 (Mitchell Library).

Australian War Memorial, List of personnel ex submarine *AE2*, Prisoners of War in Turkey 1916–1921, MP472/15/20/10349.

——Royal Navy, Royal Australian Navy records used by official war historial A. W. Jose, Bundle 49 HMA Submarine *AE2*, Lt Cdr Stoker.

——Photographic database, collection of Corporal George Kitchin Kerr, taken while prisoner of war in Turkey, 1915–18.

——Chomley, M. Elizabeth (Secretary, Red Cross, Prisoners of War Department), correspondence and personal records, IRDL/0615.

——Prisoners of war from submarine *AE2* in Turkey, correspondence with, 1915–18, MP472/15/18/9207.

——Release of prisoners of war—crew of submarine *AE2*, 1918–19, MP472/15/19/2825.

Bean, C. E. W., *The Official History of Australia in the War of 1914–18*, vol. 1, *The Story of Anzac: The First Phase*, Angus & Robertson, Sydney, 1921.

Bell, Stephen J., Typescript, Statement, Royal Navy Submarine Museum, Gosport, UK, A1991/348.

Bishop, Alan, *Gentleman Rider: A Biography of Joyce Cary*, Michael Joseph, London, 1988.

Boardman, J., Griffin, J., and Murray, O. (eds), *Oxford History of the Classical World*, Oxford University Press, Oxford, 1992.

Bott, Alan, *Eastern Nights and Flights: a record of oriental adventure by 'contact'*, William Blackwood, Edinburgh, 1920.

Bowers, Peter, *Anzacs: The Pain and the Glory of Gallipoli*, Australia Post, Melbourne, 1999.

Brackenbury, N., Becoming Guests of the Unspeakable, unpublished honours thesis, Macquarie University, 1983, AWM MSS. 975.

Bray, Cecil Arthur (*AE2* crew), diary. Original held by Mrs Gwen Simpson (daughter), Kiah, NSW.

British Red Cross, Central Prisoners of War Committee, Correspondence 1915–18, held in National Archives, Melbourne, Victoria.

Brodie, Charles G., *Forlorn Hope 1915: The Submarine Passage of the Dardanelles*, Frederick Books, London, 1956.

Brown, Herbert Alexander (*AE2* crew), diary. Microfilm No CY2662, Dixon Collection, Mitchell Library, Sydney.

Brown, James D., *Turkish Days and Ways*, Angus & Robertson, Sydney, 1940.

Bush, Captain Eric W., *Gallipoli*, George Allen & Unwin, London, 1975.

Cary, Joyce, *A House of Children*, Michael Joseph, London, 1950.

Corbett, J., *History of the Great War: Naval Operations*, vol. I, Allen & Unwin, London, 1961.

Denham, H. M., *Dardanelles: A Midshipman's Diary*, John Murray, London, 1981.

Denton, Kit, *Gallipoli, One Long Grave*, Time Life Books, Sydney, 1986.

'Exploring the Australian World War I Submarine *AE2*', *Journal of the Australian Naval Institute*, vol. 26, no. 1, Jan–March 2000.

Farson, Daniel, *The Man Who Wrote Dracula*, Michael Joseph, London, 1975.

Fewster, Kevin; Basarin, Vecihi & Basarin, Hatice Hurmuz, *A Turkish View of Gallipoli, Canakkale*, Hodja Educational Resources Cooperative, Victoria, 1953.

Firkins, Peter, *Of Nautilus and Eagles: History of Royal Australian Navy*, Cassell Australia, Sydney, 1975.

Fischer, Fritz, *Germany's Aims in the First World War*, Chatto & Windus, London, 1967.

Fisk, Robert, 'Dead Reckoning', *Sydney Morning Herald*, 9 Sept 2000, Spectrum p. 6.

Frame, T. R., *The Shores of Gallipoli*, Hale & Iremonger, Sydney, 2000.

Frame, T. R. and Swinden G. J., *First In, Last Out: The Navy at Gallipoli*, Kangaroo Press, Sydney, 1990.

Gilbert, Sir Martin (introduction), *The Straits of War, Gallipoli Remembered*, various authors, Sutton Publishing, Gloucestershire, UK, 2000.

Gilbert, Stephen John (*AE2* crew), diary. Original held by Stephen Tubbs (grandson), Inverell NSW.

Grey, Edwin, *A Damned Un-English Weapon: The Story of British Submarine Warfare 1914–18*, NEL, London, 1973.

Halpin, J., *Blood in the Mists*, Macquarie Head Press, Sydney, 1940.

Hankey, Lord Maurice, *The Supreme Command 1914–1918*, George Allen & Unwin, London, 1961.

Herodotus, *The Histories*, Book VII, 457.

HM Government, British Parliament, House of Commons Committees, *Report on the Treatment of British Prisoners of War in Turkey*, 1919.

Holland I—John Philip Holland, 1841–1914, Royal Navy Submarine Museum, Gosport, UK, no date.

Inglis, K., 'The Anzac Tradition', *Meanjin Quarterly*, vol. 24, no. 100, March 1965.

——'Australia Day', *Historical Studies*, vol. 13 (49), Oct 1967.

——'The Australians at Gallipoli', *Historical Studies*, vol. 14 (54), April 1970; vol. 14 (55), Oct 1970.

Iscen, A. Yetkin, '83 yil sonra . . .', *Focus*, Istanbul, Turkey, March 1999, pp. 62–9.

James, Robert Rhodes, *Gallipoli*, Papermac, London, 1989.

Jameson, William S., *Submariners V. C.*, Peter Davies, London, 1962.

Johnston, M.A.B. and Yearsley, K.D., *Four-Fifty Miles to Freedom*, William Blackwood & Sons, Edinburgh and London, 1919.

Jose, A. W., *The Official History of Australia in the War 1914–18*, vol. II: *The Story of Anzac*; vol. IX: *The Royal Australian Navy*, Angus & Robertson, Sydney, 1928.

Keble Chatterton, E., *Dardanelles Dilemma: The Story of Naval Operations*, Rich & Cowan Ltd, London, 1935.

Keeling, E. H., *Adventures in Turkey and Russia*, John Murray, London, 1924.

Kemp, Paul J., *British Submarines of WWI*, Arms & Armour Press, London, 1990.

Kerr, George Kitchin, Original Transcript of Diaries, Turkey, 1915–18. Translated from New Pitman's Shorthand by Jeanette Owen, Melbourne, 1995, AWM PR00953.

Kerr, Greg, *Lost Anzacs: The Story of Two Brothers*, Oxford University Press, Melbourne, 1998.

Keyes, Sir Roger, *The Naval Memoirs of Admiral of the Fleet: The Narrow Seas to the Dardanelles 1910–1915*, vol. 1, Thornton Butterworth Ltd, London, 1934.

Kinder, Henry James Elly (*AE2* crew), diary. Original held by Mr Ross Kinder (grandson), Nundah, QLD.

Kinross, Lord Patrick, *Ataturk: The Rebirth of a Nation*, Phoenix, London, 1995.

Kipling, Rudyard, *Sea Warfare: Tales of 'The Trade'*, Macmillan, London, 1916.

'Klaxon', *Dead Reckoning: A Story of Our Submarines*, Rich & Cowan, London, 1933.

Knaggs, Albert (*AE2* crew), diary. Unpublished manuscript, AWM PR85/096. Original held at Submarine Museum, Spectacle Island, Sydney, NSW.

Knightley, Phillip, *Australia: A Biography of a Nation*, Jonathan Cape, 2000.

Kolay, Selçuk, 'The Sub That Shaped Gallipoli: Subhunter at Gallipoli, *Diver, incorporating Underwater World*, Eaton Publications, Teddington, UK, pp. 59–62.

Laffin, John, *British Butchers and Bunglers of World War One*, Macmillan, Melbourne, 1989.

——*Damn the Dardanelles: The Agony of Gallipoli*, Sun Books, Melbourne, 1985.

Lee, John, *A Soldier's Life: General Sir Ian Hamilton 1853–1947*, Macmillan, London, 2000.

Manthorpe, Victoria, *Children of the Empire: The Victorian Haggards*, Victor Gollancz, London, 1996.

Moorehead, Alan, *Gallipoli*, Wordsworth Editions, Ware, 1998.

Morgenthau, Henry, *Ambassador Morgenthau's Story*, Doubleday, New York, 1919.

——*Secrets of the Bosphorus*, Hutchinson, London, 1928.

Moses, John A., with Munro, Gregory, *Australia and the 'Kaiser's War' 1914–1918: On Understanding the Anzac Tradition*, Broughton Press, Brisbane, 1993.

National Archives, Officer service records, Canberra ACT.

——Papers and Correspondence relating to *AE2* Submarine:
MP 472/1; 5/18/9207 – MP472/1; 5/19/2520 – MP 472/1; 5/19/2825 – PM's Dept CRS A2939, Correspondence 1914–17 CRS A2; Governor General's Office CP 78/24, Correspondence files 1914–20, POWs in Turkey – General Correspondence 1911–21, File No. 16/1416 MP1049/1, Melbourne, Victoria.

National Library of Australia *AE2* website: http://purl.nla.gov.au/nla/pandora/AE2.

Nichols, Alexander Charles (*AE2* crew), diary, 'Prison Life at San Stefano', Private Records Collection, Australian War Memorial, 3DRL/2965.

Pelvin, Richard, 'First Through: the Epic Voyage of AE2', *Wartime* (the official magazine of the Australian War Memorial), p. 66.

Public Records Office, London: Records on *AE2* and Crew: ADM 1/8415/718; ADM 137: 4127;4068; 4178; 4362; 4565; 2317; HS Vol. 382; 154; 179; 157; 271; 1096; 1247; 155B; 1089; 1090; 2077; 3088A. ADM 116: 178; 103; 1432; 1427; 1429; 1433; 1434; 1434. ADM 171: 78–88. ADM 196: 90. Admiralty Maps, FO 925; 3402; MP 1 Admiralty Chart 2836 B: Sea of Marmara with the Dardanelles. FO 383: 1244, 1244A; 1218; 93; 98; 101; 102.

Riza, Captain & Dulger, Bahadir, *How I Sank the* AE2 *Submarine in Marmara Sea*, publisher unknown, Istanbul, 1947, translated by Dr Gül Izmir, Sydney.

Royal Australian Navy *AE2* website: http://www.navy.gov.au/9_sites/AE2.

Sellars, Bill, 'Diving Into the Past—Australian History in a Turkish Sea', *Scuba Diver Magazine*, Jan–Feb 1999.

Shackleton, Sir Ernest Henry, *South: the story of Shackleton's 1914–17 expedition*, Heinemann, London, 1919.

Shakespeare, William, *Othello*, Act III, sc. 3.

Smith, Tim, *Project AE2, Investigation of the HM AE2 Submarine Wreck Site*, NSW Heritage Office, Sydney, 1999.

——'Return to Gallipoli: The Discovery of the WWI Australian Submarine *AE2*', *Heritage NSW*, vol. 5, no. 4, p. 24.

Smyth, Dacre, Commodore, 'The Submarine *AE2* in World War I', A transcript of lecture to ACT Chapter, Naval Historical Society of Australia, Monograph 6.

Smyth, Dacre, *Gallipoli Pilgrimage*, self-published, Melbourne, 1990.

Souter, Gavin, *Lion and Kangaroo: Australia, 1901–1919, The Rise of a Nation*, Fontana, Sydney, 1976.

Southall, Ivan, *Softly Tread the Brave*, Angus & Robertson, Sydney, 1960.

Spencer, Mark, 'The Search for *AE2*', in *Wartime* (the official magazine of the Australian War Memorial) AWM News 66, pp. 13–15.

——'Exploring the Australian World War I Submarine *AE2*' in *Journal of the Australian Naval Institute*, vol. 26, no. 1, January–March 2000.

——'Gallipoli's Naval Secret; the Search for the *AE2*' in *The Sydney Papers*, summer 1999, vol. 11, no. 1, pp. 49–55, The Sydney Institute Publications Pty Ltd.

——'The Discovery of the *AE2*—a WW1 Submarine' in *Skylife*, inflight magazine of Turkish Airline, written in Turkish and English, April 1999, pp. 26–34.

——'HMAS *AE2*—Unsung Hero of Gallipoli', in *Australian Warship Review*, vol. 3, April–May–June 1999, pp. 5–12.

——'The Unsung Heroine', in *Sport Diving Magazine*, vol 74, June–July 1999, pp. 76–81.

Stoker, H. H. G. D., *Straws in the Wind* (3rd edn), Herbert Jenkins, London, 1925.

——'The First Submarine Passage of the Dardanelles', *Tales of Hazard*, ed H. C. Armstrong, Bodley Head, London, 1932.

——Letter to C. A. Bray, 1965

——'Is Sportsmanship being killed? Wake Up England!', unpublished manuscript, BBC Radio script, Royal Submarine Museum, Gosport, UK.

——Personal papers, photographs and notebooks.

——Collection of papers, photographs and memorabilia, 8 CDs, possession of the authors.

Stoker, H. G. and Hurst, J. L., *Below the Surface*, unpublished playscript, Royal Submarine Museum, Gosport, UK.

Stokesbury, James L., *A Short History of World War I*, Morrow, New York, 1981.

Suckling, Charles, (*AE2* crew), diary, unpublished manuscript, AWM Private Records Collection, 3DRL/6226.

Swindon, Lt Cdr Greg, RAN, 'The *AE2* Graves', *Wartime* (the official magazine of the Australian War Memorial), pp. 16–18.

——'Gallipoli Revisited by RAN', *Navy News*, April 1995.

——'Navy Blue Anzacs', *Australian Sea Heritage*, no. 46, autumn 196, pp. 14–16.

——'The RAN Forgotten War Dead', *Journal of the Australian Naval Institute*, October 1990.

Taylor, A. J. P., *The First World War: An Illustrated History*, Penguin, London, 1966.

Taylor, Richard, '*AE2* Unites Former Foes', *Immersed, the International Technical Diving Magazine*, vol. 4, no. 4, winter 1999, pp. 34–39.

The Times (London), 30 April 1915, p. 77b: E. S. 'The Submarine Boat: Principles of its Construction'.

The Times (London), 12 May 1915 12, p. 8c: 'AE2 reported sunk in Dardanelles'.

The Times (London), 19 May 1915, p. 7f: Admiralty Report.

Thomson, Alistair, 'A Past You Can Live With: Digger Memories of the ANZAC Legend', *Journal of the Australian War Memorial*, 1992, p. 20.

——*ANZAC Memories: Living with the Legend*, Oxford University Press, Melbourne, 1994.

Usborne, C. V., *Smoke on the Horizon*, Hodder & Stoughton, London, 1933.

Wheat, John Harrison, (*AE2* crew), diary, unpublished manuscript, AWM PRM F0026 and 3RDL/2965.

White, M. W. D., *Australian Submarines*, AGPS, Canberra, 1992.

——'The Role of Submarine *AE2* on Anzac Day', *Royal Historical Society of Queensland Journal*, vol. 13, no. 4, Nov 1987, pp.136–144.

——'Australian Submariner Prisoners of War After the Gallipoli Landing', *Royal Historical Society of Queensland Journal*, vol. 14, no. 4, Nov 1990, pp. 136–144.

White, T. W. Captain RAAF, Transcript of diaries as a prisoner of war in Turkey, 1919, AWM Private Records Collection, 2DRL/0766.

——*Guests of the Unspeakable*, John Hamilton, London, 1928.

Wilson, Michael, *Destination Dardanelles*, Leo Cooper, London, 1988.

Woolley, C. L., *From Kastamouni to Kedos*, Oxford University Press, Oxford, 1921.

Index

T